ACKNOWL

I would like to thank everybody wh
have a wonderful family and hav
amazing close friends and loyal

CW00447277

friends. I have far too many people to thank for helping me piece the content of this book together to be able to list them individually but I'd like to thank Leo for the last two years, consisting of meeting every week in some strange places where people are giving us the funniest of looks, as we talk, act out, get emotional and most of all, laugh, as Leo makes some sense of all the detail of my life that I can remember. I would also like to thank the fantastic NHS and specifically the people in Tameside General Hospital who saved my life physically back in 1980. People clapped the NHS every week during the COVID pandemic but I've been clapping them in my mind for 40 years. Lastly though I would like to thank you, the person who has bought this book. Thank you for being interested in the story of my life.

For my Mum

Contents

Introduction

We knew we were not far short of the next checkpoint and found ourselves running through some woods. It's August 2017 and I'm about eighty miles into my first British Ultra event which is a two hundred mile cross country foot race from Southport to Hornsea near Hull. I have been running for the last fifteen miles with one of my fellow competitors who I knew only by her unusual first name 'Loveness'. It was her first Ultra event after coming back from experiencing a stress fracture of her hip and I was supporting her through some of it. It's what Ultra competitors do. You are as interested in getting others through it as you are getting yourself to the finish line, or in this case the next checkpoint. Running in a GB Ultra is as much about following map readings as it is about the physical challenge because you're not going to achieve anything running the wrong way or an extra twenty miles for no reason other than you've read your map wrong. These events have deadlines for every checkpoint and if you don't make the deadline, then forget it. You can compete in the event and get a tee shirt if you want one with 'GB Ultra 200' on the front. You'll even get the tee shirt for participating, no matter whether you finish or not or you reach the checkpoints within the time limit. If you are a true Ultra competitor though, you want the GB Ultra Belt Buckle. To be awarded with one of these, you need to reach the checkpoints by certain times and the finish line by the maximum time allowed. I'm getting that buckle and, if have anything to do with it, so is Loveness. Suddenly my phone goes and it was one of the marshals. "Right, where are you now?' he said. I tell him roughly where we are and he said 'Oh right I can see you.' I thought he may be able to see the head torches we each have to wear because large sections of this type of event take place at night across some difficult terrain. What he is actually looking at is us on his laptop as we are all carrying a GPS Tracker

7

attached to our rucksacks. That didn't quite click with me at the time though because I still couldn't see him or the checkpoint. He instructed us to keep going on the path we were on until we get to a main road and then turn left. He said that their Marshall's station, was a short distance down that road. We get to the main road that he had described and as we turn left, suddenly, this incredibly overwhelming feeling comes over me. Sometimes in Ultra Races a lack of sleep can give you hallucinations and strange experiences so initially I put it down to that but the feeling remained with me and as we made our way towards the Marshal's station, the feeling was getting stronger and it had started to dominate my thinking. It was similar to the feeling you get when you experience Deja vu but the thought was so overpowering and I said out loud "I've been here before". I'm confused because its early hours of the morning and I don't even know where I am so how can I say I have been here before? but the feeling is getting stronger. We walk towards a bend in the road and Loveness can see something is wrong. 'What's up?' she says but I'm not really listening to her so I don't answer. We walk around the bend and I'm looking down a dip in the road and there in the dip is a bridge and above it in the background I can see a GB Ultra flag. I should be excited to see the flag as it is clearly our marker for the eighty one mile checkpoint which means much needed rest and something to eat and drink but I can't take my eyes off the bridge as I go towards it. "I know this place". The bridge is made of steel amongst other materials but as I near it, strangely, I can see it in my memory as a brick bridge. I look over the bridge and there's a drop down to a railway line and I suddenly realise where I am 'Fuck off' I say out loud and then I spot the road sign 'Mottram Hall Road'. 'Fuck Off' I say again. 'What is it?' says Loveness, who by this time is beginning to get freaked out by the way I am behaving. I finally answer her, "It's a long story" I said "but I died here on this bridge in 1980".

8

Chapter 1 – Dancing at The Ritz

I had never once considered writing about my life. I wasn't academic in any way so writing was never my thing. My degree, as they say, was from the University of life, or more to the point was from the school of hard knocks. Besides, I had never viewed my life as any more interesting than anyone else's so it just had never crossed my mind. It was as I stood on the bridge on Mottram Hall Road in Hattersley in the early hours of that morning in August 2017 that a sudden realisation had hit me of how lucky I was to have had the life that I have had, given that my life had almost been taken from me at that spot thirty seven years earlier in a horrific car crash. From that moment on I have been like a man possessed and compelled to tell my story. A story of family, resilience, determination, funny moments that I can laugh about and serious moments that I'd prefer to forget about but can't be left out. Overall it's a story of battling against the odds to carve a life for myself and pursuing a constantly moving goal. It contains stories of happy times and also life's inevitably sad moments, of which I have had my fair share. Ultimately, I believe it to be the story of a lucky man. Me! Later in the story I will get the chance, together with the help of my mum, to tell you what happened to me in that crash on the bridge and how it affected my life but for now I want to start where I think everyone should really start, at the beginning and where and who I come from.

One of the effects of the crash in 1980 was my memory. I can remember some incidents as far back as when I was two years old in 1962 as if they were yesterday but there are some simple things that really everybody should remember about themselves that I simply don't. Like where I was born. I should know that shouldn't I? I think I probably did know it at one time but I certainly don't know now so I have had to enlist the help of my mum and others to fill in some of the gaps for me as I talk about my family background. I was the first born to Mum, Alma Duoba (nee Ross) and Dad, John (Jonas) Duoba on 6th September 1960. Dad was a Lithuanian immigrant who had fled from the Russians to England after the war and initially found his way to Matlock in Derbyshire. He'd later moved to Manchester and lived in the Lithuanian community club / house in Crumpsall, Manchester next to the Belmont Hotel on Middleton Road with fellow Lithuanian immigrants. My dad had come from a farming family who had their farm taken off them by the Russians. Most of my Dad's adult family at the time had been marched off to the Gulags in Siberia which were forced labour camps established during Joseph Stalin's long reign as dictator of the Soviet Union. The word Gulag comes as a shortened version of 'Glavnoe Upravlenie Lagerei' which meant Main Camp Administration. They operated from the 1920's until shortly after Stalin's death in 1953. Millions of people had been put through them. Each camp held up to ten thousand people and you were sent there if there was any indication of you challenging Stalin's way of doing things. Initially the camps were used for criminals but then more and more they were used for everyday citizens and their families. Thousands died in the process either from illness and malnutrition or were murdered by guards. Their only crime was that they had been accused of being 'enemies of the soviet state' by the Russians. My Grandad and Nana lost a baby as they were marched hundreds of miles to one of these camps which were in Siberia. Younger members of the community, like my Dad, managed to escape the Russians but were eventually swept up by the Germans and taken to Youth Camps. Dad managed to get away from there and fled across Europe to eventually land here, after war was over, in England. When Lithuania gained independence after Stalin's death, the people started to get all their land back. Dad's nephew and my cousin, also called Jonas, came over to

Manchester to see dad many years later to ask him did he want to stake a claim on a share of the land that they had been given back but Dad said no because he felt that the land was his family's future in Lithuania and he was building a future for himself in England and had no plans for going back. The sad thing is that I have little more to say other than that about my whole Duoba family. I don't know what happened to most of them and it wasn't my Dad's style to tell me stories about his past or his family. My mum says the same. The past was upsetting for my Dad so it wasn't spoken about. My mum tells me that Dad got a letter once from Lithuania. It was to tell him that his sister had died and a photo fell out of the letter and it was a photograph of his sister in her coffin and some of his family stood around her. There were more letters around the time but Dad never spoke of them. I'll come back to this much later in my story. I was a child when all this was happening and I thought nothing more about it but as I got older and with children of my own, I realise that some of the traits that I have and my children have, will have come from both my mum's and dad's side of the family but I have little to tell them about. In fact the only story Dad ever shared with me about his life in Lithuania was about Chilblains. As a boy, he had once fell through ice into frozen water near his home. After managing to get out of the water he had run to his house and tried to warm himself up with hot water and his father had stopped him and carried him outside and removed his outer clothing and rubbed him down with snow. I've seen it since on a television programme that the snow soaks up the water and warms the skin gradually to prevent chilblains which are swollen red patches on the skin caused by exposure to the cold and made far worse be warming them up quickly. So that's all I know about the Duoba part of my family. Perhaps this book with reach that far and one of them one day will contact us. Or maybe I need to make the journey one day to Lithuania to look for them. People have asked me about my name 'Duoba' many times and where it originated from. Apart from being Lithuanian, the name also has links with America and has several meanings one of which is 'wood'. To me I felt it was no coincidence that I loved working with wood growing up and wanted initially to be a carpenter and was fascinated with the different colours of wood. Duoba is a big farming name in America in the Michigan area and has been for nearly two hundred years. It's also a province of China. It's clearly a well-travelled name and one that has held me in good stead over the years being one that people tend to remember due to it being unusual.

On the other side of the family, my mother, Alma, who was born Agnes Alma Ross, was the third child of my grandparents, Walter and Margaret Ross. She had two older sisters and a younger brother called Joe. Joe was someone who I looked up to tremendously because of the things that he had achieved in his life in the merchant navy and the police which I will talk about later. The two sisters were Catherine, who was the eldest of the children, and Myra. Myra died when she was only nine years old of Diphtheria. A child's death was far more common in those days than it is now due to the many diseases that medicine had not yet got to grips with but the loss of Myra must have been very hard on my mum and her parents, particularly my Gran. As with many people of that era. People changed their names for various reasons My mum took her middle name, Alma, after her and mum got fed up of people referring to her as Aggie. Mum's sister Catherine became Doreen (her middle name) for many years until she got fed up with people pronouncing it incorrectly as 'Dureeen' and went back to being Auntie Cath. I thought she'd changed her name by deed poll or something. I didn't realise that this was her name all along. I wonder how many people nowadays do that sort of thing. I bet it's a nightmare at passport control going on holiday My Gran and Grandad, Margaret and Walter, had been married in St Chads church in Cheetham Hill in 1928 and they all lived in a flat in Collyhurst, Manchester to begin with on Burgan Drive. My Gran had always wanted a house but none was available through the council so they settled for a flat. My Grandad, Walter was a highly skilled man and worked at Cary's steelworks near Angel Meadow in central Manchester. Walter was my granddad and one of my heroes. He was somebody who I looked up to tremendously. He was a man's man to say the least. He used to be able to bend those big thick square nails with his bare hands and it amazed me. In 1949, one of his close colleagues left Cary's and opened his own little engineering business in Leyland, Lancashire, about thirty miles away. He pestered Walter to go with him but Walter resisted and stayed on at Cary's. In the end the temptation of being able to move his family out of the smokey dark streets of Manchester and into the rural area of Leyland with the countryside all around them was too much. In addition it became clear to my Gran and Grandad that as my Grandad was classed as a 'Key Worker' due to his tradesmanship, they would qualify for a council house over in Leyland and would have their own place. My Grandad made the decision to accept his colleagues' offer and went to work for his pal. My mum was about fourteen when the family made the move and she loved it. Initially it was like being on holiday from Manchester but they settled into the house and loved living 'out in the sticks'. When she reached eighteen there was nothing she enjoyed more than going dancing at the weekend at the various venues accessible to Leyland. One week they would be at the Winter Gardens in Blackpool and another week they would travel to Rivington Pike where they had converted a barn into a dancehall. Manchester was also still close enough to make the trip in on a train on Saturday nights and they used to go dancing at The Ritz, The Palace and Belle Vue. The train line ran from Manchester to Blackpool and back via Leyland so they felt they had great choice. The train would be packed with young people going to the various dance venues on a Saturday night and the train was nicknamed 'The Cattle Wagon' for obvious reasons. My mum wouldn't think twice about getting a bus or train to Chorley if necessary and walking the 5 miles home, carrying her shoes, after a night out. There was no thought of taxis or being picked up by a family member in those days. In 1956, just before her 21st birthday, life changed for the family when my Grandad, Walter, suffered a stroke. My mum is convinced to this day that it was pure excitement that brought the stroke on because my Grandad had just received a fantastic offer from his boss. Their small engineering business had gathered some reputation for the quality of their work primarily because of Walter's precision and toolmanship. At the time they primarily made grills for cars but in the August of 1956 the business had a visit from a potentially new client. The two gentlemen representing the client had a short tour of what they did on the shop floor and then watched Walter at work. They questioned him about how precise he was being when he didn't seem to be measuring his work. They assumed it was because he was so used to the work he was doing but Walter told them that he could simply judge certain measurements. They tested this by asking him to cut a length of metal to an obscure and precise measurement. He gave it a short assessment and then simply cut it. The gentlemen measured it and It was exactly right. Walter thought no more of this visit until the following day when the owner called him into the office to tell him that they'd got the contract off the visitors. They were from the Blackpool Tram company and the contract was an extremely lucrative one to manufacture leaf springs for the suspension system for their vehicles. This was great news as it was but then the owner announced to Walter that he was going to make him a partner of the business and share the profits with him. He thought that my Grandad deserved to own half of the business he was contributing so much to and so said to him that he could have fifty percent of the business. Walter

14

was so excited and when he came home he immediately announced to my mum that he was going to treat her to driving lessons and buy her a car for her 21st birthday. My Gran said to him 'have you won the pools or something?' My Grandad was so excited about it all, he explained to my mum that his plan was to buy her a car and then on Saturdays she could drive them both over to Manchester so that my Gran could visit her family in Manchester every week and my Dad could go and watch Manchester United. Plans quickly changed on all fronts though as that same week Walter suffered a severe stroke. My Gran and Mum were convinced that it was the excitement at the prospect of owning half the business and finally reaping the rewards for all his hard work that brought on the stroke. By that time my mum's brother, my Uncle Joe , was in the merchant Navy and my Aunty Catherine was married and had two children and was living in Manchester. So that left my Gran and mum to look after my Grandad. His stroke was so severe that they had to wash and shave him because he couldn't do anything for himself. Catherine came to see him at home over several weekends and realised that the situation was very difficult so she moved back in with them for six months and mum was able to go back to work. This was a difficult period as Catherine's husband, Cyril, and her own family were back in Manchester. After six months Catherine returned home and started coming back for long weekends to give Gran and mum a rest which helped a lot. Walter would only let my mum wash and shave him though. He insisted on it. He would get very frustrated because there was so much he couldn't do and he would swing his arms around in anger. Gran thought he was acting aggressively and getting violent but my mum understood that he wasn't angry with them, It was purely the frustration of not being able to do things for himself. He was a very determined man and would not use a bedpan. He refused point blank to use it and insisted on maintaining his dignity and using the toilet which was at the

15

other end of the landing upstairs. This meant that either Gran or mum had to help him get there and this was not easy. He was a heavy man and one of them would have to support his weight as he struggled to get just a few yards along the landing but they did it and he never did use a bedpan ever. It sounds quite simple but every time they made that trip along the landing, if Gran or mum had have let him fall then they would have never been able to pick him up as they just didn't have the strength so they made sure that he never did fall. The doctor would come and see my dad and say to my Gran 'how on earth are you coping getting him to the toilet and back?' My Gran said 'we just are'. Mum didn't know it at the time but looking after her Dad through this difficult period put her in good stead for many years later when I was allowed home from Hospital with severe psychological problems. It also explains some of where both my mum and I got our determination and never say die attitude from. Not all of it though because I'm convinced that the inner strength and character came from my Mum's mum, my Gran, Margaret Ross was the person I was most scared of as a kid. She seemed about two foot two inches tall and would frighten anybody. She was absolutely fierce. One time, when my mum was about nine years of age, she was playing out with her friends in the afternoon and she came off a scooter, the sort that you put one foot on and the other pushes you along. She had gashed her left knee badly.(make a mental note that the injury was to her left knee and I'll come back to that later in the book). Gran cleaned the cut and wrapped it up to keep it clean. Walter, my Grandad came home early evening from work at about 7pm, takes one look at the knee and decided to take her straight to Ancoats Hospital, which sadly isn't there anymore. The doctor examined my mum and said immediately that it needed stitches. As he started the stitching procedure, my mum winced a bit and the Doctor said to her 'Don't be so soft girl". I don't really want to tell you what My Grandad did next but after it happened, the Doctor straightened his shirt and tie and resumed stitching mum's wound. I shouldn't mention my Uncle Cyril who married my mum's sister Catherine without telling you about his background too. Their surname was Brown. Cyril was from a very well known boxing family and was related to John (Jackie) Brown from Collyhurst who was British and European Flyweight champion and eventually won a world Flyweight title in 1932. That's quite a story to be able to tell people but there is a more significant thing in my life about my Uncle Cyril and Aunty Catherine in my life and that was where they eventually moved to live in Hattersley. One of the main roads out of Hattersley is Mottram Hall Road and where they lived changed my life considerably. I'll get back to that later though. Between 1956 and 1958 mum's family remained in Leyland but they did eventually move back to Manchester to be nearer her family after she saw an advertisement in the paper regarding the possibility of exchanging houses with someone in Middleton at the top of Wood Street. This was the kind of thing that was possible in those days when you lived in council/rented houses. You could swap the houses you were living in. So their house swap was arranged and they moved back to Langley in Middleton. My Grandad Walter never really recovered sufficiently enough to return to work fully but took a temporary job at the Daily Express in Manchester, He eventually died aged 64 after another stroke whilst getting ready to go out to a boxing match at Belle Vue. Again this came at a time in his life that he was enjoying and excited about. Mum said he was so looking forward to full retirement at 65 and was all excited about going to Belle Vue to watch the boxing. He died instantly though. He had a blood clot on his brain and so didn't suffer. He never did get that chance to buy mum a car and mum didn't even pass her test until many years later when she was 42. She tells me that my Dad took her for her first couple of lessons but that didn't work out. Apparently he kept telling her to "put her foot down" and she told him "I'll put my foot somewhere in a minute!". Dad told her not to be too disappointed if she failed her first test as he had taken 5 tests to pass. She passed first time and loved the expression on his face when she told him. My mum (Alma) and dad (christened Jonas but referred to as John) met while out dancing. Going out dancing on a Saturday night was a regular feature in young peoples' lives at that time. They thrived on the opportunity to go dancing in different venues every week and now living in Manchester meant that Alma could go dancing at Belle Vue, The Palace on Oxford Road or The Ritz on Whitworth Street. It was at one of those dances at The Ritz in Manchester that she met my dad. She'd known him for quite a while as you would get to know a lot of people by dancing with them every week. They would dance all night and would dance with different dance partners as the night went on. She'd known him for about twelve months when one night at the Ritz, a young Irish lad was making a real nuisance of himself. Alma was getting more and more cheesed off with him interrupting her dancing with other partners. Alma and John were dancing and this lad just grabbed Alma. He was a hefty sort of lad and she did not like it one bit. John just stood there in shock as this sort of thing just didn't happen, as we were used to everybody behaving properly and treating the girls with respect. The dance finished and Alma just walked off the dance floor and told him to stay where he was. She'd decided to go home as she wasn't in the mood anymore after the way he had behaved. She bumped into John as she walked off and he asked her if she was okay. She told him that she was going home early as she just didn't want to bump into that lad again. She went to the cloakroom and got her coat and left. John came after her and said to her "I will walk you to the bus stop". He walked her to where she got the bus and they chatted and arranged to go dancing at Bellevue the next week and so it began. That evening led to the creation of our Duoba family.

Chapter 2 – Early Duoba Life

Jonas and Alma married at St Aidens in 1959. He was nine and a half years older than her which didn't even enter their heads at the time and they got their first home on Sawyer Street in Monsall, a terraced house. Alma was working at a place called Pattreiouex in Middleton which made 'Players' cigarettes. She worked on the conveyor line catching the cigarettes and quality controlling them, selecting any to be rejected. John was working at Booth Hall hospital as a porter but eventually went on to get a good job at Connellys in Blackley village. Connellys were a huge firm who made telecommunication cables. Eventually mum was to work there too as a Quality Controller. Dad was initially a farm worker (like his American namesakes) and told me once that not only could he have claimed a share in the original family farm in Lithuania, he could have also had his own farm down in Matlock in Derbyshire, as the couple who owned the farm he worked on treated him as the son they'd never had . He could have stayed there as they offered him the farm when they were gone because they had no children but he was keen to be more adventurous and wanted to come to Manchester and live and work in a big city. That's something I associate with today as I am constantly wanting to challenge myself and never happy to accept the norm or what is comfortable or the easy life. He spent most of his working life in Manchester firstly at Connellys in Blackley (which later became BICC Telecommunications Ltd) and then at Johnson's in Beswick, who were also manufacturers of cable, eventually returning to Connellys. Both of these companies produced cables that went all over the world. He was a grafter and had worked his way up to Charge-hand at Connellys and the management wanted him to be a foreman. He resisted that because he just didn't want to be a foreman because the last thing he wanted to do was get involved in sacking or disciplining people. He was also an

19

entrepreneur and my memory of his car was that it was always seemed to be tilted towards the boot. You see he knew the security man really well and there always seemed to be a lot of weight in it when he left work! Suffice to say it was like having a branch of Connellys in our shed at home. As I said, Mum also worked at Connellys but was also a fantastic mum who worked hard at home to bring the family up. Home for me as a toddler was Sawyer Street, Monsall. Life is full of amazing stories and coincidences and sometime those coincidences make you step back and think quite deeply. Is it really a coincidence or something a lot more meaningful? I was cutting one of my regular customers' hair one day and approaching him about getting his help to write this book. His name is Leo and he and I have known each other for over thirty years. I must have cut his hair well over two hundred times in that thirty plus year period and I just happen to mention to him for the first time that I grew up on Sawyer Street, Monsall. 'Where's that?' He said. I explained exactly where it was. He stopped me cutting his hair and said 'wow' and then explained to me that he was named Leo after his dad's cousin who was killed in War by a German bomb during the Manchester blitz when he was only fifteen years old. The bomb made a direct hit on their house in Monsall only a few yards from where I was describing to him. I said to him then ' You've got to help me write my book' and immediately he just said 'OK I will'. So back to the early sixties. Here I was on Sawyer street and one of my earliest memories set the scene for the rest of my life. Dad bought me my first bike for Christmas. I was only three years old and it obviously had stabilisers on. I immediately took it out and went on what we described as the 'concrete velodrome' at the back of where we lived where the kids raced their bikes in a circle around a space between all the houses. I was that competitive even then that I realised the stabilisers were preventing me from banking the bike so that I could take the corner quicker. I ran in and said to dad. "you need to take my stabilisers off". He just looked at me as if I was crazy. I was only three years old and already had a need for speed and competitiveness that was frustrating the hell out of me. He said "but you've only just got it". I said "Dad - take them off". So he took them off muttering "you're a crank son". Soon I was out there racing like a mad kid trying to be the fastest on the estate. I don't need to add that I paid the penalty for this. I became on first name terms with the A&E department at Booth Hall Children's Hospital in Blackley with all the accidents that I had, on and off the bike. I still have the scars to prove it from back then when I was only a toddler. Like the time when I was about four years old and I caught the skin of the back of my calf on a big square nail sticking out of the door jar of the house at Sawyer Street as I rushed out to play and ripped a huge gash in my leg. The scar is as clear as day now as it required ten stitches. This marked a very strange process across my life of injuring the left hand side of my body and was my first introduction to Booth Hall A&E. I loved bikes straight from the start. Dad used to take me to school at St Edmunds primary school in Monsall on his crossbar before he went to work and I absolutely loved it. This is what really got me into them and to this day my interest hasn't waned one bit. To date I've probably spent in excess of £35,000 on bikes and equipment to feed my hobby that started as a crazy three year old wanting to go the fastest I could on the estate all the way to competing up to my sixties and hopefully beyond in Triathlons and Iron Man events, all started by those lifts on dad's crossbar to school.

We were catholic and attended church at St Edmunds just up the road from our house every Sunday. We had very little money and were clearly struggling to make ends meet and yet we put money in the collection tray every week. I couldn't get my head around this as a child. We were poor but giving money to the church for other people. I remember it

21

vividly as it didn't seem to make sense to me. Sometime later when we moved to Crumpsall, I was at St Annes church and didn't put the money in the collection. I kept it. I spent the rest of the day waiting for lightning to hit me. I was sure it was going to happen and that any minute 'boom' and that would be it - but it didn't and I was still in one piece at the corner shop with my money. My mate Leo advises me now that God is just biding his time and recommends I don't go wandering near St Annes Crumpsall too often especially if there's a storm!

Life on Sawyer street in Monsall taught me to be streetwise and I became a lot more grown up for my age very quickly. The family behind us were bikers. To me they were Hells Angels with their leathers on. One night there was a fight in the street and one of the lads got hit in the face with a bike chain and his face was a mess. It was seeing things like this that made you grow up quickly. You had to be street wise to survive in an environment like that without getting into scrapes that you couldn't handle. The bikers were great with me though. I was a young daredevil on my first bike who they obviously saw as an aspiring biker flying around the streets like a nutcase. They always acknowledged me with a nod or something even though they were much older than me. Weird that, but I felt accepted by them even as a little kid. They saw something in me that they liked and I think it was my fearless approach to anything or anybody even at that age.

My last memory of Sawyer Street was my dad coming home with a stand-alone tin bath. Luxury! No more baths in the sink! It's funny the things I can still remember after the crash and I do remember vividly that tin bath. I remember my thoughts exactly at the time too. I remember that I was amazed that I could get in it from every angle. When you've been used to climbing into the sink for your bath in the same way every time

22

this was amazing to me. I paraded around that tin bath several times like I was a king and I owned the place!

By the time we moved from Sawyer Street to Cravenwood Road in Crumpsall in 1965 when I was five, my sister Olwen had arrived in the family in 1963. My mum tells me now that literally days after we moved, my dad, me and Olwen all got the mumps. Mum laughs as she recalls it. She was really worried at the time because she'd heard that Mumps could leave people with lasting disabilities. She had gone to the doctors and asked if it was true that it could make us all fertile. The doctor apparently burst out laughing and said "no not at all. There is a remote chance that it could make males 'infertile'. Well mum and dad had two more children after that and Philomena and I had four so my mum might have been right in the first place! There was three years between me and Olwen, my sister when she was born in 1963 and six years exactly between me and my brother Eamonn who was born in 1966 on my birthday. We shared the same birthday but are like chalk and cheese other than that Then in 1968. Simon our younger brother came along to complete the family. I had always try to set an example as the eldest but I guess they might challenge that because I did do some crazy things. Olwen was like a mother hen and very protective, especially of Eamonn and Simon when they were younger. I was the same with her and carried on being protective of her into her late teens and early twenties. She once complained to mum that she couldn't get a boyfriend. Mum told her not to worry and that a lad would ask her our soon. Olwen said to her "I've got loads of lads asking me out mum and some of them I'd like to go out with. That's not the problem. Its Chris! When the lads hear what my surname is they back off for fear of having to deal with Chris". If she could have changed her name by deed poll at the time, I think she would have. Olwen was clever academically too. She was really bright but struggled at exam time as she was a worrier. I notice that most qualifications nowadays incorporate course work into student's marks and qualifications. If that had been around for Olwen when she was at school she would have swept the board. She was a very independent person and not long after leaving school, she landed a job as a private secretary. Needless to say, she was much better behaved than us lads of the family. Olwen now lives in Dubai with her husband Peter and her two children, my niece Georgia and my nephew Joseph. Eamonn just has the one son, my nephew Mason, who is very similar in age to his cousin Joseph and they are great pals. Simon and his wife Sheila, who used to run a beautician's service from a unit within my shop, has two girls, my nieces Ellie and Gabby and with our four my mum proudly boasts that she has nine grandchildren with a great grandchild on the way very soon (see chapter 11 for details of that great news)

So back to my childhood. It was around 1969 when I received my next upgrade on my bike from my mum and dad and this bike was to become a legend on all streets up and down the country – The Raleigh Chopper. What kid in the late 60s and early 70's didn't want a chopper? There was the poor relative for smaller kids, 'The Raleigh Chipper' but the Chopper was the bike to have and was to be a forerunner for bikes like BMX's and kids doing amazing stunts on small bikes. As any serious bike enthusiast will tell you, owning a bike gives you a level of independence that others don't have. Even as a kid, your bike meant you could go further afield if you wished. Later in life my bikes would carry me thousands of miles in total and all over the world. I don't own a car now at aged 60 but I feel I could go anywhere I want to go on one of my bikes. Moving to Cravenwood Road in Crumpsall when I was five years old held new challenges. New neighbours, new friends, new enemies, new memories, some of which I have unfortunately lost since my accident. The ones that stick are weird though. We didn't have a television at Sawyer Street but I remember us getting one at Cravenwood Road and even the simplest thing on the box would fascinate us. For instance, I remember the Queen coming on at the end of the days television on BBC to say goodnight and the National Anthem being played. We'd rented the television, as most people did in those days, from Wilsons on Lansdowne Road. Can you imagine that nowadays? TVs are ten a penny now and you get more channels than you can cope with. Our family was quite friendly with Wilsons and I got my first record deck from there aged about eleven years old. It had a cassette and radio built into the main part which of course was a turntable. They called them music centres in those days and this one was made by a well-known company for electronics, Grundig and cost £96. I was able to tape things off the radio and off records and build up my own music collection. The system cost far more than I earned from my paper round. I had a certain amount of money saved up and my dad lent me the rest and I paid him back weekly.

Chapter 3 – A Mancunian Education

I always seemed to be in a spot of bother at School. From aged four to five I went to St Edmunds Primary School on Monsall Road. This was only a short walk up the road from where we lived. I wasn't too badly behaved but I do have a memory of wagging school (playing truant) on my own one day. On the spur of the moment in the playground I just decided that I'd been to school that day so I'd had enough and wanted to go walkabout. I just sneaked out of playground and went home. My dad was in bed as he worked permanent nights at the time because it paid more money. I can't remember where mum was but I ended up leaning against our back wall in the entry when all of sudden there was my dad just stood there in a really colourful dressing gown. I know he wouldn't have been happy because I was only about 5 years old but I can't remember any detail of what happened after that - I just remember I froze when I saw him and thinking the word 'busted'!

When we moved to Cravenwood Road in Crumpsall, I went to St Annes Primary school, also in Crumpsall and my teacher was Miss Beastie. I didn't like her one bit. Mrs Wood was one of the dinner ladies there and I didn't like her either. She had a moustache and I remember she didn't seem to like me. I always seemed to be getting the strap for talking or misbehaviour of some sort. My other overriding memory of primary school was school dinners. I absolutely hated custard and semolina and it put me off them for the rest of my life. I couldn't really avoid trouble as it seemed to follow me around but amazingly, I was never in trouble at primary school for fighting. I didn't get into that until secondary school.

Again the memories of that time are in snippets. Like the picture house on Queens Road where I went with my dad to see a dinosaur film. I hid behind the back seat of the cinema as this was the first time we'd seen anything like this and I absolutely shit myself. I'm not sure of the film. It may have been the Raquel Welch one "one Million Years BC' which came out in 1966 when I was just six years old.

I didn't have many close friends. I was a bit of a loner. I was always encouraged by my mum not to be a follower. She used to say 'never follow anyone else - make your own mind up' and that was what I was like and that's how we brought up our kids too. I did my own thing and didn't need anyone to hold my hand or be with me. If I wanted to do something I just did it. I didn't need anyone to endorse or support my ideas, I just got on with it. I didn't need support from anyone. I felt like I was a leader and not a follower or one of the sheep. There were other kids that I might call mates over the years but I wasn't close to any of therm. At Sawyer Street, there were other kids living across the road and their house backed up to railways lines. They had a garden which fascinated me as we had a back yard and in their living room they had Hornby Railways so that meant to me that they had money. I didn't get especially close to any of them and wouldn't know them if I fell over them now. At Cravenwood Road, there was one lad, Martin, who lived above a chip shop owned by his mum and dad. He was an only child and he had everything. He was the same age as me roughly and I can remember he had curly hair . What better reason to befriend someone as a kid growing up in Manchester than the fact that he lived above a chip shop that his mum and dad owned? He was not adventurous enough though so that was no good to me really. He was ok and I got on with him but he was typical of the friendships I had back then. They weren't close friends and I wasn't bothered about that. Later in life I developed some fantastic friendships but when I was in my early teens this didn't seem so important to me.

These are the random memories of my childhood but the biggest step I think at that time was the change from St Edmunds to St Annes primary school. Even though they were both primary schools, the transition from one to the other was huge for me. It went from a (ah) b (ber) and c (curly ker) to A, B and C. It was a whole new vocabulary for me and threw me off my spelling and my English education went rapidly downhill. When I went to St Annes Crumpsall primary school I was introduced to the strap, a form of punishment in schools back in the 60's and 70's. The strap at st Anne's had a nickname 'Cat of Seven Tails' This was based on the punishments given to those on ships in history who were punished by being flogged with a 'Cat 'o' nine tails" Our strap at St Anne's used by the headmaster, Mr Travers, was made of leather and had seven leather strands leading off it so we called it the 'Cat 'o' Seven Tails' and its reputation went before it. It was known to hurt a lot so the kids at the school feared it. My first introduction to it was for answering back to Miss Beastie in her English lesson. I can't remember exactly how it panned out or what I said but she reported me and I was sent to see the Headmaster the following day and he just went to a drawer in his desk and said 'get your hand out'. I didn't quibble or try to get out of it I just put my hand out. I was only nine or ten years old but I remember thinking defiantly ' just get on with it'. He hit me twice across each hand and I just stared right into his eyes and sniffed arrogantly as if it had no impression on me whatsoever. Although it hurt of course, it didn't bother me enough to even change to expression in my face. It was one of the first signs of my reluctance to conform and certainly not show any weakness to anybody. I was nine or ten years old and was already becoming, in my own mind, unbreakable in spirit.

Punishments got more severe as you got older. In secondary school I received one of the most dramatic punishments I ever suffered when I was caned in front of the whole school when I was just 12 years old. To be fair the lead up to this was pretty spectacular in itself. I was at St Andrews High School and was in the science lesson with a teacher called Mr Burke. I had I only turned to another pupil in the class to ask a question and all of a sudden the board duster hit me on the head. I reacted instantly and picked up my wooden chair and threw it back at Mr Burke. The whole class was stunned at what looked like a violent and reckless reaction from such a young pupil. I hadn't actually hit him with the chair. Even within the speed it happened I did have a split second thought of logic. In the seconds it all took to happen I had registered the fact that the board duster had hit my head, that it was Mr Burke who had thrown it, that I wanted to throw something back, that the only thing I could quickly grab was the chair then the logical thought of 'hang on if this hits him full on I could be in big trouble' so when I threw the chair I threw it very accurately to just miss him by inches and hit his desk with great force. It was close enough for him and the class to think I was aiming for him and missed which is what I wanted. Nothing happened initially other than a very quick bollocking from Mr Burke and so I thought he'd let it pass. Then the next day in assembly in front of the whole school of about five hundred pupils, the headmaster, a guy called Mr Grundy, was standing on the stage in the main hall and unexpectedly shouts out my name. 'Duoba up here please'. Although none of the kids said anything you can hear their excitement and everyone is looking at me as I walk up. You've got to remember I was only twelve years old at the time and assembly was full of eleven to sixteen year olds. The only thing that really surprised me was that I was not scared at all. The fact that all the older lads were looking at me with looks on their faces of 'what the fuck has he done' made me feel proud of myself. I don't

29

consider myself a real nutter, either then or now. I've never gone looking for trouble and I certainly have never picked on anyone who didn't deserve it in some way although I did scare myself a few times later in life and I will tell you later about those incidents. Mr Burke had thrown something at my head and the law of the land says you can defend yourself. Then of course there's the law of living in a place like Manchester where if you let people walk all over you, then get ready to be walked over some more because they will just carry on doing it. I didn't regret for one moment what I'd done, I just accepted the fact that I was going to get punished and quickly walked up and climbed the few steps to the stage. I was grateful it was Grundy as he was a weasel of a man. He looked like butter wouldn't melt in his mouth and a bit of a snide (Manchester word for someone untrustworthy and sinister). It could have been worse. It could have been Mr Mahon, the deputy head. He was a big bloke and far more powerful. Grundy looked like he particularly enjoyed dishing out punishment and inflicting pain on the kids but he was a weakling in comparison to some of the teachers. He didn't go into any great detail, he just said 'this is for your behaviour yesterday' I knew what he meant straightaway but all the kids in assembly, other than those in my class, didn't. He just said 'hold out your left hand'. I thought 'oh well at least he is going to strap the hand I don't write with'. He hit me six times (they called it six of the best) on the left hand with a wooden cane. Then immediately he said 'now your right hand' and instantly, without any hesitation whatsoever, I held out my right hand and he duly gave me six of the best on that hand too. I was proud of myself that I didn't flinch one bit. I just took it. It hurt alright but again I felt I could handle it. I'm 12 years old and I'm now realising that pain is something that isn't nice but it's not something I need to fear, as I can switch off from it. Having said that, I couldn't hold my pen all day and going for a wee was an interesting challenge.

When I first went to St Andrews High School which we referred to initially as 'big school', I didn't really know anybody. I had failed my '11 plus' which was the examination all primary school 10/11 year olds went through to help decide what secondary school they could go to. I had suffered greatly with the transition from St Edmonds to st Anne's and it had set me back educationally and that had carried through to my 11 plus so I failed it. I remember my dad saying to me around the time that 'you're that thick you won't even become a bin man'. This was in the days that Bin Men carried the metal bins on their shoulders to the cart and emptied them. There were no bin liners so the bins used to stink and bits could fall out if they were too full. With the greatest respect to the lads that were bin men in the 70's, It was a rotten job that people thought was a low level job. Now the job is super-efficient and the lads who do the work leg it from one wheely bin to the next to the next and I get the impression that they might even be 'job and finish' (when you've done your work you go home). My dad intended it as an insult though, saying that I wasn't studying hard enough at school. He had a point though and he was right about how many qualifications I would get as I left school with no formal qualifications. However, I was proud that I was the only pupil in the school that Mr McGee, the woodwork teacher, trusted with the key to the woodwork room and all the machinery as I was that good at carpentry because I enjoyed it that much. Mr McGee was someone you didn't want to get punished by. He made his own canes and they were designed to make an impression on you in more ways than one. All that said about qualifications I was so happy that my dad got to see me in later life become a business owner and make something of myself. I remember the day I bought the business and I told him. It was so satisfying that he knew I'd surpassed his expectations of me. After the crash, which we will talk about later, I was offered money to settle for

31

my injuries, which I took. They gave me the money because they said that I would permanently have limitations due to my injuries. I took the money but eventually I proved them wrong too. Limitations? What limitations? I've done more physically in my life than most people would ever think about doing.

Thinking back to attending St Andrews, going there and back every day had its challenges too. I lived in Crumpsall and St Andrews was in Higher Broughton. To get there and back using the quickest route would mean that I would have to run a gauntlet every day between the housing estate and the Jolly Roger Chippy. I came close a few times but I never got into an altercation with the gangs from the housing estate. Now and again it meant that I was being chased by groups of lads. I enjoyed the challenge and the jeopardy of having to face groups of lads if they caught me. It never happened though as I was always too quick for them and had the stamina to outrun them at a pace. As much as this might sound crazy, they didn't realise it but they were lucky that they didn't catch me. I had already planned what I would have to do to the first lad to try and put the others off. The only thing that frightened me at the time was the fact that I didn't seem to dread them catching me. I was comfortable either way but thank goodness I was competitive enough to outrun them every time.

Back to punishments at school and in the Science lab on the top floor at St Andrews, Mr Lawrence, who was a big bloke, didn't use a cane or a strap. He had a cricket bat instead. One day I was in the science lab and saw a plastic tupperware container on the windowsill. I went over to it and opened it to see what was in it. As I lifted the lid, what appeared to be millions of flies flew out. The container had maggots in and Mr Lawrence had it there to show how they turn into flies. There they were

32

flying around the science lab as I jumped over tables to avoid Mr Lawrence hitting me with his cricket bat. It was like a scene out of a comedy.

One of our teachers, Mr Nono, played basketball for Manchester Giants. He was our PE teacher. Can you believe that I, as a person who would go on to be an extreme athlete, did everything within my power to avoid doing PE at school! I invented letters from home, I deliberately forgot my kit and all sorts to get out of doing it. I didn't mind the punishments they dished out either as I hated PE with a passion. One PE teacher used to get a size 15 trainer out and make you bend over while he smacked you across the arse with it. You could tell any kid that had been punished in this way, they had a massive imprint of a size 15 foot across their arse all day. To me it was well worth it to get out of PE. Having said all of that when it came to sports day, I was having some of that. I loved it when it became immediately competitive and there was an edge to it. I did the javelin and ended up throwing the second furthest distance in the school. Not bad for someone that never really practiced. I also did high jump, long jump and the 100 metres. From school sports day I competed in the 100 metres for the school against other schools at various venues including taking part in a schools finals day. I ran just under 12 seconds that day in a stadium near Altrincham. I came second to a black lad who was incredibly fast and smashed me and all the rest of the field. He must have run close to sub 11 seconds that day and we were only about 14 years old. I checked all this out recently in case I was remembering it wrong but in 2019, the fastest 14 year old in the UK ran 11.04 and the kid I raced that day was super fast. I look back and find it strange now that I did hate PE but loved competing in the sports that PE covered. What's more is that I wasn't competing for trophies or for any of the spoils. It was purely the adrenaline of competing that was the buzz. I

33

found out sometime later that I got this from my mum's side of the family. My uncle Joe Ross was apparently an amazing athlete and was a track runner and did lots of different sports but did not enjoy the limelight. I'll tell you more about Joe later in the book as he was an amazing character and it was no accident that the both of us in different timelines had the drive to compete but not for the spoils, just purely for the competition itself.

I was stubborn too and wouldn't let people get the better of me. Coming out of science lab one day after lesson a lad called Alan Mitchell punched me in the back of head. Alan was second 'cock of the school'. For those that don't know what this means, Cock of the school is the hardest lad in the school and someone you didn't mess with if you could help it, or did mess with if you fancied a few days off school. That was Paul Delaney who was one big bastard. Second Cock, Alan Mitchell, was not far behind so you don't normally mess with him either. As he went past me after punching me, I hit him in the back of his head too. As I did it, Mr Lawrence came out and grabbed me. He hadn't seen Mitchell punch me. He gave me a bit of talking to and then sent me on my way. As I followed the whole class out into the playground it was like a scene from a biblical epic. The playground full of 400 to 500 kids parted like the Red sea parted for Moses and opened up this path for me to walk through. I just thought 'what's going on here?' And then I see Mitchell waiting for me at the end of the parted pathway. I think 'fucking hell - shit'. I had no real choice so I thought 'well here we go' and I ended up just walking up to him and starting fighting. We fought for a few minutes and ended up over near the cookery room windows which were at ground level. As we carried on fighting, I was punching him and all of a sudden his younger brother, Brian Mitchell, came steaming in. The momentum of Brian steaming in carried us towards the cookery room windows and like some kind of magician's act, Alan disappeared. One of the windows had been left slightly open on a swivel and Alan had gone straight through it. I ended up fighting his younger brother and then it got broken up by teaching staff. From that moment on I became the recognised second Cock of the school which I wasn't the slightest bit interested in. That said, if anyone wanted to start trouble with me my aim always was to finish it.

What I was more interested in was my attitude to the pain I experienced during fighting. I didn't feel it. It wasn't playing on my mind at all.   I was giving this more and more thought as I developed new experiences of it. I come to realise that when I was being competitive, I switched off to pain. I didn't know why this was happening but it was a genetic gift I had always had. When I was about 14 when we lived on Cravenwood Road, my dad had a Black and Decker metal disc sander. He had a piece of wood that he wanted to sand down using his sander and he asked me to put my foot on it to hold it. He was busy sanding it down and the next thing we know he's hit a knot and the sander came up and hit my left knee. Out of the corner of my eye I saw a chunk of flesh from my knee fly past. My dad only faints and is on the floor and I'm left holding on to my knee to stem the blood. I just calmly shout my mum. There's blood squirting all over the place and I'm trying to hold it back and mum comes and shouts Ralph who is the only neighbour who had a car. She came in with a towel and wrapped at around my knee. I said 'just get me a plaster, it'll be alright'. Ralph got us to the hospital and it needed 14 stitches. I remember when we arrived at Booth Hall that time one of the staff just said 'Hi Chris' because they knew me so well. A nurse tried to administer a local   anesthetic so they could stitch it and the needle was bending because she just kept hitting bone as the injury was around my kneecap. I just said 'Nurse - forget the needle just stitch it' and so they did. I'm looking at the scar now and can close my eyes and can see the nurses face when she was running out of needles. If I could have carried on regardless of an injury like that, I would do but clearly some injuries would still stop me doing things as it would 'normal' people because for example, if I let something bleed out then I might pass out, if I walked on a broken ankle it would give way. What I am saying here is that just being able to resist pain doesn't make you invincible but it does make you a strong competitor in a physical challenge of any nature. The trick would be not to take it so far that it became reckless.

My first experience of real recklessness was when I diced with death when I lived on Cravenwood Road in Crumpsall. As most kids do, we got up to mischief and living near Railway tracks was always going to be a recipe for something dangerous for someone like me who loved a challenge. When we were about ten years old, a few of us, myself and two kids called John and Ralph, used to play chicken with the trains. The competitor in me meant that I always had to win. That meant standing on the tracks the longest as the train was hurtling towards you and being the last to jump out of the way. One day I'd left it that late that I'd only just made it. The train missed me by inches and as it screamed by behind me, I felt someone physically pulling me back into the trains path. I shit myself. I can only describe it by saying that I was trying to run away and something was pulling me back towards the train and then as the train completely passed they let me go and I fell forward. I now realise that what was pulling me back was the suction of air from the train as it sped by. I was so close to the train that I was caught in the airflow. It was far too close for comfort and I could have easily lost my life. But I won!

Chapter 4 – The Crank Versus Jean Claude Van Damme

There's no doubt that I've always been a little unstable. My accident in later life made things worse but people who know me say to me that from an early age I'd always been a 'not right' and that my wiring in my head was already a bit tangled. My Dad summed it up well. He had always said that I was a 'Crank'. It was his affectionate way of describing my unusual behavior growing up and my behavior was very unusual. I sympathise greatly with anyone with mental health issues. In my life, I have been to the depths of despair and have been lucky enough to have experienced some of the massive highs of life like getting married and having children. That scale is a ridiculously slippy path. You can fall so easily towards despair if you are that way inclined and those people that do, I have a lot of time for. They deserve speedy assistance because the path back is still within sight and all people have to know in many cases is how to deal with these bouts of mental health and who is there to support you to get you back in a place that's OK. If you have never had a mental health issue then you will be looking at this book with that look on your face like "what the chuff is he on about?" Those who have had mental health issues will know precisely what I am talking about. It's the first time it happens to you that is the killer as it is so unnerving and you feel it must be irreversible but it isn't. Anyone that might be reading this book who is unsure about that, please know this. You can be ok! Just accept some help and take it from someone who knows, you won't believe this now but it will be OK.

I'll be talking about my dark times later but for now I'll admit that I had a screw loose from birth. I don't quite know whether our Olwen, Eamonn and Simon found it exciting or crazy or even frightening living with me. Our house on Cravenwood Road only had three bedrooms, so mum and dad had one, Olwen, my sister, another and all us boys in the third bedroom. I was in a single bed in the room as the eldest and they were in bunk beds with Eamonn in the bottom bunk. One night I went to the bedroom an hour before they would have to go to bed. It sounds unhinged now but it seemed like a right hoot at the time for me to lie under the bottom bunk so they couldn't see me and in my hand was a live wire. I had a plug with a wire coming out of it, probably for a radio or something, and I'd cut it with scissors so that I had live bare wires at the end of it then plugged it in to the socket. They came up and both went to bed. After a few moments of them chatting, which included them talking about not seeing me for a while, I put the bare end of the wire to the metal base of the bottom bunk. Fucking hell - all hell broke loose. Eamonn goes into spasm and his right leg shoots upright and kicks Simon clear out of the bed and he comes flying down onto the floor. The noise of the shouting and bang as he hits the floor brings my dad racing up the stairs. I jump into my bed and as dad comes in the room I sit up and say 'will you two stop messing about I'm trying to get an early night here'. Dad gives them both a crack for messing about.

It gets worse though. The bare end wire trick starts to get extended to my friends. One of my best mates is John Hughes who lived in moss bank. Our mates tended to come to our house rather than the other way around. I'm guessing that's because their mums and dads had been warned about my pranks. John arrived at our house and he gets sent by my mum up to where I am in my room. As soon he walks in I say "will you hold this for me mate?" and he's just grabbed the live wire. I didn't realise that he would just grab it but lucky for him it throws him back and he lets go of it. I am in fits of laughter and he's just sat there wondering what the fuck has just happened. I was nicknamed 'loose wire' by John not just because I had played this trick on people but because I definitely had at least one loose wire myself.

If Simon and Eamonn thought I was a crank then they gave me a fair bit of competition. I don't remember how old Simon was at the time but he was only a kid and he had a bow and arrow. Now it wasn't Olympic standard but it wasn't a sticky end one either. It was a big bow and it shot makeshift arrows that could stick in. One day a kid on the street said to Simon "I bet you won't shoot your Eamonn with your bow and arrow". Simon wasn't going to lose any bet so he immediately turned and fired an arrow into Eamonn's chest. Eamonn simply pulled the arrow out and said to the local kid "you lost your bet". It all happened in a few seconds but it was hilarious. Luckily Eamonn wasn't really hurt so it must have only just gone through his clothes and into his skin.

Our house on Cravenwood Road faced other houses which were more than 150 yards away so it felt quite private not being overlooked, or so I thought. I was about 16 or 17 years old and my mum comes home one day and tells me that the woman facing us has complained that I walk past the window naked from the bathroom. She's fucking 150 yards away. She'd have to be watching with bleeding binoculars to see me. So the next time I'm coming out of the bathroom stark bollock naked I help her out. I jumped up on the windowsill and stood legs apart like a Sumo wrestler does facing out to her house and waving. I thought 'get a load of this, you nosy cow" There were no more complaints as far as I am aware!

I hope my mum and Anne next door will see the funny side of this but also on Cravenwood, when I was about 16 or 17, I did have one romantic encounter with my next door neighbours' daughter Denise. I fancied her and thought she might fancy me. One day we found ourselves in my house on our own and one thing led to another and we were kissing when all of a sudden there's the sound of a key in the front door. Denise and I straighten ourselves out as we bomb into the kitchen. It's the only thing I can think of so I open the fridge door and grab a bottle of milk and shove it in Denise's hand. As my mum walks in I say "hiya mum, Denise came to borrow some milk". Denise says "yeah thanks Mrs Duoba" and toddles off to her own house. Phew I think, that was a close one. About ten seconds pass and mum opens the fridge door as she's making a brew and says "we don't have any milk!" She turns to me with that knowing look a mum can give you and says "Will you nip next door son and see if Anne will borrow us some milk?" Busted or what? Especially when Anne next door gave me a bottle and said "funny that, our Denise has just brought a bottle in and we've got loads!!"

When Simon was 10 and Eamonn was 11, Dad made a go kart for us which had Silver Cross Pram wheels. Silver cross was like the Rolls Royce of prams and having Silver Cross wheels on your go kart meant speed and a smooth ride. The mechanism for steering was by putting both your feet on the piece of wood that had the front wheels on and it was fastened on with a bolt that allowed you to steer left by pushing with your right foot and so forth. We lived on a hill that bent to the right at the bottom. One evening Eamonn and Simon were going down the hill on the kart and as they hit the bend they must have been doing 20-25 miles per hour and all of a sudden there's a tramp walking past. They hit him from behind and the tramp was launched into the air head over heels and hit the ground really hard. We were all laughing our heads off and he sprung to his feet and goes for them. I grab a massive car tyre out of our garden which my dad was going to make into a plant holder and I run towards the tramp and I throw it over his head so his arms are trapped by his side and I pushed him over. He starts to roll down the hill and we legged it. Teach him to mess with us. Please believe me when I tell you I am not making this shit up. Incidents like this were every day for us. It was like we were the real life version of something out of 'The Beano' or 'The Dandy' and I guess that's where we got most of the ideas from for our bad behaviour. Having three young lads in the house, things got broke. I lost count of how many windows or glass ornaments that we broke over the years. We had a kitchen door where the bottom panel of the door was made of glass. This may sound like an exaggeration but it is my mum that counted that it was 48 times it had been fixed or replaced because it was cracked or had broken completely. With it being a bottom panel it could have been football, marbles or just throwing things at each other that might crack the window or put it through. Mum got absolutely fed up of it and announced one day that the next person to break a window would be leaving home. After all the years of me. Simon and Eamonn smashing that door, It was my sister, Olwen, who was only 13 years old at the time and wearing some wedge type shoes, that simply bent down to do something and her back foot banged against the glass and broke it. Well you can imagine what us three lads made of that. I was the first to say 'Ooooooooooh Olwen, you'd better pack your bags and then let me know when you've finished because I'm having your room'. Olwen seemed to just accept it and packed her bag and wrote a note for mum (who was out at the time) and left. Like the caring brother I was, I quickly got my stuff and moved into her room. We were amazed at how she'd accepted it and just gone very quickly. All three of us were asking each other "where's she going to go?' The first mum heard about it was when Dad turned up at Connellys at 8.00pm, an hour before mum's shift was due to finish. When he walked in, Mum said "What are you doing here?" Dad blurted out "Olwen's left home. Look, she left a letter". The letter simply said "I'm sorry Mum. I've broken the glass in the kitchen door and I know I have to move out so I've left home. Love Olwen xxx. PS Chris said he want's my room". Mum said it was heart breaking to read and she knew that we'd had a hand in it. Although Dad didn't have a clue what to do, Mum knew straightaway as she remembered that Olwen had told her that there was a trip organized for that evening by The Brownies group that Olwen went to. The group was being taken to Blackley Fire Station for a talk about Fire Safety. Mum and Dad went straight there and as Mum walked in, there was Olwen sat listening with the group. Mum took her out of the talk and told her she wasn't in any trouble and that she hadn't issued the ultimatum to her, it was to us three brothers. Mum also let me know in no uncertain terms that Olwen was to get her room back immediately. Can't blame a lad for trying Can you?

I'll cover my working life as a Barber a little later on but as I settled in to my first year of work on the princely sum of £6 per week, I got a little too comfortable earning my money and getting into a routine of doing my job and drinking beer in the Belmont pub and doing very little else. Then one night I am in the Belmont having a beer playing pool as usual and I saw a side view of me in a mirror. I had the start of a beer belly. 'fucking hell" I said out loud. I've got a beer belly and I'm still seventeen years old. I got hold of my pint, drank it and then walked out and got home said to my dad 'Dad I need to get a hi fi, not just a normal hi fi, a proper music system'. I asked him to meet me at a shop called Zeniths in Cheetham Hill precinct the next day. The music system I wanted was a Panasonic. It's got a turntable, a cassette deck and an amplifier and glass cabinet for your LPs and it cost £400. Bearing in mind this was 1977 and I was on £6 per week, my dad got it on hire purchase for me. I couldn't get it, given that I'd worked less than a year and I was only on £6 per week but he could because he had a steady job at Connellys in Blackley. I gave him back £1 per week. As we completed the purchase in Zeniths, the guy that sold it to us said to me 'You do realise son, you are hooked on music for the rest of your life with this?' He was right too. The unit was out of this world for its time and had great sound both through the speakers and through headphones which I used most of the time. Music became important to me and I used it to either train to or relax to. I built up my music collection using the cassette tape recorder and listening to our new local station as it was back in the 70's, Piccadilly Radio. Piccadilly was a fantastic Manchester based radio station playing a wide range of brilliant music and had proper presenters, many of which went on to bigger and better things and some of whom I still listen to now. The likes of Andy Peebles, Gary Davies, Chris Evans and Timmy Mallett passed through Piccadilly Radio in their early years and DJ's I still listen to today like Mike Sweeney and Becky Want who work for the BBC now as presenters, I have seen live doing their thing back in the day. I saw Becky Want when she was a DJ at 'Carriages' in Droyslden which was a Nightclub and Becky may well have been playing the music on the night I met my Mrs there. I saw Mike Sweeney along with his band The Salford Jets on the opening night of a pub/ restaurant in Rochdale but that night didn't start too well for me and I hope Sweeney didn't notice what was happening. My sister, Olwen, worked for Whitegate taverns at the time as a private secretary to one of the directors. We were invited to the opening of one of their pubs and went along to have a meal before The Salford Jets took the stage. My eyes were bigger than my belly as they say and I was even picking at other people's food as well as my own. We then go down into what is really a big ballroom with a bar and we are sat in the middle of this room of round tables. I've got a pint in front of me and I take one swig of the drink and I all of a sudden have this almighty feeling of needing to be sick. It's not like I'm getting a two minute warning or anything like that so that I can make my way calmly to the toilets or even leg it very quickly to the toilets. I'm going to be sick and I am going to be sick now!! I stood up and put my hand to my mouth in a futile attempt to try and make it outside the ballroom but as soon as I stood up I spewed all over trying to hold it in as kit sprayed through my fingers. It was bloody awful. I wish I could tell you that nobody noticed but what had happened as soon as I stood, the people in the tables around me realised what was happening, so they had also stood and scattered away and it looked to me like people were backed against the walls of the ballroom. It was all over in seconds and I immediately went to the bar and got paper towels to clean things up. As I started the clean up process and people started to get back to their seats, the announcer shouted 'please welcome The Salford Jets" and Mike Sweeney came running on and things returned to a form of normal. I wonder if Mike knows that his warm-up act that night was me? Having said all of that about Piccadilly Radio back in the 70's, that is not the main connection with myself. The DJ that had such a profound effect on me and my music tastes was a guy called Mike Shaft. I remember listening to Mike's show and the soul music he played and thinking that was the music for me. One night I was listening to Mike's show on my headphones and he was playing a track from the band Earth, Wind and Fire. All of a sudden I could hear Donna summer in an extended version of 'I feel love" and he is mixing the two tracks. I thought I was having a stroke or something. I could hear two different tracks on each side of my head on the headphones. What's going on here I thought. When I realised it was Mike deliberately mixing the tracks I thought wow this is unbelievable. It's the first time I'd heard anything like that before and I thought Mike Shaft was a genius. The style was revolutionary and still has a place in today's music mash ups. Mike's show was on a Saturday night at the time so my Hi fi was doing exactly what I had bought for. Instead of being out boozing on a Saturday night adding to my beer belly, I was training and listening to Mike's show. My love of music was motivating me in many ways and I was enjoying getting fitter and fitter every week. I started studying martial arts and trained every night. I went from doing nothing to running, stretching and doing Shotika martial arts at Ardwick. I built the training up that much that on a typical weekday, one of my early morning runs was up Cravenwood Road where we lived, up past The Edgerton arms, down to Woolworths on Cheetham Hill Road, right up to the Half Way House pub, then down Middleton road to Blackley New Road and then along there, past The Millstone pub and start to go up to Delaunays Road. About halfway up there I would pass my Dad walking home after finishing his night shift at Connellys at 6.00am. As I ran past him I'd shout 'Morning Dad'. Without fail he would always respond with the shout 'You're a bloody crank son' There was a reason he would say that. Not because I was out running before 6am in the morning. He'd call me a crank because I was running in my bare feet. He'd be walking home and he'd see me doing that run every morning in bare feet. By the time I'd arrived back at Cravenwood road, I'd run about 6 miles (10K). When I got home I would stand in the garden in a bowl of my own piss to harden my feet up. When Dad walked in past me he just said ' You're off the bloody scale you are'. I had read somewhere that to make your feet tough, you needed to do more with them barefoot to harden the skin and that treating them with your own urine would also make the skin of the sole of your feet tougher. I'd shower and then cycle to work and then do a day's work as a barber on my feet all day and cycle home. My training was getting extreme to say the least. I had to keep challenging myself and was always looking to get better and better either by making things harder for myself or doing things faster. I'd do things like putting a wooden sleeper up and punching it then when that became easy I'd start punching a brick wall. I was toughening up the nerve endings so

45

that it didn't hurt anymore. A lot of kick boxers do it with their shins. I'd do sit ups and press ups for fun and all while I was listening to my music. Talking about it now makes it sound like I was a bit loopy even at that stage of my life but at the time it all made sense to me to be training like this. I just didn't do things by halves. I had to go all in or nothing with everything I did. Little did I know that the level of fitness I was achieving would eventually go a long way to saving my life.

My idol as I hit my teens was Bruce Lee so I got very interested in Martial Arts. I heard about a Shotokan class at Ardwick. Shotokan is a form of Karata that focuses as much on the mental side of things and the discipline as it does on the physical side. It was long way to go and one lesson per week didn't seem enough for me so I practiced at home a lot. I took it very seriously and did lots of exercises and disciplines at home as well as in the classes. My two brothers Eamonn and Simon were happy to assist me for money. Initially they did it for nothing. They would hold a foam pad to their chest and I would do sidekicks and launch them into the air. I was 17 and they were 11 (Eamonn) and 10 (Simon) and they took it well and appeared to be enjoying it, although to be fair, you'd have to ask them. I'm saying to them 'come on another one' and they are just lining up for another one. Mum's not there, she's at work and I'm in charge which was probably not a good thing. After a while they are getting wise to what's in store for them and like mini businessmen they come out of their two man boardroom meeting and tell me that they want 10p each to do it. So a negotiation takes place and I say to them "If either of you can drop me I'll give you 10p each" I've hardly got the word 'each' out of my mouth and I'm on the floor looking up at the ceiling. Simon, who is the youngest has clobbered me over the head with a full bottle of Milk. The bottle was behind his back during the negotiations and he let me have it. The bottle smashed and there's milk all over the carpet and blood gushing out of gash above my eye into the milk . I've grabbed him to give him a suitable clout and he's struggling to get out of my grip of him and all he kept shouting is 'Where's me 10p?' I still have the scar today above my eye and a chipped bone next to my eyebrow that feels sharp to the touch. Brotherly love!! We took boisterous to whole new level. I can still hear him now 'Where's me 10p?' I might have looked angry at the time but I was thinking in my head, good for you Simon, putting me on my arse. I love the fact that he came into a negotiation for money with a bottle of milk as his weapon of choice. And I'm the Crank?!

Years later, when Simon himself was about 16 years old, he was working as a shopfitter. We had a dog called Benson who was a Rottweiler and was as solid as they come. He was huge and must have weighed 13 or 14 stone. At the side of where we lived there was a Croft. Simon had come home wearing a parka and I was in the garden with Benson. One of the things we would do regularly would be that Simon would run into the field with his parka on over his head like a robber and I would unleash Benson just like they do in the Police dogs training to take a perpetrator down. Benson runs like the wind after Simon and pulls him to the deck and they are wrestling which was part of the fun for the dog. If it was a burglar, Benson would have ripped them to shreds but this was Simon and he was playing. On one particular night there was a cop car with two coppers in going past the house and the two coppers saw the dog take Simon down and start wrestling. They thought it was a mad dog attacking a member of the public and shouted "don't worry son we've radioed for help' - I'm in the garden pissing myself laughing. The coppers were scared stiff and wouldn't get out of their car and go and help him and just kept shouting words of encouragement to him. As

47

Simon gets up and the dog follows him into the house the coppers shout 'you're fucking mad you lot'.

Once I had got into martial arts I loved it. I loved the discipline it was giving me but I had difficulty progressing through the various belts because I had started work full time by then and that involved working Saturdays and that was when the belts were completed and awarded. I knew where I was though and was on track towards a Black Belt eventually. One evening, I was at the Shotokan class at Ardwick and when we got there we realised there was to be an event that evening instead of the lesson itself. Some guests had turned up from another club and the idea was that you will spar with someone from the other club. I got myself ready and spotted this guy about my height and who looked a lot like John Lennon. To be honest he didn't look like he was up to much so I went over to him and said 'you and me sparring?' He seemed unbothered and said ok. So we found a bit of space as there are now a good few pairs starting to spar. I had been practicing my roundhouse kicks which I'd started to master and I figured that one of these would give this guy a proper wake up call. I positioned myself perfectly and executed the roundhouse kick towards the side of his head. All of a sudden I felt someone from behind slap me on the side of the face. I turned around and said "be careful' to the other people behind me as I thought they had hit me by accident. Ahead of me John Lennon hadn't moved at all. It happened a second time and as I tried the roundhouse, the guy behind me slapped me again. This time I turned around annoyed but the two blokes behind us were a good distance away now. It suddenly dawned on me that John Lennon had done it. He was so quick he was like fucking lightening. Then out of nowhere - bang! I didn't see the kick coming I only felt it. The pain in my solar plexus was like no other I have felt before and I am on my arse and I am done. I can't hardly

48

breath. Our master comes over and starts to help me up and as he does so I see John Lennon go over to his bag and get something out of his bag I see 'GB coach' on the side of it. He then puts on his black belt with four red stripes on which means he is a black belt fourth dan. It was a great lesson to me. Never judge a book by its cover as they say. It was around this time that I thought if I was ever lucky enough to have children, I would make it a compulsory part of their upbringing to introduce them to martial arts and the good discipline it brought with it.

Another thing that came out of the bout with John Lennon was that he had asked me where I was from. When I'd said Crumpsall, he asked me why I didn't go to the Abraham Moss club. I hadn't realised that there was a Shotokan class at Abraham Moss which was literally around the corner from where I live. I went and joined almost immediately and started attending lessons there twice a week. Soon after, I was participating in a last man standing Martial Arts competition being held in Abraham Moss Hall. The participants were to be whittled down from thirty contestants down to the last two. We paired up with somebody of the same size and at the start of each contest you would face your opponent and bow and then start to fight. At the time I was winning bouts by simply getting into a start position where I would go straight into a head-butt into my opponent's solar plexus and that would weaken them straight away. I went through each round doing just that, I was winning all my bouts and reached the final. At the final I faced my opponent and one of the masters stepped in. He'd seen what I had been doing and asked my opponent to step aside and he gets in front of me. I suspect he knows what I am going to do but I do it anyway. He immediately gets me in a head lock. Now we are fighting on the floor and I am conscious of the fact that he is a master. I got him pinned down with my feet on his body and his arm in a submission position very close to the wall. I think to myself 'I've got you now you bastard' and at that moment he bites my testicles. I'm not just talking about a nip. I am talking about a full bite and I jumped up making a noise that I had never heard come out of my mouth before. What are you supposed to do when faced with that? There is nothing that you can do. He has won and I had to accept that. He is the master remember so he knows how to win a competition. This was a Thursday evening. The Sunday came and I went back down to Abraham Moss and he is there with his arm in plaster. What I didn't realise was that as I jumped up from his bite, already having him in a submission position with his arm, I've jerked up and the movement had broken his wrist. I didn't notice him nursing his arm as I was too busy nursing my two friends.

One of the highlights of my time in martial arts came along purely by chance when I was still recovering from the incident when I was bitten. A few weeks later, John Drogan, who was the organiser, picked twelve of us to attend a special exhibition session. We were told that a world champion at Shotokan was visiting us to give an exhibition for us. These two guys turn up and one is a world champ at his weight and the other guy, we were told, was the guy that he beat to be world champ. I think the second guy was an Australian and I can't remember his name but the world champ was a complete unknown to us called Jean Claude Van Damme.

We were in this big room like a school gym with a wooden floor and there was the twelve of us in our karate suits and these two guys. We all had to introduce ourselves and are lined up facing the two visitors. Next thing I know Van Damme drops down on the floor by doing the splits facing us. He's not doing the splits by putting one leg forward and the other leg behind him, he does it with his left leg going to his left side and his right leg going to his right side like he does on the Coors adverts now with his feet turned upwards. He didn't just go onto the position gently either. He hits the floor with a massive thud and the floor vibrates. We are all shocked and think he has just voluntarily crushed his testicles because we'd never seen anything like this before. It looks impossible to do this. He hasn't even warmed up that I've seen. He's just sat there looking at us and I cannot get my head around it and I'm starting to panic now and the thought that enters my head is 'He surely doesn't fucking want us to do that does he?' I'm already nursing my mates downstairs to full health again, they won't take that kind of abuse' I can just about do the splits with a good warm up but no way can I do what he's just done. After that I can only remember that he made us all lie down on our backs about two feet apart and then so that your elbows couldn't touch the next person. He had our legs straight out and our toes pointed back towards our face and our feet about six inches off the deck. He said 'I just want you all to focus on something'. Now this is about 40 years ago and I can still see the single brick in the wall that I had focused my mind on. So there we were, the 12 of us lined up on the floor, fairly close next to each other with our legs straight and six inches off the floor and our stomachs taking the strain and very tight. What we didn't expect was for him to run across us using our tense stomachs as stepping stones and fairly quickly too. As he stepped on to our stomachs your legs shoot into the air and then come back down and hit the floor. And as he's running across he says I'm not stopping until you can all hold your feet 6 inches off the floor and he kept running across us.- it seemed impossible but with the group willpower and the focus distracting us from any discomfort, I can't remember how many times it took but we eventually did it and the sense of achievement from the team created a brilliant atmosphere.

We followed that up with a sparring session and as I was one of the tallest in the group, I was initially lined up against the Aussie guy. He proceeds to kick the shit out of me. I couldn't get near him as he was so quick and he took full advantage of the situation. He's taking a liberty really as he is world runner up in his discipline and I'm an amateur from Crumpsall but I keep trying nevertheless. Next thing I know, Jean Claude Van Damme stops things. We stand back and he calls the Aussie guy towards him. We think they are going to show us some more exhibition stuff and in a way he does. It's an exhibition of how to make sure a guy gets his comeuppance as he proceeds to show all his best moves on the Aussie guy. At one time he knocks him to the floor and almost knocked him out. At the end of this little session Van Damme winks at me. I took it that he's acknowledging that the Aussie guy took advantage of me so he's put him in his place. After the session is over we all head to the bar that is upstairs in Abraham Moss and my stomach is hurting like mad, not through the kicks but through the training. At one time in my life I've been capable of doing 500 crunches or 500 sit ups before I went to bed but at this time I've not done less than half of that probably as low as 100 and it's had its effect on me. We are having an orange juice and Van Damme is telling me where he is from in Belgium and all about his background. He told us that he initially trained as a ballerina as his mother had him at dance classes and then he progressed into martial arts later but that is why he is so supple. Many years later I saw him in what I think was his first film 'Blood sport'. I don't think I registered it was him at first but then he was in a scene as a solder in a fight to the death and all of a sudden he drops into the box splits and I realised it was him. He obviously looks different as an actor now and I can only go off how he conducted himself that one day and a half hour chat in the bar but I can tell you he was a really nice bloke when we met him.

52

Chapter 5 – Work and a Second Father

I was planning to leave school when I reached 16. During the last year at St Andrews High School in Cheetham Hill, we had a Careers Officer. The Careers Officer was actually our History teacher too. When I was fifteen and just about to break for the summer holidays before my final year, The Careers Officer started talking to us for the first time about potential jobs and he handed out a piece of paper that was a tick box form with lots of career choices on it. You were supposed to put your name on the form and tick the jobs/ careers that you might be interested in pursuing. I remember it like it was yesterday. I ticked the box next to 'Carpenter' as that was something that I'd always been interested in and felt that I was good at. I just liked the idea of working with wood and making things out of the different types of wood. I felt that was the only calling I had, if you could call it that and as I said earlier, I was the only pupil in the school who had the key to the Woodwork Room so Mr McGee, the Woodwork teacher, rated me in the subject. As I ticked it as my choice I noticed the title of 'Hairdresser' below it. Now I am keen to stress that I am not homophobic in any way but being a jack the lad in those days and a bit rebellious, I wrote across the box next to Hairdresser "Puff's job' and we handed the forms in. Yeah I know. How daft? But how ironic? Not just in relation to the career I ended up pursuing but also because both my Grandad Walter and mum Alma both cut hair for the family but my Gran, Margaret, put a block on them pursuing it as a career for some reason.

During the summer holidays before my final year at school, all I heard about was how Formica was replacing wood for cabinets. The amount of times that I heard that this fantastic new wipe clean product would mean no more varnished wood was worrying me. It seemed to me that being a carpenter as a trade was going to be extinct eventually which would mean no apprenticeships and possibly more factory jobs mass producing Formica. I didn't want a factory job. There was no chance of that. I wanted to make tables and chairs and things like that. There was no way I was going to be working next to a conveyor belt. Around that time I was going for my haircut in Cheetham Hill precinct at a place called 'The Modern'. It was called 'The Modern' because they had a men's barber shop downstairs and a women's hairdressers upstairs. This was the first signs that I had seen of a Unisex salon and why they called it 'The Modern'.

The Jewish guy that ran 'The Modern' was called Hymie Goole. My decision to go there to have my haircut one day when I was 15 was to map the rest of my life out. I asked Hymie whether there was any chance of a Saturday job sweeping up hair and that sort of thing. Amazingly he said yes straightaway but then told me that they were about to move premises because they'd been served a compulsory purchase order by Tesco. They had decided to move to somewhere much smaller on Middleton Road and were buying a place called 'Louie's'. He said I could start work there as soon as they moved in and could work after school and on Saturdays. I took the job and the following year when it came to leaving school they gave me an apprenticeship. Just before we left school, our careers teacher asked the class if anyone had secured work yet. Those that had, put their hands up. I was reluctant to put my hand up as I suspected what was coming. In the end I thought 'Fuck it' and was one of the last to put my hand up. As soon as he saw my hand, he came straight to me and said 'Yes Duoba. So you've got a job. Tell the class what you will be doing. He was doing exactly what I thought he would do. I said 'A barber sir'. There was a little pause and then in front of the class of about thirty pupils he said 'Oh then you're a puff then Duoba?' "No sir - I'm a barber' I say. 'You're a hairdresser' he says. 'That means that you're a puff son'. He's paying me back for what I put on the form being a smart arse almost a year before. He keeps at it too and I'm saying 'No sir, I'm a barber' and he's saying 'oh no you're a hairdresser and a puff.' I can't count the amount of times over the early years of my career as a barber that I've chased people down Middleton Road and battered them for shouting into the shop and calling me a 'Puff' or other homophobic names because I'm a barber. It shows you though, how your attitude can change with a bit of education. How much I had learned in that last year at school. It was a lesson I never forgot. I have a much more open approach now to meeting people from all walks of life and take people as I find them and don't pre-judge them. Back in our teens, the world was a different place and we said and did different things that looking back were offensive and discriminatory but most of us have woken up now. I'm very happy to have a wide cross sections of friends and customers that show just how diverse a city Manchester is and I like it that way. So I left school and went full time as a trainee barber. Initially I didn't enjoy it at all. In fact I hated it and I was convinced I'd made the wrong decision. The Modern had been owned by Hymie Goole and his brother Louis Goole and they employed a barber called Henry Rich. As they had to move out because of the compulsory purchase, Henry and Hymie decided they would buy a shop that was up for sale on Middleton road in Blackley. Soon afterwards Hymie got offered a job by his brother in law working in baby wear in a Cheetham hill warehouse, so he didn't make the move to Blackley but remained a part owner with Henry. It wasn't long before Henry eventually bought him out though. I thought at that time that Henry might offer me a part interest but I realise now he probably thought I was too young. I was already ambitious though and I would have pursued it if the opportunity had arisen.

So that left me working with and for Henry Rich and initially we were not getting on. I was giving him too much respect like a teacher and he was abusing it and playing on it. Now here's a thing. What I am about to say is a memory of mine as clear as anything. I came home one day crying about it and my uncle Joe Ross was there and my Grandad, Walter Ross who I looked up to immensely. He was a man's man and like a god to me. I was sixteen years old at the time and my Grandad who was huge, good looking and strong man picks me up with one hand and sits me down in front of him and says this. "So you don't like your job? Let's say you're on the other side of the world and you've got no money and you're in a bar but you've got your scissors and a comb with you and you end up cutting a couple of peoples hair and in return they give you a beer and some food and a roof over your head for the night cos you've got no money. As a barber, your money is in your hands not in your pocket or your Wallet". He carried on " What I want you to do now is stick out the four year apprenticeship and learn your trade and then go and do whatever you want to do after that". How was that for great advice to a sixteen year old. Only my mum says that all of that did happen when I was 16 but my Grandad had been dead for years. She tells me that Joe was there but it was her who said all of that to me saying that 'your Grandad used to say.. etc.' I can see it as clear as day so either I've forced the memory of my Grandad saying it instead of my mum saying that he said it or something very spiritual happened that day. Either way, this year, 2020, I celebrated 45 years in the trade in the same premises on Middleton road.

I've remembered that chat with my Grandad (or my Grandad via my mum) ever since then because it's also an example of taking advice from someone who you are comfortable listening to. When your dad gives you advice or I give advice to my sons, it's taken as a lecture rather than sensible advice. Recently I was talking to a customer who had just completed his law degree. He is spitting his dummy out because he can't get a job as lawyer. I'm cutting his hair and said "Let me tell you something - when you apply for your next job in a law firm - tell them you want to be the tea boy - if you get the job you will be the most over qualified person in the law firm and your foot is firmly in the door. Then you can aim to be chief exec in that firm in thirty years time" The lad says to me 'That's what my dad said" I said to him 'Well surely one of us is right". Hearing something from someone other than his dad helped focus him and had a bigger impact. My mum and Dad will probably have given me sound advice that went in one ear and out the other but I'd listen to my Grandad all day long and maybe that's the reason I remember it as my Grandad's advice.

I worked alongside Henry Rich for many years. Sometimes he treated me like the son he had never had and sometimes I looked up to him as a second dad. I had certainly spent more time with Henry than I had with my own dad. I don't get emotional often but when I think of the working relationship that I had with Henry and how it ended its one of the few things in my life that I would go back and change if I could

Henry and I stood side by side cutting hair for twenty years and I learned my trade partially through his guidance and partially through my determination to succeed both as a barber and as a businessman. Henry was set in his ways and had an old fashioned approach but the best parts of him rubbed off on me. I also identified the things I would do very differently to him but that didn't mean that I didn't respect him and what he had achieved himself.

Casting my mind back now to the many years I worked with him I see the two different sides to him. The father figure that taught me a lot and that I had loads of laughs with and the boss that would sometimes embarrass me in front of customers by telling me I had done something the wrong way. He would quickly go from shouting at me for a mistake to us both doing a barbecue in the back yard of the shop and him talking to me about life in general and treating me as his successor.

Like I said, he was like a mixture of being a second dad and a teacher. I basically did as I was told. I remember one day going back home and talking about how he was treating me. My mam said 'just stand your ground when he has a go at you' My family had always brought us up to stand up for ourselves when necessary. I thought my Grandad Ross was 7 foot tall because he always gave that impression and stood tall. The same with my Uncle Joe and the same with me. I was not 6 foot tall but people thought I was because I stand tall like I have always been taught. My mam's final advice about my problem with Henry was ' you're not at school anymore just answer him back one day and tell him to sweep up himself'. So this one day came and he told me very abruptly one day to sweep up and give me the brush. I just came out with it 'you fucking sweep up' and threw the brush at him and walked out. I was going to walk home but changed my mind and walked across the road and got a Mars bar from the newsagents. As I came back into the shop he said 'do you want a brew?' and I said 'Yes – do you want half a mars bar? And he said yes and we acted like nothing had happened. I noticed though that he had swept up.

He was a very good barber and he had text book rules. So if it was an inch on one side it was an inch on the other side. The way I addressed it was down to the needs of the customer. If you came into the shop and you've got a dint in your head on one side of your skull then I'm going to cut your hair to hide that dint for you even if it meant I was cutting a slightly different length to the other side. This meant going against Henry's golden textbook rules. My rules were if the customer looks into the mirror and goes out of the shop happy as Larry, then job done.

So one day I do this and the customer has gone out of the shop and Henry has given me a bollocking. He tells me that I've done it wrong and I say if I've cut it to hide a dint in his skull and he is happy then what have I done wrong? Five weeks later and same guy comes into the shop and Henry grabs him and says 'here you go' pointing to his chair and the guy only says "Henry is it ok if Chris cuts my hair?' 'Yeah no problem' says Henry. The guy sits down and says to me 'Same as what I had last time Chris.' I gave him the same haircut and he paid me and walked out. Now Henry might show me up in the shop in front of customers but I wouldn't do that to him. I waited till we didn't have anybody around and I said to him 'It's amazing isn't it how that guy keeps coming back and paying me for fucking up his haircut' and Henry just says 'Right'

In early 1978, there were lots of barbers to choose from and some of them like Mackey Davies and Cecil's were famous in the north west for proper cutthroat shaves. I am about 6 months into my apprenticeship and Henry's back goes. It's a slipped disc and he cannot possibly work. He had only bought the business months earlier and had invested a fair bit of money transforming the place and was still building up the clientele in the area. So yours truly was thrown right in at the deep end big time. Overnight I became head Barber and businessman. I had to handle all the running of the shop and the finances and then cycled to Henry's house at the end of every week and delivered the takings to him less my wages. I did that for around 6 months and kept the business going in Henry's absence. I also managed to further develop the customers base. Just six months before that I couldn't even cut hair and now I was running the shop. It was probably this that gave me at a very early age a taste for having my own business. Before Henry came back to work, the shop was getting busier and busier so Henry asked someone he knew, called Cecil, to come in and help me out on Saturdays when it was at its busiest. Cecil had a reputation for being one of the biggest gamblers in the north west. Big money lost and won. We are talking thousands of pounds. He came in to help me out but he also told me some great stories about big card games. in one of those card games he had won enough money to buy a house. Then he needed to have it all carpeted so he played in another big card game to win the money and lost the house. He was a fantastic barber and one of the best in the North West for shaving. He turned up one day to help me out and walks into the shop with four cans of special brew. He puts them on the shelf and says 'That's breakfast, dinner and tea' and opens and drinks the first can. He gets to lunchtime and he's on his fourth can when a customer comes in and asks for a shave. He gets the guys face and throat lathered up and then gets the cutthroat razor and I am talking about a proper cutthroat razor, the sort that Sweeney Todd used. I'm watching every bit of this while I cut the guy's hair in my chair. He goes towards his customer's face and his hands are shaking uncontrollably. I'm thinking he's going to cut his face off. The guy in the chair is oblivious and lathered up and relaxed. Cecil takes another swig of his beer with his hand still shaking all over the place and all of a sudden he swipes down the guys face and then another big swoop of the blade and then about 5 or 6 more and the guy is perfectly shaven and not one nick. He pays and leaves and I said to Cecil, 'You can go now if you want Cecil' I was bag of nerves and gave him everything he took in terms of money. It was a favour to us so I gave him the lot and was relieved when he left even though I knew it meant more hard work for me.

We had so many diverse customers. Syd Addleman was a guy who owned a shop on Leicester Road in Cheetham Hill called Brackmans. I still cut his hair today. One day he rocked up in a blue Rolls Royce. Its late in the day so I cut his hair and ask him could he drop me off in Cheetham Hill when I've locked up. He takes me up Middleton Road and I think I'm going deaf because I couldn't hear a thing. What a drive, it was pure silence. You felt as though you were flying or more to the point, hovering just above the road because it was so smooth. I was 17 or 18 years old and I was in a Rolls-Royce going down Cheetham Hill Road. I asked Syd to drop me outside Woolworths so I could get the maximum exposure from getting out of this fantastic car. Would you believe it? There was no bugger around. I thought where is everybody when you need them?

When Henry came back to work we would always go out for lunch and sometimes he would take me weightlifting. He had an incredible physique for a man of his age. He had 18 inch biceps and a chest of about 48/50 inches. This for a guy of only five foot seven in height gave him a solid physique. I tried to emulate him. This was the early influence on me to eat the right sort of foods and the first signs of my ambition to be healthy and look after my body.

Eventually I was training seven days a week and had also become a workaholic. I had got myself a Saturday night job in late 1977 collecting glasses in a Manchester night club called Pips. Nowadays, people who went to the Manchester Hacienda in the 80's boast of their experiences in

61

one of the most iconic night clubs ever. Pips preceded The Hacienda by ten years and is looked back on as the place to be in Manchester during the 70's. I had lied about my age as I was only seventeen. I was still doing my martial arts early every Sunday morning at Abraham Moss in those days so sleep deprivation became a weekly event and was an experience that held me in good stead many years later when competing in two and three day events. I got sacked from Pips after only a short time working there. I'll explain why I got sacked in a later chapter.

After I lost the job at Pips, I got another job while I was still 17 at a place called Lynwood Lodge in Crumpsall. This was a well-known one stop shop for weddings or any other large celebrations. It was a big detached house that had been converted into some large dance rooms, bars and dining areas. It also hired out wedding cars and drivers hence the one stop shop bit for weddings. I worked there after work on Saturday evenings when the evening functions and buffets for the weddings made things really busy. I was trained in silver service and worked both in serving food and helping out in the kitchen. The experience and pressure of working in such a fast paced business with such high standards was second to none. I had two years of that and the money I earned helped me pay off my dad for the loan for the hifi system I had bought and the occasional bit of clothing just like any teenager.

Zowie's was a men's boutique on Cheetham Hill Road. It sold Ben Sherman shirts and all that kind of stuff. I liked to spend a few bob and I always remember looking at a shirt in their window that I really wanted but I couldn't afford the £12 price tag. I thought to myself I'm going to have that shirt one day. I looked in the same window at the same shirt for weeks and then on one occasion, the owner Zowie come out, as he had clocked me every week looking at this shirt. He said 'why don't you come in and try it on?' I said "I haven't got enough money yet'. He just came back at me with 'Come in and try it on'. I went in and tried it on and it was a great fit. He said "Just give me a quid a week until it's paid'. I must have looked initially reluctant and then He said ' if you had given me a pound a week since you've been looking at the shirt, you would have paid half of it off by now. He was right and I bought the shirt. I still cut his hair today and his dad and his nephews all come into the shop. He had a vision back then of being like Topman and his display was always way ahead of its time.

Back at Lynwood Lodge, we worked our socks off on a Saturday night. The food being served was fantastic and sometimes, having already worked for more than 12 hours, the temptation to sneak a sandwich was too much. As soon as I did, the owner, Sam, collared me. 'These are for customers not for staff'. I explained that I'd worked since 8.30am in the morning and was starving. He said we could eat anything that was left at the end of the night. The trouble was that the food was so good there was rarely anything left. One night I got a bollocking for dancing with this girl during a wedding. I was working and had brought food out to the buffet table and on the way back across the dancefloor a girl started to dance with me so I joined in. Sam, spotted me and when I'd left the dancefloor he said 'what the heck are you doing?' and I said 'what am I supposed to do if a guest asks for a dance? I can't be rude' All the staff were laughing as I went further and said 'Is it my fault if I'm attractive ?' Sam stormed off still rollicking me but the staff were in uproar. I told my family that they were now paying me to dance at the Lynwood Lodge!

Around this time, I was getting fitter and fitter doing all this work and training so many days per week. My ambition had become to try and get into the GB squad in martial arts – Karate. I wanted to get to a standard that meant I could compete at the highest level. One day after work, Henry took me to The Village squash club where we were to do some weight training together. To be honest I was trying to show off when I immediately opted to lift the weight I knew I could lift without building up to it or warming up properly. I heard this crack like a gun shot and I'd ripped a pectoral muscle across my chest. I would be out for a few months or so I thought. This was only weeks before the crash, where an injury to my pecs would be the least of my problems.

Throughout my time with Henry in the shop on Middleton road he had promised me that he would sell the business and the property to me when he was ready to retire. We had discussed it many times and the general agreement was that when the time came, I would pay £30,000 for the business and the property, Lock stock and Barrel. This went on for a while and when I told one of my trusted customers that I had a gentleman's agreement with Henry, the customer had said to me that it was not wise to have an unwritten agreement and that I should get it in writing. Henry and I went for lunch regularly because he liked to close the business at dinnertime. It was one his rituals that I didn't agree with and planned to change once I had bought the business from him. One day we were sat having lunch in a Chinese restaurant on The Rock in Bury and I put the suggestion to him of drawing up an agreement. He went absolutely ballistic. He was throwing his arms around shouting at the top of his voice "What do you take me for? I am a man of my word.' Everybody was staring at us in the restaurant. I left it at that as he was so offended. I was worried that the whole thing could go pear shaped if he changed his mind so I couldn't risk raising it again. I suspected that this would become an issue at some stage but I had little choice and had just hoped for the best that he would honour his word when the time came.

Henry unfortunately wasn't investing in the business or trying to grow it. So here's me looking forward to buying the business from him and watching it die slowly in front of me. I had made loads of suggested changes to Henry both in terms of the way that we did business and the shop front but he knocked them all back or ignored them. It was clear to me that I had no chance of making any changes while he was still the owner. He even said to me once when I suggested a change 'you can do whatever you want when it's yours.' I simply couldn't make any changes because he was in charge. I decided to bite the bullet in July 1996. A shop on the same row as ours on Middleton Road, that had been a greengrocers, became available. I was on it like a flash. I spoke to the guy selling the place and lined up the purchase for myself. I went back into our shop and immediately told Henry that I was moving out and into the new place on 1st September unless he was ready to commit to a deadline for selling me the business. It didn't need to be too soon, I just needed a date that I would be working to. Henry could have called my bluff but I was ready to set up business on my own if he did. He committed to the 1st September 1996 and the deal was done. One major headache for me had been resolved and I had a date. The problem then was that Henry created a whole new problem when he decided not to tell his wife about the deal we'd just made or in fact the deal we had for many years and this was to cause a massive rift between myself and Henry's family. It also didn't go down too well with the guy who owned the greengrocer building as I'd strung him along for a while before telling him that I was pulling out. He understood in the end as he was a businessman.

Now that Henry was tied to a date with me and he still hadn't broken the news to his wife and family about what was planned, it was making him ill. I could see that the pressure was building up on him. He had no problem in selling the business to me and had no change of heart about the date that we agreed but he was petrified about breaking the news to his wife. As far as she was concerned she knew that Henry was selling the business to me but for some reason Henry left her with the impression that they would be retaining the property and the income from that. This all took its toll on Henry and in early 1996 he spent a lot of time away from work unwell. I worked hard in the meantime as I knew that I was now building the business up for myself when the sale eventually went through. I was going to Henry's house in Whitefield weekly with the takings minus my wages and Carol, his wife, would take the money off me, I knew she was just looking at me as a loyal employee and she had no idea about the deal we had done. She eventually found out as Henry told her just as the deal was going through. The next time I was at their house she walked straight up to me and called me a 'piece of shit' and spat in my face. I didn't do anything. I just stood there really not knowing what to do. Henry had let me down terribly and had made me look to his wife like someone who was conning him out of his business when that clearly wasn't the case. This was all because he hadn't been honest with her and shared with her about our arrangements right from the start.

Henry eventually did explain to Carol that it was his fault that she didn't know the full facts about our actual arrangement and we arrived at the date that we had agreed for the transfer in September 1996. I met with Henry to finalise things as he was still off work. I told him that I wanted him to come back to work after he recovered. I didn't want him to leave. I wanted him to work for me. Although he had handled this poorly I still had a tremendous loyalty to him and wanted to see him right after the sale. Very late in proceedings, we eventually came to a financial arrangement which differed a lot from the original plan. Despite the fact that these late changes put me under additional financial pressure, I agreed them to finally get the deal done without any further fall outs. The original arrangement was that I would pay £30,000 for the business and the building. In the final agreement Henry demanded £40,000 instead of £30,000 and he wanted to carry on cutting hair doing four days a week and him keeping the money he took, less 10%, that he would give to me every week to pay for the chair. I didn't have a problem with the deal in principal but it really put me on the spot as I had only just raised the £30,000 capital by telling a few white lies to the bank manager. I had told the bank manager that my wife and I were divorcing and that I was allowing my wife to keep the house as part of the settlement. I said to them that I would be living back with my parents rent free and that I would be renting out the flat above the barbers to create an additional guaranteed income. This allowed me to borrow the £30,000 because with the picture I had painted, I had little or no overheads or other debts. I couldn't now go back to them and increase this to £40,000.

So what I decided to do was to continue with the arrangement with the bank and source the additional £10,000 another way. In the end I managed to borrow £5000 off my sister, Olwen, and agree with Henry that I would pay him a small amount every week equivalent to the 10% of his takings until the £5000 was paid off. This would mean that although he paid me 10% of all the money he took every week, I would let him keep it until the debt was paid. He agreed to this and I decided to keep a ledger to track exactly what was happening with all of these payments. This ended up my wisest decision in the whole matter as that ledger and its accuracy helped me in a further situation that developed with Henry later.

The charade of the bank believing we were getting divorced and that I had no maintenance to pay did have some consequences. I was paranoid that somebody, a neighbor or somebody else, would grass me up so I used to sneak into the family home commando style every night after work. I'd told the bank that I would be living back with my parents rent free and would rent out the flat upstairs in the shop. These arrangements would easily see me paying the bank back £200 per week with no bills and rent coming in from my property but all of that would go up in smoke if the bank knew I was still living in the marital home and had misled them.

Ironically, this time Henry did want something in writing. I agreed because it was the wise thing to do. He asked Michael Sedgwick from the law firm Sedgewick Phelan and Partners to draw up the agreement. Michael was one of Henry's long standing customers who eventually became one of my loyal customers even with Henry still in the shop. The agreement had four main aspects. The first was that I could never fire Henry as an employee. The second part was that I would give him £30 per week until the £5K debt was settled. The third was that he could leave anytime of his own volition. The fourth and final part of the agreement and the most difficult for me to swallow was that while Henry was alive nobody could know that the business was now mine and that Henry wasn't the owner anymore. This agreement would remain under the table but would surface if reneged on. So he could leave anytime but I couldn't fire him and I was not allowed to tell anybody that the business was mine while he was alive. I could change name providing this didn't infer that I was the owner and I could develop the business in any way I wanted providing it didn't reveal that Henry was no longer the owner. Although it was probably the wrong kind of agreement to make I knew what I wanted to do short term did not go against any of these terms and longer term, I was confident, would look after itself.

So back to me buying the shop. I had to apologise to the guy who owned the Middleton road building, he was a bit annoyed but wished me good luck. I now had to get stuck into the appearance of the shop. It was dated and behind the plaster and under the floorboards the electrics and the pipework were archaic. The gas boiler that tried to give us hot water (it tried hard but didn't) looked as though it could blow up at any time. I had taken on all these liabilities and didn't have a carrot to my name. I simply couldn't afford to do anything with the shop and it looked as though it hadn't had any attention since it was built in 1936. I was determined to succeed in at least developing the place where it desperately needed attention even to bring it up to a reasonable standard but I couldn't borrow any more money. I sat and cried with frustration at the thought of having the business and not being able to do something with it. Thankfully my brother in law Chris come up with a plan to help me. He knew the place needed gutting but that I had no money to gut it. He said to me " I'll sort the shop out. I'll gut it and do it right and you can pay me when you are back on your feet. So that's what he did. He took it back to just the shell and started to build it back up again. I remember the feeling of satisfaction when it got to the stage where it started to take shape. Through Chris, we'd managed to get it back to good working order but without developing the place in terms of design. I accepted that this was an early chapter in the development of the shop and the vision I had for the future. The shop looked a little like a building site but my vision was clear. I wanted a barber's shop that offered something different and that was steeped in sport and well-being. The sort of place where you could go for a haircut have a massage and get some physiotherapy if you needed it and share stories of sport and fitness

69

and possibly even seek advice. Most of all though it was to be a place where a people with similar interests or wanting to know more about sport and general fitness could chill and feel relaxed.

If I listed the many types of customers I've had in the shop I could fill a book just on that alone. One day a sports car pulled up outside. The guy comes in and says 'can I have a haircut mate?' I was in the middle of labouring for Chris at the time and the shop is just a building site. I'm looking at this guy and his car and I'm thinking "are you for real?" but I just say to him "it's not open mate the place isn't finished yet" So he comes back with 'So you're not going to cut my hair? There's a socket right there what more do you need?' So, I put him on a piece of wood for a chair and without mirrors or any of the usual fuss I cut his hair how he wanted it. He gives me a tenner and as the guy walks out Chris snatches the tenner from me and says 'I'll have that'. In a nutshell that epitomizes the way my finances have worked ever since. As fast as I could earn it or obtain , my money would go in different directions almost immediately. I have never craved being rich with money but I have always craved having everything just right for my family and getting the bank and the tax man off my back. It's not something that worries me now but I would still like to achieve that. At the time when I first became the owner of the business and a business loan plus a house mortgage, it was of major concern to me.

So, Henry is still recuperating at home. Our deal had been finalised and gone through but he hadn't returned yet. In total he was off for about five months. In the Jewish community everyone still thinks that Henry owns the shop and can see that money is being spent on it. I heard comments coming back to me via my own customers saying that people were saying 'Have you seen what they are doing with Henry's" It did hurt a little that they were not saying 'Have you seen what they are doing at Chris's place or "The Barbers'. It was getting to me a little but I stuck with the agreement.

One day, after Henry had come back, I'm cutting hair and at the time I was having some spotlights fitted outside out the shop on the new sign. I'd renamed the place 'The Barbers' because I felt it was right. It was simple, it said what we were about, it didn't breach our agreement and it fitted in with my long term vision. The spotlights that were being fitted would come on at night and light up the new name 'The Barbers' for all to see. The spark (Electrician) that was doing the job shouted for me to come out and have a look from across the road. When I looked at it, I could see that it needed another floodlight between the two of them to light up the middle of the sign a lot better. 'I'll be around tomorrow' says the spark. The next day, I'm in the shop cutting hair as usual and this guy comes down as promised and puts the third spotlight in. He shouts into the shop 'Right Chris have a look now'. I walked across the road and look back and its perfect. As I walk back into the shop and leave the spark tidying up outside, this Mercedes pulls up at the side of the shop. It's a guy called Stuart, a wealthy businessman who sells silk and lives on the south side of Manchester. To give you an idea of how wealthy this guy is, he'd recently sold a little unused square of his garden to a developer for £100K and I'm going back nearly twenty five years here. As soon as the Merc pulls up Henry drops what he is doing and runs out of the shop and grabs the spark and looks up at the sign. The spark looks a bit puzzled but looks up at the sign too and Henry says 'Yeah. Yeah, that's alright now that' I'm in the shop looking at this and just shaking my head. It would be easy to get angry about it but I found it amusing that Henry was determined to keep all of his customers in the dark about the fact that he's not the owner anymore. Whenever he did pull stunts

71

like that, I ignored it because I was happy with how the business was taking shape. If I ever let myself get angry about it, I calmed myself down with my long term strategy and that it wouldn't be forever. This was still not my long term vision for the place but we now had three barber's chairs, three electric showers in three sinks with three mirrors all engraved with the name 'The Barbers' and we'd managed to get rid of the death trap that was the boiler. I was happy enough for now.

I kept to my word and never told any of his customers about the sale and allowed them, no matter what was said, to think that Henry was the owner. One day I was working in the chair next to Henry just a few months after he had returned to work following his breakdown. I'm cutting hair and he's cutting hair. He is attending to the guy with the Merc who only a few weeks earlier, he had put the show on for with the 'Spark'. The guy bends forward to have his hair washed and as Henry is washing his hair he says 'wow Henry that's great, you've got instant hot water now' and as he says it, he turns his head slightly towards me so that he catches my attention and under the sink that his hair is being washed in he gives me a thumbs up and mouths to me "Good Luck'. I realised then that a lot of people knew that I was behind the development of the business but allowed Henry his pride.

The business started to build and it got to the stage where at the end of the week, Henry was giving me £30 based on 10% of the £300 he was earning and he was only doing 3 days per week in the shop. When Henry wasn't working there, I was working alone and still had lots of customers waiting. When Henry had the shop he closed all day Wednesday and between 1pm and 2pm for lunch every day, even Saturday and then when it became mine his hours became 9am to 5.30pm. I was opening the shop from 8.30am and closing 6pm with no closures for lunch from Monday

72

to Saturday with the only exception being Wednesday where I would shut half day. Henry was actually working Thursday, Friday and Saturday and still having his dinner hour and then at key times when we were massively busy he would simply go into the back and have his lunch and leave me cutting hair on my own with five or six people sat waiting. I would be left to keep those customers happy or possibly lose them. That was the point really, they were my customers. I made sure that I kept the ledger on his takings and my payments to him. Henry was very money oriented and what he earned and what he showed the taxman were two entirely different things. It's one of the reasons I couldn't get a sizeable loan when I worked for Henry initially because according to Henry's books I was only earning £50 per week. I wasn't of course but some of it he gave me in cash. The business of him keeping his own hours and letting customers down had to come to a head at one time or another and it did. One Saturday afternoon his takings for his three days had reached £400, We were massively busy across the three days and still were when all of a sudden at 2pm on the Saturday he says 'Chris can we settle up. I'm going now'. There were four people sat there waiting for haircut and he announces that he is going. One guy who had been waiting actually stood up and sat in Henry's chair and Henry says to him 'I'm going now'. So on the front of our shop it says we are open to 6pm but when he's reached what he thinks is his quota he leaves and is happy to let down the customers who are waiting. This happened a few times so I decided to get another Barber in. This was when Steve Bowker joined us.   He'd come into the shop looking for work just at the right time. His dad was a well know barber in the industry and worked, I think, in Broughton. Steve had floated from job to job so I took him on. Henry did not like that at all. Steve's family was Jewish and Henry was obviously worried that, as I had made the decision and offered Steve the job, it would get out in the Jewish community that I was running the business and Steve was working for me and not for Henry. What I didn't realise at the time was that this was the least of my worries and that World War 3 was about to start between Steve and Henry.

Steve Bowker is about two foot two and Henry was about three foot three. I'm exaggerating of course but they were not big men at all but could they work side by side without bumping into each other? Could they fuck! They were at each other's throats right from the start. The tension in the shop was incredible. Henry was mostly the instigator and boy did Steve bite. At the time I'd already paid the £5K off to Henry and so I was no longer in debt to him. It had taken me three years to pay it off but the business now was mine without anything hanging over me from Henry. I decided that I had to do something as the row between them was building and building and was potentially losing us customers. I had to make a decision who was to go and unfortunately this was a clear decision for me. Henry was already losing us customers with his attitude at work before Steve arrived but things had got worse after Steve arrived and nearly all of it was instigated by Henry. I made the decision that Henry would have to go. I am not sure that people would appreciate how hard this was for me once I had decided it. This was the man who was like another father to me. I had spent over 20 years working by his side and he had given me my opportunity to own my own business. I felt an awful lot of loyalty towards him but knew that my decision from a business perspective to let him go was the right one. No matter how many times I said that to myself and I knew I was right , It didn't stop me from feeling disloyal and emotional. I also knew that Henry would take it badly and that my ties to his family would be severed permanently. Despite all this flying around in my mind, I did the deed.

It was a Saturday and Henry had gone home and I'd paid up his money for the week. I've reflected on this a lot over the years and I've come to the conclusion that I should've done this face-to-face but I took a decision at the time to ring him at home. I was in my kitchen at home and I phoned him up and said 'Henry it's Chris - don't bother turning up for work on Thursday' and he said 'what do you mean?' and I just said 'I'm sacking you' and he said 'you can't sack me – that's one of the terms in the letter that we both agreed through the solicitor' I said ' Yeah it is" and he came back at me with "Well you can't sack me then' I'm sure that he then thought that this would be the end of the matter but I said to him " OK, well then, I'll sack you and you take me to court using that letter and I'll bring the ledger with me that I've been keeping for the last three years. It outlines all the money that I've paid you over the last three years in wages and in additional moneys. I hope you've told the tax man how much you've taken out of the business over the last three years' He stuttered a little 'What do you mean ?' 'Well' I said 'I can see that you've taken about £16,500 per year out of the business so I hope you've told the taxman that's how much you've earned in the last 3 years'. 'I've earned that' he says. 'Yes' I said 'That's right – that's how much you've taken – so when we are in court over me sacking you I'll be bringing this up with the judge so I hope you've told the taxman' The last thing that was said between us was him shouting down the phone " you piece of fucking shit' and he slammed the phone down. Deep down I never wanted to do that but I always knew that in my head that I had a safety net of his own greed. He wouldn't have given the taxman a penny if he could hide it. I couldn't let him ruin the business for me. It had become unimportant to him and was just there for his £300 per week or so. He was destroying the business and everything I was trying to achieve and still living a lie that he owned it. I felt shit for a while about what I had done and we never spoke again. I tried not to think too much about

Henry over the years because, although I didn't regret the decision that I took, I did regret the way it had all ended and I wished it could have been different. I still get emotional about it now but it was 110% the right thing to do at the time. This was a man that gave me my trade, saw me through the car crash when I was struggling to cut hair properly because of my arm injury. He still kept me on board and treated me like a son. I had only one time in the early years with him that he'd treated me very badly and that's still a painful memory too. I had asked his daughter Lyndsay out and had arranged to go to the pictures with her on a Saturday night at the Mayfair cinemas in Whitefield. This was just after the crash and emotionally I was still a wreck. Spending time with Lyndsay had helped me through that period of time and initially we had just spent time together as friends but it had turned into something more and on this particular Saturday I realised that I was looking forward to seeing her and I knew I was going to discuss this with her that night and declare that I wanted it to be something more than a friendship. Henry's wife knew all about it but Henry apparently didn't. Carol had said to Lyndsay 'tell Chris to come for tea after work with Henry and then go to the pictures from here. At the end of the working day Henry had said to me 'I'm going now'. I said to him 'I'm coming with you, Carol has invited me for tea as me and Lyndsay are going to the pictures tonight at the Mayfair'. As soon as I said it I saw a barrier come down as clear as if he had pulled a metal shutter down between us. He clearly didn't approve.

Carole was an invigilator for school exams. She'd be off work on a Saturday and she had the car to pick Henry and I up to take us to their house. I was so disappointed when I saw his reaction and really didn't know what to do. We made the journey in his Ford Cortina on the way to his house in silence. The atmosphere didn't get any better when we got

76

into the house. I remember us going into the house and that Carole had already prepared the meal which was ready on the table. He walked in and said 'put my tea in the oven I'll have it later' He didn't sit with us at the table. He just went and sat in another room. I was made to feel very uncomfortable. We had something to eat and went to the cinema as planned. I can't even remember the film we saw that night because the night had been ruined by Henry's reaction. I used to see Lyndsay when she visited the Jewish community centre / Youth club further down Middleton Road opposite the Belmont . It was called the JBB which stood for The Jewish Boys Brigade. I think that girls were also allowed in under the Jewish Girls Brigade which joined as one organisation eventually. She used to get me in as I didn't qualify for entry into the place. She told me that her dad had said to her that it had to end. He had actually said " I'm having no daughter of mine marrying a barber'.

This was when I was about 19, after the crash, and when I was his employee. He had three daughters; Jackie and Elaine who were twins and two years older than me and Lindsay. So I was the only son like person in his life. We went to the gym together and lifted weights and did things that felt like dads and sons did together but he felt I was not good enough for his daughter. The only time he ever admitted that he was wrong about anything was just before I brought Steve in. We were in Bury one day. I don't know why we was there but he said to me 'I have to apologise to you' and he shook my hand. 'You are a businessman'. He was admitting that I had done well in the three years that I'd had the shop. It was never in my mind at that time just before Steve came in that I would be letting Henry go in just a few months. He gave me no choice. I'd borrowed £40,000 to build a business and had I allowed it to continue, eventually I would have had little or no business left to pay the bills. His behaviour was badly damaging the business and threatened to

77

destroy it and I couldn't accept that. I had to make a decision and couldn't drag it out. I could have let Steve go but then some other poor bugger who came in would have been the brunt of Henry's attitude problem. It was probably the most difficult decision I had ever made but it was the right one at the time without doubt. Steve did go on to cause me a problem years later but this didn't alter my thinking on the decision about Henry. All that said, it saddens me now to write about what happened as he had become a second father to me and I wish we could have remained friends after he retired. Although I am sure that it was the right thing to do, it hurt me as much as it hurt him and it still bothers me today some 20+ years later. My business also allowed me eventually to borrow money from the bank to make improvements on our house. One day I went into the Royal Bank of Scotland and the bank manager says to me "Chris do you want to borrow any money?' Now this wasn't a question I had ever been asked before. Normally you have to beg Bank Managers to lend you money but this time, because I had proved to be a safe business investment for them, they were proactively offering to lend me more money. As it happened at the time I did want to borrow money but not for the business. I had just bought a house on Mainway in Alkrington at the time and I had an extension partly up and running but not finished yet because I needed the money to finish it. So I answered the Bank Manager 'Yes I need £25K but it's not for Middleton Road, it's for my private property' Surprisingly he said " OK you can borrow on the strength of the shop but it will actually go into an extension at home – a business loan for finishing a house improvement off' "Yes, that's right' I said 'That's clever' he said 'you will get tax relief on a business loan and spend the money on a domestic property, well you can't do that". I said "yeah ok" but went ahead and I borrowed the money anyway, I filled in the forms saying it was for the business but I put the money into the house extension. The bank never paid me an official visit on the matter. The bank manager however always came in regularly for his haircut. He made a point of commenting on the improvements he saw in the shop very tongue in cheek. At one time he said " is that a new shower Chris" "yes I said' He continued ' that   shower is the most expensive shower I've ever seen. I can see where you spent the £25K in here.' The main thing to me in becoming a business owner was that my dad knew it had happened before he died. Lily never met my dad and Jourdana and Rhys can vaguely remember him while Arron remembers him well. I wanted him above anybody else to know that I had become a business owner.

Chapter 6 – The Crash & The Missing Weeks

My last full days memory before the crash itself was actually a month before it happened. I had been given Money by my then boss, Henry Rich, to put a bet on for him and I'd not made it in time to the bookies to put the bet on before the race started and fuck me, the horse only won. Henry was really pissed off with me when I told him I hadn't made it in time. There was a full month between then and the crash and my memory of that month still hasn't come back to me other than snapshots of things from the day of the crash and the moment of impact itself.

I'm told it happened on 25th March 1980. The rest is all that remains of my own recollection of the lead up to the crash. I was nineteen years old and working in 'Henry's' as a barber. I had saved money and had just took possession of a new car, a 1700 cc Triumph Dolomite Sprint. It was more body filler than metal and it had those 'go faster' stripes down the side. I remember feeling excited and wanting to show my cousin Adrian the car so I drove to his house in Hyde. He wasn't just keen to see it, he was keen to have a drive of it so we went for a spin with me as the passenger.

Adrian was opening it up and accelerating whenever he could to show me what the car could do. My last memory of that day was that when we reached the bend on Mottram Hall Road in Hattersley we were going far too fast. I'm told since that we were doing at least sixty miles per hour on a thirty mile per hour road and instead of turning with the road, Adrian simply lost control and the car turned sideways and skidded off into the brick wall of a bridge. As I spun with the car I remember seeing the wall coming towards me as we were going to hit it side on into my side of the car. From my injuries they worked out that I had put my left arm up to

80

try and protect myself as we struck the wall. I was later told that the fact that I didn't have my seat belt on probably saved my life too as I would have remained more upright. As it was I was able to put my left arm up and bend down a little probably trying to brace for impact all in that split second. I remember about five years later when I lived on Cromwell street I jumped out of bed one night and was sweating that much that it looked like someone had chucked a bucket of water over me. I'd had my first nightmare of that wall coming towards me again.

My injuries were severe and life threatening and I am told that I died for a few seconds both at the scene and at the hospital but on both occasions they were able to revive me. How my left arm remained attached to my body is difficult to comprehend as all my main bones and my elbow had shattered and my left arm was dangling from me. I'd then been thrown by the impact into Adrian himself and I'd fractured two of his ribs. I had completely cracked my skull open on my left side and my brain had been damaged in the impact. It was this injury that had caused me to stop breathing at the hospital on arrival and my heart stopped but they'd managed to bring me back and as always I was a fighter even if I was unconscious. Adrian must have got out of the car and got help as the car was partly hanging over the edge of the bridge with me inside. My next memory was then one of waking up in the hospital several weeks later and realising that I was alive.

I know I am a fighter and that my mum would have known this too as I lay there in a coma for about two weeks. I was in bad way and my mum said that my body was like a pin cushion as they tried to get a reaction from me at all by sticking me pins now and again and giving me blood transfusions. If there were any doubt that I was in any mood to fight for my life, that doubt would have disappeared when the doctors met my

81

mum. I'll let her tell you her version of events as she remembers those critical days of my life far better than I do.

Before I do that though I need to acknowledge something. My decision to write about my life has created a path for me to be in contact with my mum again as we had become estranged over the last fifteen years after an unnecessary row. It's not something that we both would have wanted but we are both very strong characters and sometimes that can lead to a break down in a relationship. Writing about my life has made me revisit how I feel about my life and my family and look for some explanations regarding why I am the person I am now. For that I am grateful as it has allowed me to appreciate my family even more than I did before and being in contact with my mum again is something that I now realise I wanted all along. So I will gratefully pass on now to my mum, Alma Duoba, whose memory has not faded of the day of the incident and the weeks I spent in Hospital.

Chapter 7 - The Crash & The Missing Weeks (by Alma Duoba)

Chris was born on 6th September 1960 at Crumpsall Hospital in North Manchester. He was in a rush even then arriving early at eight and a half pounds and he's been rushing around ever since. I used to say about Chris that when he arrived anywhere, his head and shoulders arrived first and the rest of his body would arrive later as he was always looking like he was in a rush. The police saw it differently because as he reached his teenage years he was brought home by the police at least three times that I can remember. When I asked them what he had done, they always said they didn't know but 'he was acting suspiciously running away'. One day I actually saw the police holding him on the bridge near us and I shouted to them 'what's he done?' and they shouted back 'we don't know but he was definitely running from something'. I shouted back 'he's running to get his bloody dinner'.

He was always running and yet he didn't really do sport at school. He would come home to Crumpsall for his dinner from his school on Leicester Road in Cheetham Hill and didn't have much time to eat it before he had to get back so he would always be running to be on time. I remember one year I had bought him a new winter coat and he went to school in it and had it pinched. He came home instead in a filthy disgusting coat. He told us that a teacher had told him to put it on when he discovered his own coat had been pinched. I'd thrown better rags out.

He was a bugger for playing pranks on his brothers. He would happily hide in a cupboard for hours and hours just to spring out at the next person who opened that cupboard and give them the shock of their lives. He couldn't do things by halves, he had the patience and the dedication to apply 110% effort into anything he did, even playing pranks.

Thankfully, it was this determination and his application that was something that was to later save his life.

He was into his martial arts in a big way. He was fanatical about it and like everything else he gave 110% in his training and in his events. It was the day before he was due to get his Karate Black Belt that his accident happened.

It was 25th March 1980. He was nineteen years old and had just bought his first car and had gone out in it over to his cousin Adrian's house in Hyde. Both my Husband, John, and I were both working at Connellys in Blackley, who produced telecommunication cables and were living in our home on Cravenwood Road in Crumpsall, Manchester. I worked shifts 2pm to 10pm at the time and when I finished at 10pm that night, I came straight home to be there for the kids, as John would start his shift at Connellys at 10pm. I had been in the house for just a few minutes chatting with my other three children, Olwen, Simon and Eamonn, about school and how their day had gone when there was a knock at the door. I sensed something was not right straightaway. When I opened the door there was a policewoman stood there. In that second I looked back and saw that all the children were all there except Christopher and immediately I thought the worst and before the policewoman could say anything I shouted his name out loud "Christopher". The policewoman said to me that Christopher had been in an accident. My first question was "where is he?" My next question was " Is he alive?" The policewoman told me that he had been in an accident and was in hospital in Ashton. There was no information about how badly he'd been hurt or whether he was in any danger or not. I had to organise things quickly. I was thinking I needed to get John and get a car to get to Ashton immediately.

I sent Olwen to our trusted next door neighbours, Ann and Ralph Webb. They both came immediately to help us. Ralph said he would go and get John and he jumped into his car and drove down to Connellys. Apparently when he got there the gates were shut because it was the nightshift. The security man was nowhere in sight and Ralph was left standing at the gate not knowing what to do to try and get the message to John. Then by pure chance John came out of one of the buildings and started to cross the road in the complex to go to another building and Ralph shouted him. Thankfully, John heard him and run to the gate. Ralph told him that Chris had been in an accident and John immediately climbed the gates and came back with him in the car to get me. Ralph then drove us both to Tameside Hospital in Ashton while his wife looked after our children. They were wonderful neighbours and we were very grateful to them.

All I could think of on the journey was 'please God don't let it be his head'. We went into the hospital and saw our nephew Stephen, who was Adrian's brother, who was there with his sister Fiona and Adrian's wife, Karen. Stephen told us that Adrian and Chris had been in a car accident and that Adrian had broken ribs and had punctured a lung but was ok and was just down the corridor but that Chris was in a bad way and they were working on him around the corner from where we were stood in the accident and emergency area. Stephen said that the doctors had been in and out of there and were rushing around but would not let anyone in to where they were with him. Stephen also said that he'd made it very clear to the people looking after Chris that he was fit, didn't smoke and was a fighter so to give him a chance. Looking back, it was so important that Stephen had said that because it made sure that whatever Chris's injuries, they would give him every chance of pulling through. After a while of

85

waiting and nobody coming to see us I'd had enough and went looking for where Chris was. I remember walking around in almost a complete square before coming across a room where there was some activity. I pushed the door open quietly and peeped in. The room looked like an operating theatre but was probably a treatment room and as I looked in they were transferring Chris from the table that they had been working on him on to a trolley to transfer him somewhere. He was in what looked like a big cradle as they carried him from the table on to the trolley. I walked in and nobody stopped me. I could only see one side of his face as the rest of his face and head was heavily bandaged. Where the bandage ended his face and forehead was bulging with swelling. He looked in a terribly bad way. His left arm was also very heavily bandaged and he had injuries that I realised later that I couldn't see under the covers to his ribs and his body which was heavily bruised. I asked someone could he not be given anything for the pain and they said he was unconscious and couldn't feel anything. I leant in and said to him I'm here now Chris. There were no signs initially that he understood what I was saying. I stayed with him and kept talking to him. At one time, I said to him 'Don't worry Chris you are going to be okay' and although I could only see one of his eyes and it was shut, he squeezed his eye as if to wink at me. I knew then that he could hear me.

They transferred him on to a ward and eventually they told us that the registrar wanted a word with us and John and I went in to a room with an Indian doctor. It was a very strange conversation. The doctor refused to look at me throughout the whole conversation and just looked John in the eye. I'll never forget the words he used. He simply said "Take your wife home and we will give you a call when he dies." John was struck dumb by what he said. I said 'What do you mean?' He ignored the fact that I was asking the question and continued to speak to John. He went on 'It's a waste of time you being here'. I responded angrily and said '"The only time we are wasting is talking to you". He still didn't look at me and said to John "Can you control your wife". I was furious and walked out and went to find Chris. I wasn't leaving his side until I knew he would be ok.

Chris had eight blood transfusions. It was the loss of blood that had nearly killed him at the scene of the crash and we were told that they had to start his heart again just after he had arrived in the hospital. He'd lost that much blood that they were pumping transfusions into him urgently and it was clear that they thought he had little chance of survival.

The rest of the story I pieced together from Adrian's account and speaking to the actual Ambulance crew, who came to see Chris when he was on the ward. The two paramedics who attended the crash scene and had brought Chris back from the brink of losing his life had nicknamed him 'The Rubberman'. Adrian had fortunately not lost consciousness after the crash and had managed to flag a car down. The police and ambulance crew arrived quickly and Chris was trapped in the car. The paramedics were concerned immediately as they could see that Chris was losing blood fast and they couldn't get him out of the car to help him. They told me that the police officer was reaching in to the car and desperately trying to apply pressure to Chris's wound to stem the flow of blood to give him more time until the Fire Brigade arrived with cutting gear to release him from the wreckage. The paramedic's guidelines on this sort of thing were that they couldn't risk further injury by trying to get him free from the car and that they should wait for the fire brigade to arrive to use their tools and machinery to free him safely but they both said that they knew if they did that, he would die. So they bravely took the decision to get him out even if it injured him. As they pulled him out his foot was still trapped and it looked likely that if they yanked him out

87

they would break his ankle but it was so urgent that they were able to stop the loss of blood that they said that they decided to take the risk. They used brute force to pull him out and just yanked his foot out. Amazingly his ankle didn't break. They both said that they had cut it fine as his blood loss was so serious and his pulse was weak that in their opinion he may have been only seconds from it being too late. They worked on him at the scene and saved his life in getting him from the scene to the hospital as quickly as they did. He was still fighting for his life when he arrived at the hospital and his head injury caused a second life or death scare when he stopped breathing but he was revived a second time. The paramedics had nicknamed him 'Rubberman' because of how his leg and ankle had bent to allow them to yank him out of the car without breaking anything. The fact that they both came to see him afterwards meant a lot to us and we were so grateful to them but I understood the seriousness of the situation. Without spelling it out for me, it was clear that they were amazed Chris had survived the crash and his injuries. Adrian explained the accident to us. He had lost control of the car and the car had spun to the right and the left hand side of the car and the passenger seat that Chris was sat in, had taken the full impact of the crash against the bridge wall. Chris had been lucky in one sense not to fracture his skull but his head had been split open and he had a gaping wound at the left side of his head. His left arm was very badly broken and his elbow had been shattered into pieces as he had lifted his arm to protect himself from the impact with the bridge wall at the last minute. He had fractured ribs and literally hundreds of small wounds from shattered glass that had embedded in his head, his face and his arm and other parts of the left hand side of his body. He remained unconscious for two weeks wired up to a panel above his bed with various lines going into and on his body. The doctors never gave us any further indication at that time whether or not he was going to be okay. I sat by his bedside and talked to him constantly and I knew in my heart that he could hear me.

One morning a doctor came to his bedside along with some junior doctors doing the rounds of the wards. The senior doctor said to the students "this man is unconscious after a serious car accident. He doesn't hear anything and he doesn't feel anything" I said straightaway 'yes he does'. The doctor moved towards Chris lent forward and pinched his cheek quite firmly and said to his students "see, he doesn't feel this at all". I spoke up again "he does so don't do that" and he replied quite firmly 'I can assure you that he doesn't'. I turned to Chris and said loudly 'Christopher' Chris replied 'yes mam' and I said 'Sorry for disturbing you but just tell the doctor that you felt that and Chris, who still had his eyes closed and looked asleep, said very quickly and very abruptly without moving anything but his lips "Yes I fucking did'. The doctor was left open mouthed and eventually said 'well I never'. Chris remained unconscious for a further week and a half and never responded to anything else other than when I insisted. It was as if I was the only one he felt he had to communicate with. He remembers nothing of this now. I kept mentioning to the nurses and doctors a large swelling in Chris's throat and neck area. It looked worrying to say the least. One doctor eventually explained it to me. He quoted Winston Churchill 'Never in the field of human conflict was so much owed by so many to so few'. Now Churchill was referring to The Battle of Britain' and the RAF whereas the doctor was referring to the blood cells in Chris's body. He'd had so many transfusions and so much of other people's blood that his immune system was fighting to allow the new blood cells to be accepted. The doctor explained that the few cells of Chris's own blood was having to work hard to accept the new alien blood cells into his body and that was the swelling around his throat. When he eventually regained

89

consciousness after two weeks, his memory had been severely damaged and it was heartbreaking to see this young lad who was so active and bright now sink into a shell and struggle for a while. When they said he was well enough to leave the hospital several weeks later they gave him what they thought was the prognosis for his injuries. They said to him that he had life limiting injuries. They said that his arm would never be the same again and it was unlikely that he could hold down a manual job in the future (which was referring to his occupation as a barber). They also said that he had suffered some brain damage from the impact of the crash on his head and that this may also hold him back from working again. At nineteen years old this was a devastating prognosis but they hadn't planned on Chris and his attitude. Telling him that he couldn't do things was the best medicine you could give Chris as he would refuse to accept that.

I had many dreams in the past about my children when they were in danger or something serious that was going on in their lives but not Chris. I never dreamed about anything that happened to Chris including the crash. I had a dream while I was away on holiday once about Simon and Eamonn having an argument in the house and one of them punching a hole in the wall. I rang home and asked what was wrong and what had they done and they said 'how do you know?'. Another time I'd had a dream about Olwen being out late in a van and woke up worried. Olwen was supposed to be staying at a friend's that night but had stayed out late and had been given a lift in a van. She couldn't believe that I knew about it. But I never dreamt at all about Chris. Chris used to call for a coffee and sit with me and we had some long chats but when it came to my dreams we both agreed that we were both tough and stubborn and would never let each other into our heads. We were both the same – single minded. It's that single mindedness that drives him now in what he's doing and it's that single mindedness that got him through the injuries he sustained and the dark times he experienced afterwards. In my opinion, there was only one person responsible for Chris's recovery and that was Chris. We could all say we helped but it was him that got him through it somehow over a much longer period than those two months in hospital. The physical effects and his recovery from them were difficult enough but the psychological recovery was to prove just as difficult and just as worrying.

Chapter 8 – Coming Home

It's an understatement to say that I had been lucky to survive the crash. In fact, it is true that the crash could have so easily cost me my life three times over. The first was as I was bleeding to death in the wreckage. It was the paramedics who clearly saved my life there. The second time was as I arrived at hospital still losing blood and with a serious head injury. It was the surgeon's turn to put me back together again, get my heart going again, save me from bleeding to death and fix me as best they could. The third time was some weeks later and it was my mum who stepped in to save me from a fate much worse than death itself as I was in danger of being committed to a local mental hospital.

The human brain is an amazing thing. Most of us take it for granted as it's there for us every day doing its job to keep us alive and helping us survive and develop ourselves in different ways. I know I didn't think about it too much until after well after the crash and I realised that mine wasn't quite working properly. I've since learnt that one of the most common effects from a traumatic brain injury is increased aggression. That was true of how I was reacting and it got progressively worse.

Initially, I was so grateful when I woke up. Being alive felt so good. I didn't even think to check all my limbs I was just grateful to wake up. I did end up very lopsided due to the damage on my left hand side and my head required more than 40 stitches to a wound that I am told created a huge gap in my head and the scar is pretty brutal but I was alive and I was living to fight another day.

They had operated on my arm and had done an amazing job of rebuilding my elbow given the extent of the damage and the lack of co-operation they had received from me in allowing the injuries to heal. They had to plaster from my wrist to the top of my shoulder and my arm was set into an L shape. I couldn't sleep with it and it was getting right on my nerves so are used to karate chop it and snap it so that I could rest my arm more comfortably. Three times within the couple of months I was in hospital, I actually karate chopped it and ripped it off and three times they did it all over again but every time putting more plaster on thinking I wouldn't be able to get it off this time. I was still confused of course and didn't realise that this wasn't helping my arm heal. One day, one of the nurses said to me 'why do you keep doing this?' and I replied 'I'm fighting Joe Bugner tonight'. I was deadly serious too. I was convinced at the time that I was due to fight him. It sounds crazy but I thought it was true. They were losing patience with me because they had reconstructed my elbow and needed things to be held still. Eventually I did conform and things healed well and I have a fully functioning arm now although it is heavily scarred and it was a bit of a journey for my arm to get there.

I was so elated about being discharged from hospital that I didn't notice the discussions that were going on around me about why I was being discharged. Since they had said to me that I had 'life limiting' injuries and that it was unlikely that I would be able to hold a job down or go back to my barber's job, I had already made my mind up to prove them wrong. It had been two and half months since the accident and I had started to go stir crazy and needed to get out. I was very impatient and thought it was about time that I was sent back out into the world to continue my recovery

To me, their decision to discharge me meant that they obviously thought I was well enough to leave the hospital and go home, Even that is a distant memory as I remember very little detail about returning home and for a while after that. I suffered with post traumatic amnesia at the time and some of the memories of the weeks and months after returning home have simply not come back to me. What I realise now though, is that it was not about me being sent home having recovered from my injuries, it was more about the hospital needing me out of their ward because of the way that I was behaving. Whatever it was, I have little recollection of those times and they remain missing weeks from my life. Many years later when a compensation claim for my injuries was being assessed, I saw in one of the doctor's reports, obtained as evidence, the following words;

'Mr Duoba's personality change has been held in check in part by the devoted attention of his mother and I think we must view with some hesitation the suggestion that Mr Duoba could cope on his own'

My mum clearly played a major part in getting me home instead of what the alternative was. The hospital was happy with my physical recovery and saw my mental recovery from the brain injury as something that should be looked after by another hospital. It was my mum that prevented that from happening and took it upon herself to care for me. It is well documented that when someone suffers a traumatic brain injury, dependent on what part of the brain is injured and how badly the brain tissue is damaged, they may experience different problems. Clearly I was functioning well physically but emotionally and behaviorally, I wasn't. The part of the brain that is associated with this is the frontal lobe and when that is affected, it is typical for the person to get quickly frustrated, depressed, irritable and aggressive and experience dramatic mood swings amongst many other problems. What's more, is that the person will not realise that this is happening to them and will be in denial of the problem. I now know that this described my behaviour for the first few

94

years after leaving hospital. Slowly getting better but initially extremely difficult for people to manage and my mum took all this on herself. So, there was me thinking that they were satisfied with my progress and were sending me home but the truth was that I was becoming impossible for the hospital staff to manage as I was reacting aggressively to everyday things and had started threatening people. As soon as they felt they could discharge me they did but they had already decided that mentally I was also too ill to go home. They had arranged to transfer me to a ward in Prestwich Hospital. Prestwich is well known in Manchester for caring for adults and youngsters with varying levels of mental health issues, some of whom might be violent or have committed violent crimes. There is no doubt now that their assessment of me at that time was accurate and I was struggling mentally and was becoming more and more aggressive to anyone who interacted with me but there was no way that my mum was going to allow me to be transferred to Prestwich so she stepped up and my life was saved for that third time in just a few months. She forbade the transfer and said that she was taking me home. She knew it was going to be extremely tough, but she is a tough woman to say the least. Writing about it now fills me with emotion as it is because of me writing this book that I am reunited with her after a stupid row meant that we hadn't spoken to each other for the last 15 years. Like I said, I have always known that my mum was tough, but it is only now that I realise how tough she had to be as I come to understand how difficult it was for her to look after me. The books and medical articles on this sort of thing all concur on the fact that mood swings and aggression are the biggest strain on someone recovering from a brain injury and on those that are caring for that person. My mum took that upon herself rather than let me get admitted into Prestwich.

I say, with no exaggeration at all, that if my mum hadn't taken me home and let them send me to Prestwich then there's a good chance I wouldn't have made it. I'd have been stuck there for years getting violent with the staff , being put on stronger medication and getting worse rather than better. I would never have met Philomena and would never had the children and the fantastic life I have had so far. So when I say that my mum saved my life I mean it. I later fell out with her about money. They say that money is the root of all evil. I agree with that. I only now realise what she went through to save me from being lost in the system. What I'd put her through. I'm grateful that I'm getting this chance to say these things and to finally thank her for what she did for me. The next few years after returning home were difficult and I'll share some of the things I experienced later in the book but for the moment, I've left it again for my mum to describe how difficult that specific time of me coming home from hospital was for her and the family as I only remember very brief moments from around that early time at home. I rely in this book on my mum being able to fill in some of the more important gaps between the crash and starting to get back to some kind of normality. If I dig deep, I only remember random things. I really can't remember whether Henry came to see me in Hospital. He certainly wouldn't have let his family come as I was in a right state. I remember seeing a picture of me thinking I had a tan but it was the bruising from head to foot after the crash. Back at Cravenwood Road after being discharged from the hospital. I wasn't able to return to work of any nature for a while. It was at this time that I hit my lowest period. I was depressed and for one very brief moment, suicidal. I do remember seeing a Psychiatrist on Middleton Road not far from the shop but I couldn't tell you how it went at all or whether I got any benefit from it. I couldn't cut hair in the same way that I used to, I couldn't do martial arts which I loved, I couldn't drive just yet because I wasn't well enough to and I didn't have a car anyway. It was at this time,

I got close to Henry's daughter Lyndsey who had played a big part in my recovery after I got out of hospital. She was about 16 and just about to leave school and I was 19. She was a calming influence on me and I was able to open up and talk to her about what I was experiencing. I'm not kidding when I say that the Psychiatrist the doctor referred me to cost probably hundreds of pounds a session and I can't remember any impact that had on me but being able to talk to Lyndsey about things gave me some hope that things would improve. Henry put paid to any relationship hopes Lyndsey and I might have had, as you will know from Chapter 5 so I was back with my thoughts drifting. My pal, Tony Heffernan had been to see me at the hospital and was around me at the time and Nick Lock and Dave Baldock who were two other mates that had their own cars so that they could get over the see me Tameside. Every time I got in a car for the next few years, I would tell the driver to move over more to the right as I'd get a little paranoid that my side of the car could hit a wall again. It was quite a period of time that this went on for and I developed a reflex reaction of lifting my arm up in fear to protect that side of my head to the slightest movement. Things got rock bottom for me later in the year of the accident during the course of either the November or the December 1980. I was getting lower and lower in mood. I can't recall how I got there or what I was doing there but I found myself stood on the pavement on Cheetham Hill Road. I walked to the kerb to cross the road near Woolworths and looked to my right and saw this big lorry tipper wagon with stones in the back coming down Cheetham Hill Road. The lorry was getting closer and closer and I started to feel the weight falling off my shoulders. In my head I was thinking – *'this is the answer – just step out in front of this Lorry and it will all be ok again in just a few seconds'.* I can't explain the feeling well enough but it was like a huge release of pressure. I actually felt a sudden happiness coming over me. All this took about four of five seconds. I had made my decision. The Lorry was only a second or two from reaching me and now it was just about steeping out at the right time. Then from nowhere, just as I was about to step out came another thought – **Woah - what if it doesn't kill me – I'm not going through this again** – it was as if someone was pulling me back just as the lorry passed in front of me. As the lorry arrived, so did the guts for me to continue and I decided that I had to face my demons. From that moment on I got mentally stronger every day and I never again considered suicide as a potential answer to anything. I didn't get fully better mentally for quite some time and some would say that I still haven't full reclaimed all my marbles but I never went back to that point where it seemed that ending it was the best way forward. I've only learnt this now many years later. I can deal with anything now. What's the worst can happen? I can deal with whatever is thrown at me now. I appreciate now that I'm alive and what an honour that is. Some people don't get that but I do. I'm still here. You can't kill me. I can't kill myself so how are you going to do it? I am not frightened of anything or anyone. It's ironic but once you've reached that second in your life where you are prepared to end it and you step back from it, you really start to understand and appreciate more about life itself. I live close to one of the biggest parks in Europe, Heaton Park in North Manchester and I exercise in that park most days of the week. People who live near that park do not appreciate how beautiful that park is right on their doorstep. I do, and the older I get the more beautiful it seems. The older I get the younger I get in my mind. Some people develop hang ups as they get older – some people have a 'mid-life crisis'! What the fuck is that? As I get older I get more carefree and appreciate things as they are. I started to develop a strong feeling of positivity as soon as I stepped back on to the pavement in Cheetham Hill. It was weak at first but it got stronger and stronger every year and now forty years on I'm as positive a person as anybody I've ever met. I never let any negatives outweigh the positives and I'll always put 110% into everything that I do. For example, one day very recently, I was in Heaton Park on my day off and I had just been to Hebden Bridge and back on foot which involved fartlecking 46 miles. Fartlecking Is Swedish and means 'Speed play'. In our language it means training at two different speeds and I've covered the 46 miles running and walking. I bumped into a customer walking his dog who said to me "have you just done abit of a run in the park?" and I told him that I'd just come back from Hebden Bridge. "Hebden Bridge?" he said "in your car?" "No on foot" I said. He's about five years younger than me. "On fucking foot?" 'Yeah" I said. His face was a picture. "Chris you're not 21 anymore you know" and I come back to him with "I know I'm not. If I was 21 I'd have been back a lot slower, I'm quicker now". I remember the phrase 'Act your age not you're shoe size' and I was exactly the opposite. Here's a guy younger than me already talking older than me. I'm conducting myself based on how I feel and I'm alive and I feel great. If I had stepped out off the pavement that day, the last forty years wouldn't have taken place for me. There would be no marriage, no children, no friendships, no business, no customers (who I also call friends) and no Christopher Duoba, just a headstone in a local cemetery – Christopher Duoba 1960 – 1980. Well bollocks to that! To anyone in the same position as I was on Cheetham Hill Road that day, I do sympathise because I know what it feels like, but please know this. The brave thing isn't to step forward in front of the Lorry / Bus / Train, the brave thing is to step back and to live. It won't be easy but you could have the wonderful moments I have had in life and more to look forward to. To the rest of the people out there who have never had that experience, then that's great but watch out for it in your friends and family, sometimes it's only about some love and positivity that's needed to ensure they don't end up in that moment. There were 6,507 suicides in the United Kingdom in 2018. Stats for 2019 are due out after I publish this book. Over three quarters of those 6,507 people were men. The current campaign to get people talking more about their mental health is the right way to go and will save lives. As men historically don't open up readily about their problems it's up to everybody to spot any signs and when we all say the automated words "How are you?" when we meet people, try and listen to what they actually say and if there are any signs of something being wrong then ask them how they really are.

Just a few days after my moment of revelation on Cheetham Hill Road, I popped in to see Henry at work and he told me not to worry as my job would always be there for me when I was ready to return. This was his opportunity to repay me for when I covered the business when he was injured. Initially I returned to work and managed to cope one handed for some time before I could use both hands again. The styles of the day were such that using clippers was rare. So scissors and comb were the tools of the trade. I can't tell you how awkward it was when my hand for holding the comb had to be re-educated as if it was a foreign body rather than an extension of my hand which it had been before and needed to be now.

Of course my recollections of coming home and what I went through leave a lot left out because of my memory issues at that time. I talk later in the book about some significant incidents where I clearly demonstrate that my mental health was still causing serious issues for me and others for some years to come but my mum remembers better the detail of what it was like leaving the hospital and being re-introduced to everyday life for me and my family. So over to her again.

Chapter 9 – Coming Home (by Alma Douba)

When he was well enough to leave the hospital several weeks after the accident they gave him what they thought was the prognosis for his injuries. They said to him that he had life limiting injuries. They said that his arm would never be the same again and it was unlikely that he could hold down a manual job in the future and were particularly referring to his occupation where they knew that the needed to use his hands as a barber. They also said that he had suffered some brain damage from the impact of the crash on his head and that this may also hold him back from working again. At 19 years old this was a devastating prognosis but they hadn't planned on Chris and his attitude. Telling him that he couldn't do things was the best medicine you could give Chris as he would refuse to accept that.

What Chris may not have realised at the time was that when the hospital had made the decision to discharge him, it was a far from straightforward decision. They had explained to me that they needed him to come off the ward he was on because he was physically strong enough to leave the hospital but he was getting more and more aggressive with the staff and fellow patients. I discussed this with them and I asked what would happen and they wanted to transfer him to Prestwich Hospital. At that time being transferred to Prestwich suggested that you had a mental illness. I told them immediately that there was no way that was happening and he would be coming home to his family, which he did. My reaction was immediate as his mother. I didn't think of the difficulties that we were clearly going to have. As a mother I knew that I could not let him be taken to Prestwich and thank god I did that, because Prestwich was the sort of place that someone could easily spend many years in once admitted and possibly even spend the rest of their life going from one institution to another and never really returning to everyday life.

When Chris did come home it was clear that things were immediately going to be difficult for him and the family but I was determined to get him through it. His head injury was causing severe mood swings and at times he was at a very dangerous level of low mood and had suicidal thoughts. At other times he was getting aggressive with his brothers and sister and sometimes myself. I could only support him as best I could and pray that he would be able to get through that at the time. I used to sit and talk to him for hours and hours into the middle of the night and if I suggested that he get some professional help he would point blank refuse. It was heartbreaking to watch him sometimes as he would always regret his actions and get upset and say to me "why am I like this mam?"

He started to become obsessed with getting himself back into shape. He would work out in the kitchen with weights for so long that I would have to mop the floor afterwards because of the puddles of sweat he left on it. It was if he'd had a bucket of water poured over him. I would say to him 'you've done enough for one night Chris ' but he would go on for hours and hours afterwards at a frantic pace. He was determined to prove them wrong. I was worried he was over doing it. He kept pushing himself and pushing and pushing. It was incessant. It used to make me cry watching him as I thought he was losing his mind.

There was also a significant physical recovery needed from his accident but this was being overshadowed by the mental issues he was facing. In the meantime he had to attend lots of hospital appointments particularly because of his arm and the way that they had to rebuild it using screws and bolts. After a few weeks at home he came to me one day and say 'mam, what the hell is going on?' and when he held up his arm I could see two pieces of metal sticking out of his arm. We rushed him to the hospital and the doctor said 'perfect – Just bring him back for his next appointment which is in two weeks' time. Chris went crazy at the doctor's reaction as he was in agony with it but the doctor explained that his arm was knitting well and rejecting the screws and bolts and that eventually he would get rid of them. We thought it all sounded a little odd but maybe because it was his elbow, this was the way it worked. He'd had several operations to repair the arm during his stay in hospital even when he was still asleep. A surgeon actually asked me one day while Chris was still asleep, what he ate at home ? I thought why is he asking me this? I thought it was for a menu or something but he was trying to ascertain how healthy Chris's growth was generally before the accident and how much he was eating and his growth rate. He told me that some children shoot up early and stop growing at 15 or 16 but others started the growth spurt at 15 or 16 and it goes on into the late teens. Chris fitted into category 2 as he had shot up since he was 15 so the surgeon knew then that he had to take his future growth into account when fixing his elbow joint. Stephen also stepped in at that point again and made sure the surgeon knew just how healthy Chris was and how strong and fit he was. Talking of growth, all of my children got height from somewhere. All three of my lads shot up like beanstalks. I used to say tom them "don't stand behind a lamp post or nobody will see you'. Chris was 6 foot one, Eamonn was over six foot one and Simon was Six foot three. Even Olwen was touching six foot. They didn't get this off me or their dad but my brother Joe was very tall so possibly from that side of the family. Chris also made the most of his height by walking tall. He'd always walked with his shoulders back as if he'd been in the army.

His physical recovery continued gradually and amazingly for many months he was still shedding small shards of glass. I remember sat by his hospital bed, while he was unconscious, picking bits of glass out of his face and his arm and his left hand side. I had a small container full of them on the bedside cabinet in the hospital. This carried on when he got home and you would be amazed at the size of some of the pieces of glass that must have healed under his skin and then decided to break free at a much later stage. He shed them regularly for what I thought was months afterwards but Philomena told me one day that she had picked a piece out of his arm for him and that was probably two years afterwards.

With regard to his mental recovery this was much slower. Over several months things got harder for us all. Chris would turn on people for the slightest thing and he was getting more and more threatening and potentially violent. As he did this I started to question whether I had done the right thing in bringing him home. I knew that the alternative would have broken my heart but he was making life extremely difficult for all the family and his aggression towards his own brothers and sister was making things impossible. I was the only person that he didn't turn on in that time. I would be the one to calm him down and encourage him to listen to his music which I knew calmed him but things were progressing to dangerous levels and I knew that I was the only person that was between him and being committed to Prestwich Hospital. If he turned on me then that could be it. Then came the day that I had to tell him that in no uncertain terms. My friend and next door neighbour, Ann, was in the house with me and was very worried for me as she saw first-hand Chris's temper as he turned on me. What he wasn't going to do to me was nobody's business. He was shouting obscenities and threatening me and he had followed me into the kitchen. I knew this was it. This was the key moment in his recovery. If he hit me I would have to have him admitted to Prestwich. I was the only one who could get through to him and if that failed then he was completely out of control and we had no choice. I went right into his face and said 'Go one then Chris. Do it! But if you do, understand this. I will wash my hands of you and that will be it'. There were a few seconds where I prayed that I'd got through to him because I knew I meant what I said. He backed off and it was a breakthrough. I knew then that I could influence his recovery and that despite his mood swings he would listen to me. Apart from the crash itself, It was one of the most significant moments in both of our lives.

Luckily there was soon to be another woman in Chris's life that would influence him, Philomena. When he met her I pulled him to one side and told him that his mood swings had to stop because a girlfriend wouldn't tolerate them but thankfully I had no need to fret over that because they got on like a house on fire and it wasn't long before they were married.

Chapter 10 – Soul Mate

I wonder how many blokes can say that their first date with their future wife was in a hospital restaurant where the deal was 'All you can Eat for a Quid'. Yes, that's right an unlimited amount of food for £1 pound in a local hospital, which ironically was the very hospital that my mother had protected me from, Prestwich, the hospital renowned for handling mental patients. Let me explain.

I was 22 years old and playing football for a local pub called The Welcome Inn. My physical injuries were much improved and I was already flying in the face of the doctors who had said I had life limiting injuries. In fact, whatever I did, I put 110% into, not just to prove the doctors wrong but to prove to myself that nothing could hold me back. What I didn't quite realise at the time was that it was my mental health that was still suffering and it was this that was partly driving me forward to try that bit harder in any activity that I felt could prove everybody wrong.

I played Centre Forward for the team and I'd been scoring a few goals. My simple strategy in every match was that I would flatten their goalie as soon as possible after the kick-off, which would either take him out of the game or at least let him know I was there and then he'd be wary of me after that for the rest of the match. One day we were playing in a cup final and I went to take the goalie out as usual and bounced off him. I looked at him and thought 'fucking hell! I have met my match here'. He was a man in his late twenties and I was a young kid in comparison. He had a bottle of whisky in the goal behind him and just stared at me without saying a dicky bird. My usual strategy wasn't going to work. I had no regard for my own safety and I was flying in to tackles. Early in the second half, I went full blooded into a tackle with one of their players. He had also come in hard and to be fair we had both gone for the ball and there was nothing unfair about the challenge but he came off far worse and broken his leg. I just heard a sound like a gun going off and didn't realise what had happened. There were never more than a couple of dozen of supporters at these games but it seemed to me that all of them had invaded the pitch because they thought I'd done it on purpose but I hadn't. I was just 110% committed to winning the ball. Eventually everybody put their handbags away and we concentrated on helping the ambulance crew get the lad sorted. Luckily there weren't many moments like this and I loved playing for this team as my personality totally fitted in with them and it did pay dividends for me too. One day in a Sunday County Cup game away at Darwen, I scored twice. The first was with the outside of my right foot and the second was a half volley. I connected with perfectly and the ball flew in. I'd hit the sweet spot on the ball and caught their goalie off guard. Everything seemed to be going in my favour for this team and after the major misfortune I'd had, I was enjoying it.

So what's all that got to do with meeting the love of my life for the first time and then taking her on a date to Prestwich Hospital? Well, our Goalkeeper at the time was my mate Miren Bates who we called Miz. Miz could eat for England. He was a big lad with a 52 inch chest and looked as hard as nails but he was as soft as fuck. Him and I used to go to a Greek place close to where he lived called The Umbrella. We would both order half a chicken and salad and go back to his mum's house in Prestwich. That wasn't all though. Miz would order steak and kidney pie, chips, peas and gravy which he ate in the chippy while waiting for our order of half a chicken each. Another example of my strangely inconsistent memory. I can't remember what road he lived on in

Prestwich with his mum but I can remember exactly what we ordered and also that we were with another team-mate, at the time, who was a top guy called Dave Ashworth, known better to us as Ashy!

It was at this time that I found out about Prestwich Hospital. Miz took me there because he'd heard that they did an 'all you eat' meal for one pound. I didn't believe it at first but it was true. Miz would sometimes fill a tray with food twice and then still have an appetite in him to go to The Umbrella afterwards for his half a chicken.

On the night I met Philomena for the first time, Miz and I had been drinking, We'd had a few beers in the Grapes in Prestwich and got slowly drunk enough to make a pact that we would never get married and just go for the ugliest birds ever. We went on to Carriages (a nightclub in Droylsden) and got as drunk as skunks and we were being right pains in the arses, literally. I was crawling around on all fours and biting girls' arses. This was a Thursday night and there had been a happy hour where it was two drinks for the price of one so we were proper shitfaced and were annoying a lot of people. I spotted Philomena later on in that evening and I was being a real arsehole mithering her for her phone number. She was desperately trying to get rid of me so I managed to get her home telephone number off her best mate, Lorraine, which she wrote on the back of a fag packet.

All I knew was that her name was Philomena and I couldn't get her out of my head. I waited for just two days, until the Saturday evening, to ring her. I was working all day Saturday and my stomach was churning all day about making the phone call. Despite my behaviour on the Thursday evening, I knew I was in love. I remember making the call on the type of phone where you put your fingers into the holes and dial the number you want. You don't see them anymore. I rang the number off the back of the fag packet and a guy answered which I later found out to be her brother Harry. I said 'Excuse me is Philomena there?' The guy responded 'Sorry mate. No one here called Philomena.' My heart sank. 'Bastard' I thought. She's deliberately given me the wrong number. I'm in bits. I've just met the love of my life and I've got a bogus number for her. It's a massive kick in the balls. 'Are you sure' I said ' No mate. There's Mena' he said. I still didn't twig that it was her. I just thought she might have a sister called Mena. "Yeah' I said 'I need to speak to her'. When she came to the phone and started talking, I realised it was her. We arranged to meet on the next Saturday night outside the Dolci shoe shop in city centre Manchester in Piccadilly.

When the time came to meet her, I was outside Dolci's and I couldn't remember what she looked like. Two girls had already passed by with me smiling at them like a not right and them staring back at me probably thinking I was weirdo or something. Third time lucky and it was Mena. It was September and she'd only just returned from Florida on holiday with her best mate, Lorraine (who had given me her number on the night we met) and she was tanned and looking gorgeous.

They say that when you meet your soul mate it completes you and that it feels like you were meant to meet. I just felt immediately comfortable her and was grateful that my drunken antics on the Thursday night had not put her off. I had a Ford Capri at the time and we walked back to my car and got in. I had the car radio tuned into Mike Shaft who was the DJ on my favourite radio show on Piccadilly Radio at the time. Mena was a proper prude and it didn't help me at all when I turned the radio on in the car before we set off and Mike Shaft was playing 'Sexual Healing' by Marvin Gaye. It looked like I had set it up so I was already in the bad books within a few minutes.

We drove towards a well-known more rural area of Manchester called Daisy Nook. It was popular area for young courting couples away from the busy traffic and looked more like you were out in the sticks. It was just reaching dusk on a beautiful summers evening and we parked up. We took the opportunity to talk and find out about each other and I can say now that talk was the only thing in my head. I was smitten with her and wanted to know more about her. We talked until it had gone dark outside and I'd found out that her name was Philomena Winstanley and she lived on church street in Newton Heath with her mum, Lillian, and her older brother Harry. Her father John lived in Clayton where she had grown up as a child and he lived there with Blaise her brother and Pat her sister. Philomena's other sister Margaret lived on Graymere lane close to Openshaw market. Her eldest brothers John, Anthony and Chris all lived nearby to her in Newton Heath. Just as we were getting into exchanging information with each other, a car pulled up in front of us. All we could see was the bright lights of the car and the next thing I know I see this person walking towards us with a torch. We can't see who it is holding the torch. We can't see anything but the torch light. Very quickly the person is at the side of my car and taps twice on the window. I semi-wind my window down and say 'Yeah!' 'What are you doing here' the voice comes back. I can see just about that it's a copper who is now shining the torch in my face. 'I'm just talking to my girlfriend' I say. He is now sounding like he is accusing me of something as his tone changes 'What are you up to?' he says. 'Nothing' I say he quickly follows up with 'Where are you going? 'Nowhere' I respond. 'Oh right' he says 'Have you got your scissors on you Chris? I immediately realised who it was. It's Frank, one of my customers who is a sergeant in the Greater

Manchester Police. He's spotted my car a mile off and decided to wind me up. 'OK' he says, 'I'll see you Monday Chris for my haircut' We are still sat there laughing when another cop car pulled up. Frank has only radioed ahead and told the patrol cars to pay us a visit every five minutes. We got the message and moved on. It was an eventful first date. I decided next time it would be a proper date and I'd take her to Prestwich Hospital. She reminds me now that it wasn't just me and her either, I brought my mate Miz along for the grub and only he and I ate, Mena didn't have anything to eat. I think she should have known then that life with me would be interesting but thankfully she wasn't put off. It was only about a week or so later that I was at her house meeting her family. Incredibly my youngest Son Rhys has just bought the house that his mum Philomena was brought up in over in Clayton which I think is brilliant. I'm sure his mum must love it too.

Mena and I got on like a house on fire. We got on with each other's friends and colleagues and enjoyed each other's company. We spent a lot of time with Mena's friend, Lorraine and her husband Steve as we were all on the same wavelength and had great times together with both them and Mena's employer, Dave Bowker and his wife at their house near Hollingworth Lake.

I'm sure Mena would confirm that It never entered our heads that we wouldn't get married. I honestly can't remember ever proposing and I'm pretty sure Mena didn't propose to me. We planned a wedding for April 1986 and a honeymoon in Portugal. On my stag do amongst others was Miz, Dave Ashworth who we called Ashy and Tony Xavier who I grew up with and was my best man. Back then our stag night was a pub crawl from Bury to Prestwich pub to pub. I'm one of the smallest in this group and as we walk into every pub, the landlord clocks this group of big lads

111

and says 'shit – here's trouble'. So in every pub the Landlord approaches us and goes 'Right lads' The lads then point out it's my stag do and the landlord then says "What's he drinking?' By the time we get to Prestwich Village and The Grapes I am proper steaming drunk. My cousin Steven Brown had a house at the back of the Grapes on Clifton Road. It was big Victorian house with a cellar. I was in no fit state to go to town so Tony took me back to Steven's house. There's absolutely no point tying me to a lamppost naked because they know I really don't give a fuck and it wouldn't bother me. The morning after I'm downstairs and all I'm feeling is my back and shoulders. I moan out loud about the pain. Tony is making breakfast and he comes up to me and says 'Are you for real? you went missing last night and I'm in the house shouting you and the next thing your head appears over the banister on the top floor and says "Yeah I'm coming" and you just threw yourself over the bannister and hit the bannisters and pinged off the sides all the way down the winding staircase'. Apparently I've then hit the deck and slept so Tony said he put me to bed. No wonder my back is sore. I don't remember it at all but I've just done the first skydive of my life without a parachute. Do you see now how I think I am lucky? It's one thing surviving that crash but now I'm surviving throwing myself off banisters. I thought it wise not to mention it to Mena!

We got married on 12th April 1986 and went to Cascais, a beautiful fishing village near Lisbon in Portugal, on honeymoon. Back in them days Mena had blond hair . Everybody there was tanned and Mena and I stood out like a sore thumb. We were at a restaurant and getting ready to order when three smartly dressed English guys, who were sat adjacent to us, said "would you like to join us?" We said yes and moved over to their table. They recommended that we had the Steak Dianne off the menu. I'd never had it before so we ordered it and then we introduced ourselves to each other. Two of them were solicitors and one was a Barrister. We explained that we'd just got married and then one of the guys says "do you mind if I sing you a love song as a wedding present? Or course we accepted and he went on 'I'm a bit rusty though so bear with me.' The restaurant came to a standstill. His voice was amazing – he was like Pavarotti. All the waiters and kitchen stuff came out to listen to me. He was unbelievably good and had a powerful voice. I still get goosebumps even now when I think about it. When he had finished, we were all getting very emotional and he got a massive round of applause from the diners and staff in the restaurant. It set our night and indeed our week off. I wish I could remember his name but what I do remember was that I turned to the table and our new friends and said ' And he calls that rusty!!

We had another honeymoon holiday in Sept 1986. After our return from holiday in April 86 things were hectic to say the least with both work and a busy social life so we decided to have another holiday and booked to Benalmadena in Spain. A few days into the holiday It was a beautiful sunny morning and we were having breakfast in a very picturesque place on a small promenade overlooking the beach and the sea. Mena and I had been having breakfast there for a few days as it was so close to the sea itself. Right next to where we were sat, was a windsurfing board. I got talking to the owner of the café who was German. I'd asked him who owned the board and he had told me it was his. As he told me this he said 'Would you like a go?'. I told him that I'd love to as I had never been windsurfing before and he simply said 'use it'. Now the bay we were in had some problems for windsurfers. Beyond the harbour was open sea and around the bay were rocks but you had about five hundred metres of sheltered waters before the open sea. I spent the course of the morning falling off the board almost as soon as I got on. It was taking me a little time to sus' it out. Before I knew it, it was lunch time and Mena and I got something to eat. As we settled back on the beach, Mena says ' I fancy a go myself' so I said 'be my guest'. I was almost chuckling to myself as she went into the sea with the board and was thinking about how long it would be before she fell off. She's soon up on the board and just heads straight out no messing and no falling off. I'm just sat there gobsmacked. Mena is slim and looks great in her swimsuit but she's not sporty at all and there she is getting the hang of it straightaway and heading out into the open sea. The owner of the board, who has been watching initially with a smile on his face realizing that my wife has just out done me, starts to panic a little. He comes over to me and says 'your wife Chris?' I just say to him 'she got herself out there she can get herself back' He's really panicking though and suggests that I take a pedalo and go and get her. She's now that far out that it is getting a bit dangerous. He must be thinking that he doesn't want a dead body on his board in front of his café! This is one of those places where you could get meals at any time of the day so I don't want to fall out with him as Mena and I will want to come back to it. So I get the pedalo and I get out to her. She'd rode an off-shore wind out there and had been trying to get back. She was panicking a little because she knew she was in deep water. When I reached her I said 'Come on yer dickhead drop your sail' She got in the pedalo with me and we dragged the collapsed board back to the shore. When I got back from holiday I realised I had the bug for windsurfing. Living in Heywood wasn't ideal for that kind of hobby but Mena, seeing how much I liked it, booked lessons for me with a guy called Martin Ashby who had a windsurfing shop in Bury on Wash Lane. It was to be the beginning of an era for myself, Mena and our family that saw us have many happy times and some pretty crazy ones too. I'll talk a little about those later on.

When we were courting, Phil used to itch her arm and pull at it a lot. When I asked what the matter was, she said it was to do with a dog that once pulled at her arm. This went on for a while and then when our first child, Arron, was born in 1989, she had a difficult birth and afterwards she started itching her forearm again and it was getting worse. Eventually I pestered her to go to the doctors and after a short examination he immediately referred her a specialist at Crumpsall. By amazing coincidence Mena was being referred to the same specialist that I had for my head injury after the crash and who my mum had been under when she had a brain hemorrhage just before my car crash, Miss Bannister. The coincidence got bigger when Mena's mum was referred to Miss Bannister years later when she had a brain tumour. Mena saw Miss Bannister at Crumpsall Hospital and she eventually got news that gave us all a shock. She had a tumour in her armpit and it was getting bigger and pressing on nerve endings and making her itch. They took part of it away and ran tests on the tumour and she attended an appointment at Crumpsall Hospital on her own and was given the news that it was cancer. She'd driven to the hospital but the news had floored her so she walked from the hospital to my shop which was about a mile and a half away. I went and got the car and gave her a lift home. It was a scary time for us both. I later got a proper bollocking off the surgeon for letting it go on for so long. I didn't argue back as, with hindsight, I was thinking the same thing myself. You can kick me, punch me and stab me if you want and I'll not give a shit but hurt Mena or any of my family and I will feel it far more than any other person. I felt responsible for not insisting that she got examined earlier. She had to attend the famous Christie hospital. She was only twenty eight years old when it happened and they didn't want to do anything that might mean that she lost her arm so they decided to remove the tumour and give her radiotherapy so that it didn't spread to the lymph glands. The specialist had said to her as she started

115

that the period of recovery that she mustn't mope around and to remain very positive. I interpreted this as that she mustn't be allowed to dwell on it so when I came home from work and she was lying on the settee I bollocked her for not doing things around the house. I remember at the time, my best man, Tony Heffernan, said to me 'Don't speak to her like that, she's had cancer' but I explained to him that it was tough love and I was doing exactly what doctor ordered. That same evening, I came downstairs to be on my own and I sobbed my heart out. I was over the top positive during the day putting a brave face on things and treating Mena normally and not with kid gloves as I believed what the doctor had said but then all of a sudden it all came out of me. It was touch and go for the next five years and then she was finally given the all clear. I can't describe how I felt when we got the news. I was so happy that she was ok. I'd have never forgiven myself if anything had happened to her.

Mena had always wanted a big family and having radiotherapy frightened her in case it affected her ability to have children. When she got the five year all clear, the specialist said to her 'If you want more children, I'd get cracking if I was you!' Jourdana and Rhys followed very quickly afterwards and then Lily was a lovely surprise some five years later to complete the family. I need to take the opportunity while talking about Phil and my family to say how she has been a fantastic part of my life. For our relationship to last as long as it did, she needed to have the patience of a saint and the balls to give as good as she got. She was a fantastic mother and still is. She fosters children now and does an incredible job of that and thankfully we still talk and have remained friends despite the fact that we are not married anymore. I am grateful that is the case as some couples might not have that benefit after divorce. I'll say more on that later.

Our family unit started in 1989 when we had Arron. We were living at 36 Cromwell Street in Heywood. We were enjoying life as a couple going out for meals and being very active at weekends. We were chatting one night in the house and we both came to the conclusion that we wanted to start a family. Now, from a man's point of view this is like winning the lottery. In my head after we agree this all I could hear was the word, 'Bingo'. I'm thinking that we are going to have months of love making trying to make a baby. I'm rubbing my hands together, this is win win situation. Well not for long. One week! One week it took before Phil gave me the good news that she was pregnant. Now don't get me wrong I was as happy as anything getting the news. We were going to be parents and that was both exciting and frightening at the same time. I just thought that the baby making bit could have lasted a few months longer that's all. My reaction of 'Already? Are you sure?' could have gone down better too!

Chapter 11 – Captain Fantastic's Kids

From almost having my life cut short by the crash in 1980 and the issues I faced through the early 80's particularly, it was hard to see that I would have the life that I have had for the last 40 years. I could have died, I could have been committed or I could have been locked up. Instead I have the most incredible family and sons and daughters who are capable of so much. There can't be many parents out there who are not proud of their kids in some way and I am no exception. The only thing I would say is that I have always challenged them and pushed them and that may have come across that I have not been impressed by their achievements so far. Nothing could be further from the truth. I am immensely proud of all four of them. The reference to 'Captain Fantastic' relates to the film of the same name with Vigo Mortenson. I won't spoil the film for you if you have never seen it but suffice to say that the dad in the film seems like a crank like me and his kids are cranks too but incredibly admirable. It's an amazing film and my daughter Jourdana has always said that 'It's like watching a film about our family'

The only thing that doesn't fit with the comparison of our family with the film 'Captain Fantastic' is that it's about the Dad and his children and the mum is a background figure. Before I can talk about my children individually, I want to talk about their mum, Mena. I married Philomena on 12th April 1986 in Christ The King Church in Newton heath . We got on like a house on fire straightaway from the first few minutes of meeting and I don't even think there was ever a proposal. I hope that's not my memory playing tricks on me again but I honestly don't remember ever proposing to her. We just seemed to go forward with our relationship because it was so natural. Obviously we must have discussed it at some stage but it seemed never in any doubt to me that we'd marry.

I don't think it will take a brain surgeon to work out that Mena was the most patient of wives given the type of man I am. I always put my fitness and training first. It had saved me from going around the twist and I needed it to carry on in life. I need it now 40 years later more than ever. I can't imagine a life without being able to train towards some goal or another. That must have made me a little difficult to live with to say the least but Mena was incredibly supportive and we tried to tie it in with family life as much as we could with activities at weekends, going to the coast or some lake or another. To me she is still my soul mate and although we are divorced now, we are still friends and speak regularly. It would be hard to accept if that wasn't the case because you don't just switch off love for someone that been so close to for so long. Mena is an amazing woman. She fosters children and has looked after at least seven children over the last three years which is incredible. She should get a medal for being my wife for so long never mind all the fantastic work she puts in looking after those children. I do want to take this opportunity though to thank Mena for our thirty two years of marriage and thank her especially for her putting with me and my ways. As I said in Chapter 10, she will always be my soul mate and the love of my life – and I hope we will at least remain friends forever.

So to our kids now. Arron was the first born in 1988 and is 32 at the time of me writing this. As with all first-borns, they seem to get a lot of attention throughout their early life that a second child or third or fourth, doesn't get because there are other children that need your attention too. I always encouraged Arron to get involved in sports and he was the first of our four to take up martial arts and Shaolin. He completed his various belts and was very good at it too and ended up in exhibitions and was considering at one time spending time in China and learning more about the Shaolin discipline. I mention somewhere else in the book that Arron is a drummer and wants to train to be a professional percussionist. When Mena was pregnant with him she used to make me listen to or feel her tummy when we had music on in the house, it seemed that the baby was kicking his feet to the rhythm already showing signs of what Arron would become. He first showed an interest in the drums when a friend of mine who was a session drummer called Tony Thompson was showing Rhys how to play something on the drums and Arron wanted to have a go. The trouble was Arron had broken his arm recently and had it in plaster so he could only use the one hand. Arron took the drumsticks and held them in one hand like you would hold chop sticks and began to beat out the rhythm with both sticks, Tony was amazed and said 'well I've never seen that before'. Arron is determined to be a professional percussionist and I back him 110% to succeed in anything he puts his mind to. He is a deep thinker and enjoys learning and new experiences. I managed to spend some quality time with him on a trek to Hadrian's wall recently which I talk about in chapter 25. I loved the opportunity to spend time with Arron doing something together using the trip to bond further and I plan to do this with all of them as much as possible to catch up on some lost time. I probably didn't spend as much one to one time with them growing up as I should have so if I get an opportunity to do that now I'll jump at it. I'm lucky that I have close relationships with them all already as we are all good mates but I don't think I could ever spend too much time with them. I love it.

Jourdana came along in 1993. She was our first daughter. I could never have guessed how much alike a daughter could be with me. She's just as driven and competitive and has more of my traits than I thought a daughter could have of a dad. She's a model and very good looking, again like me!!! She's also very hard working. All my kids have those Chris Duoba crank genes in them and when they were younger, and even now, I'd invite them to try and catch me off guard by attacking me when they thought I'd least expect it. For those that have seen the film, this was just like Kato in the Pink Panther films, who is Clouseau's man servant who attacks him constantly. They had never caught me off guard until one day while I was in Aldi shopping on my own, Jourdana attacked me and jumped on my back. She had me in a head lock and kisses me on the cheek and says 'Love you dad" She'd got me. One day I think around 2014 she came back from a modelling assignment and told me that she had loads of energy that she needed to get rid of and pent up aggression. She had also done martial arts when she was younger as all my children did so and I had just heard of an event in Middleton for Shaolin and it was a last man or woman standing event. We got her entered and got through all the preliminary's and eventually she made the final and she was fighting a girl a good bit stockier than her which wasn't hard as Jourdana is slim. During the bout, the girl lands a kick to Jourdana's throat and it hurt her but then you see this glazed look come over Jourdana's face because she been hurt. I'm sat there thinking 'oh shit'. Like I said, Jourdana is a lot like me and the red mist has descended and she is furious. Next thing this girl is on the deck sparko (sorry - translation from Mancunian is – on the floor dazed or unconscious). The tournament did the trick though and Jourdana had got rid of all her frustrations and pent up aggression and also went home with a winner's trophy. There were 30 + competitors in that tournament and Jourdana walked off a catwalk in Paris and won it.

Life's experiences are so important. We all get bad times in our life and we have to handle them but when the good times come we should make the most of them. I feel that I should have had more with my kids but I'm planning to do more going forward with them as I enjoy their company so much. Jourdana got her degree last year 2019. She achieved the second highest mark in the University for her subject and was to graduate at the special presentation at The Bridgewater Hall wearing the traditional hat and gown. Well before the event she said to me 'I'm not paying for this - it's too expensive.' "Jourdana" I say "You are getting your hat and gown and graduating at the Bridgewater Hall, I'll go halves with you". I've always said to my kids that if they really want something I'd always go halves with them so that they are working with me to earn it. I explained to her that in 30 years time when she is looking back and saying 'what a great day that was', the money won't come into it at all. 'OK' she finally says. Only then she said to me "I've got two tickets here and you can be back in work for 12'o'clock dad'. I say "Jourdana, don't you realise I am going on the razz that day with you, we are going to have a great day.' I've already told Faz I'm not coming in that day. I know this is a great day in Jourdana's life and I'm going to be there to see it and celebrate it with her. This achievement is a passport to life for her and this will open doors that would have been shut beforehand. Now it's a question of how far she wants to take it. Both Philomena and I were there to see it and were so proud of her. All my kids make me proud. They are all amazing young adults with fantastic potential for the future. I hope they can be as lucky as me in getting the breaks. I was fortunate enough to spend more time with Jourdana recently on one of my bonding adventures as Jourdana, Arron and myself went on a search for the monument to William Wallace (Braveheart for those that don't recognize the name - see chapter 25).

Rhys came along in 1994. Our second son. Having two lads and the way that they bounced off each other reminded me of my time at home with Eamonn and Simon. Brothers have that special bond that if it came down to it they would be there for one another in a flash but brotherly love always involves fighting like cat and dog too and winding each other up.

They are very different characters, both brilliant and special to me in their own way but like chalk and cheese to each other. Rhys was into Rugby and was playing for Eccles Under 13s down at Eccles ground and during the game a player got tackled and Rhys jumped in. It was a bad tackle and it resulted in fisticuffs. I'm on touchline with Philomena and on the opposite side of the pitch. Philomena starts panicking and says to me "Get over there and help him out". "It's a rugby union game, they will sort themselves out" I said. As I said that a guy runs onto the pitch and the Ref grabs the guy and says "get off my pitch" The Ref sorts it all out and he came over to us and gets the guy who has run on and give him a massive bollocking. I turn to Mena and say. "There you go. That's how to handle it" To be fair I wasn't just relying on the Ref to sort it out, I did also know that this was Rhys we were talking about and that firstly he didn't need me to help him sort it out, he was well capable himself and secondly the last thing he would have wanted was for me to step in. Rhys, just like all of our children, from an early age can stand up on their own two feet and I am proud of them all for that.

Rhys has already done things in his young life that most men would be happy to experience across their entire lives. He's well-travelled and has achieved an awful lot in his 26 years of life so far. He still may end up in the Marines as it has been a constant attraction to him growing up. While he was in Cardinal Langley they did an outward bound type of exercise in conjunction with the army where he had to go out and then avoid being captured and they never caught him and in the next one he had to capture the sergeant. Rhys worked out where the Sergeant was walking and he buried himself in a load of mud to get him. As the sergeant came closer another kid from another school comes along and steps on Rhys and gives him away but the sergeant knew that Rhys would have had him. Following his careers recruitment, Rhys went down and enlisted on to their qualification course which was of course basic training. He completed that but it just wasn't the right time for him. He is a daredevil that needs that adrenaline rush or a new challenge regularly. After his sky diving experience with us all in New Zealand, he must have got the bug for that as he has gone through the necessary training and qualifications you need to do a solo sky dive and has done countless solo sky dives since then. He currently works as a specialist abseiler and has worked on many projects and has had some incredible experiences. He's already well beat me in that area as I couldn't do that work with my fear of heights. Rhys has amazingly just bought the original house that his mum was raised in with her family in Clayton. Rhys and his partner Annie have just recently announced that they are expecting their first child in October 2020. I couldn't be more pleased for them and I couldn't have asked for a better partner for Rhys than Annie. And so the Duoba name continues down our line to the next generation. The term granddad might bother some blokes but I wonder how many granddads think that they can still win their next Ultra race.

Then we have the youngest of our four, Lily, who was a lovely surprise for us both in June 2000 . Lily is so self-sufficient she is incredible. Being the youngest you could end up being molly coddled by everyone but not Lily, she is so capable and independent. I'm sure all four of our kids could say that I haven't spent a lot of time with them especially when I was training hard for events but Lily is the one that I think I have given least time to and that does bother me, just as it does bother me that I haven't spent enough time with all of them. I have started to try and rectify this with them with bonding trips to different walks or landmarks and I aim to do more and more of this going forward if I can and when time suits all of them, especially Lily.

Lily has always been this independent soul. She had a habit of wandering off and disappearing from a very early age. When she was two and a half we were in a beautiful place called Russell Bay on the North Island of New Zealand right at the tip of Auckland. We were in a shop looking at clothing prices, just doing a little bit of research really. It was around lunchtime and there was a fish and chip shop next door selling local fish. In Manchester, Cod and chips represents our most popular fish and chips. In New Zealand their fish was Hoki and chips and was gorgeous. As you can imagine being a Mancunian family, you could always be drawn to a fish and chip shop especially in somewhere like New Zealand where the local fish would probably be fantastic. Mena had said to me "you look after Lily and I'll go and get dinner". So we mooched around for a bit and then met Mena at the chip shop. Rhys, Jourdana and Arron came out with Mena with their chips and I said 'Where's Lily?' They looked at me as if I was a lunatic. "I don't know" Mena said. So now there's immediate hysterics, she's missing! We are all trying to calm each other down and I'm thinking that we are in New Zealand, she'll be fine. That doesn't stop us running around like blue-arsed flies (I'm guessing that comes from the way a blue bottle buzzes around but I don't know for definite). After a few minutes we went from calming each other down to proper shitting it. It was a small bay and the police station wasn't that far away so we reported her missing and had a load of tourists running around with us trying to find her but she's nowhere to be seen. Another half hour goes by and now we are really panicking. The shops we had been in started locking up so we backtracked our steps and ended up back in the clothes shop and there she was. She was only hiding in some clothes in the shop ''playing hide and seek'. She loved the fact that everyone was looking for her and laughing her little head off. Even then she showed her little competitive edge in her own game of hide and seek.

Not long after coming back from New Zealand we were living with Mena's mum on Church Street in Newton Heath and there had been reports of child snatching going on in Manchester. Mena doesn't remember this particular occasion but it was a lovely summers day and Lily has gone missing. She'd done it again. She had us chasing around the streets of Newton Heath shouting her name and after what seemed like hours, but was probably half an hour, we were fearing the worst. Then I hear some giggling coming from our car on the driveway. I open the car and there she is in the back of the car in the well between the seats giggling away. I said 'We've told you before this is not funny" and she just laughed even more.

Lily went to Cardinal Langley High School, as did all our children, and she was a great swimmer. Her mum described her as an elegant swimmer because she cut through the water effortlessly. It was clear that she was going to be a great swimmer when she was at St Thomas more junior school. When she was 13 or 14 years old she used to swim front crawl for the school. She's always been knowledgeable about nutrition, which she must have got from me and we had a routine that if as she finished a race that we were watching from the balcony of the swimming pool, I would drop a treat / energy bar or something like that, down to her from the balcony and she would eat it and take in energy for the next leg or race. She was so competitive though that she had a bad habit of looking for her opponent which meant lifting her head out of the water to see them. Once we had told her that this was slowing her down and to concentrate on her performance, she became an amazing competitor. She used to come with me to the Middleton arena swimming very early in the morning around 6.00am to improve her swimming techniques and it was great for me to be able to spend time with my youngest before I went off to work that day. Unlike the other three, she never did martial arts. She was a natural fighter though and could look after herself. You didn't grow up in the Duoba household with those brothers and sister without being able to hold your own and I think this is what has influenced her and made her the independent individual she has become. I hope that something of both Mena and myself has rubbed off on her and I think it has as she set very high standards for herself personally. She is currently at Leeds University studying for a degree in Physical Education and Sports coaching which will hopefully open the door to many options for her going forward. Lily has been in a steady relationship now for nearly four years with her boyfriend Callum, who she has known for probably 9 years as they met when they went to the same high school together. Again, I couldn't ask for a nicer lad for Lily to be involved with. Watch out for Callum too. He has been making headlines recently as a professional footballer and plays for Barnsley scoring a massive goal for the club in a dramatic league game versus Brentford recently that ensured his team stayed in The Championship for the coming 2020/21 season and prevented Brentford getting promotion to the Premiership.

Lily once said to me "If Arron was appearing on stage at the Albert Hall playing percussion in an orchestra and Jourdana was appearing on a cat walk in Paris modelling for a famous designer and Rhys was passing out in The Marines and it was my graduation ceremony in Leeds all on the same day. Who would you go and see? My answer was 'None of you – I'd go and get your mum and persuade her to come out on the lash with me and have the biggest celebration ever because we would be so happy for all of you'. 'Good answer' says Lily.

I am immensely proud of all four of our children. Like everybody else, I just want to see our children happy and with a chance in life of a future that they can get excited about. All four of my children are at those stages in their lives where the next decision they take could possibly be the one that formulates the rest of their life. I love the end of a film I saw recently (I won't name it as it will be a major spoiler) where the main character ends up stood next to their car at a crossroad with a map out that shows that the four different ways leads to different parts of America and Canada. There doesn't need to be any script because you can see what this means to the person stood there. So it is with our four children. Which way do you go? Instead of this being a confused time and a pressured time, see it as an exciting time where you could literally do anything you want. If you go one way, your life ends up in a very different outcome than if you go another way but you are in total control. How many 60 or 70 year olds would love to be 20+ again at that crossroads with the world at their feet? I know our four will make the right decisions for them and as long as they are happy that is all we wish for them. I've never been a gushy person by any stretch of the imagination but hopefully they all know they I love them. They are the most amazing kids with fantastic and individual personalities. I know most parents will big up their children if asked about them but I just can't see any family having four more amazing and capable kids and now young adults than our four. If you haven't seen the film 'Captain Fantastic' then go and get it - you're in for a treat. Then remember that Jourdana said that no film reminded her of our family more than that film. I'll leave the last word though in this chapter to Lily. Of all the stories, my favourite is one that she actually told me. She was travelling through Rhodes in Middleton in a car with her mum in terrible weather and Mena spotted this guy walking along the road dressed in shorts and flip flops but with a big thick coat on. The weather was shocking and Mena said to Lily "look at that poor homeless guy wearing shorts and flip flops. He must be freezing. That poor poor man" and Lily looked at the guy and said **"Mam, that's Dad!!"**

Chapter 12 – Rage

I want to make it clear that aggression isn't my normal go to behavior. In my head, my idea of a great day is being surrounded by positive people doing challenging things. I bounce off positive people. I admire people who makes things happen and inspire others. If I could inspire one person positively by telling my story , I would be chuffed to bits. I had two initial objectives at the start of this project. The first was to respond to the feeling I had on that bridge in 2017. It was a feeling that I was being compelled to tell my story. The second objective was to get the message out there that anything is possible with a continued positive approach. The third objective was that if by telling my story I could convince just one person not to step out in front of that truck or abort whatever other method they are considering, then that would be some achievement. They need to know that things can change and that they can become happy and motivated again.

I feel very strongly about people, especially young people, being told that they can't do something. The human mind is such a powerful thing and if you think you can't do something then you won't be able to but if you tell yourself you can do it then you are far more likely to achieve it. I have needed that positivity all my life but especially after the accident. Things were happening in my head that I didn't understand. Things that I didn't want to be happening were happening and at times I was out of control. It took a long time of me not accepting it and believing that things would get better if I continued to believe in myself. I could never have done it alone though. Firstly it was my mum that showed faith in me and supported me through it and then my wife, Mena and my four children showed great understanding of me as a person and allowed me to pursue my sporting ambitions to compete at a high and extreme level.

I will always be grateful to all of them for that as I know it's not been easy for them at times. I want to share with you some of the incidents that made me such a difficult person to understand and that could easily have seen my wife turning away from me. Instead she didn't and she showed great faith in me for many years through these incidents.

It was plain to see that I was in a bad way in 1980 and others were talking about my 'life limiting' injuries and my mental state. Now though in 2020, although I don't think I have 100% recovered from my brain injury, my injuries have not prevented me doing anything that I really wanted to do. Physically, it is clear how far I have come and in the next few chapters I will talk about some of the amazing things I have experienced in the last 40 years since the crash. What is harder to see is how far I have come mentally. Here I am sat here thinking about this chapter on a park bench in Heaton Park in North Manchester at 60 years old with my long and wild grey beard and a huge rucksack on my back. People passing by either think I am homeless or a nutter and they tend to steer clear of me. They couldn't possibly know that now I am a perfectly approachable guy who is always up for a chat with anyone. I love meeting new people and bouncing off someone through the art of conversation. Don't get me wrong, woe betide anyone who has a go at me or anyone close to me as I think I am still quite capable of doing anything I need to do to protect myself or anyone I love but I have changed a lot in the 40 years since the crash. Back in the first 10 years of my recovery, things could get very dark and I could be aggressive at the drop of a hat. My increased aggression started in the hospital just after the crash and was fueled by my frustration with my recovery. I wanted to get better faster. When I got home, my mum was tested to her limits with my continued aggression against family members. I was taking the usual arguments brothers and sisters tend to have to new extremes but luckily my mum showed great patience with me and helped me bring that to a head. I know that my brothers and sister also had a hard time with me and I can only apologise to them for that. Outside of the home, my increased impatience with people didn't change for many years and if provoked, a red mist descended and I could get out of control very quickly. It wouldn't take much for me to react to a situation in an aggressive way and then soon afterwards go through the feeling of guilt about how I had behaved. Just as I had asked my mum that day, I asked myself after many serious incidents 'Why am I like this' I remember the Incredible Hulk being on the TV and when he got angry he went from mild mannered David Banner to this raging green powerful giant version of himself. What I identified with this was that David Banner didn't want to be the Hulk. It just happened when he got angry. I hated what I was becoming too. I couldn't help but overreact to things and get very very angry. I'd always regret things afterwards though.

The worst cases of this came out while in a car. It didn't matter whether I was the driver or a passenger, believe me, you didn't want to end up in a row with me. I'm not joking when I say that I think I helped define the term 'Road Rage' which was first used around 1988.

There are many 'Road Rage' incidents on our busy Manchester roads but I'm pretty sure that your average person doesn't get themselves involved with as many as I did personally. Drivers having a go at me or any of my family members would push my buttons immediately.

One evening I came out of work to go and pick up a video from a shop on Bury Old Road before setting off for home. It meant taking a short detour from my usual route which I did but as I indicated to turn into the narrow road that was set back from the main road in front of the shops, I realised that I was about to make a mistake and I was entering the narrow road at the exit. It was a one way system and the entrance was about 50 yards further down the road. It was an honest and easy mistake to make but no harm done. Just as I decided to maneuver the car and go to the entrance, I heard the sound of a car horn and two guys in a car came past me and gave me the finger. I gestured to them to pull over and they did. Because there were two of them they initially got cocky and were acting tough but when I actually got out of the car their bravado waned and the driver started his engine again. I booted the back of the car and put a dent in it. He made his next mistake of stopping and I opened the back door and dragged him into the back seat and give him a few digs. I remember I was shouting things about him being a dead man in temper. I expected his mate to join in but he just sat there petrified. I stopped what I was doing and walked back to my car. I immediately regretted it and went back to the car and offered to pay for the damage to his car but the driver, who by now clearly had a busted nose, said it was ok and drove off. I felt bad but if I had been a lad who wasn't able to take care of himself would the two of them bullied him or waded into him? I thought that at the very least they might think twice about having a go at people from the safety of their own car in future. To be fair I was trying to justify my actions to myself as best I could.

A further incident was after Mena and I were married. My temper raised its ugly head again on a day that Philomena picked me up and was bringing me home from work. I was around 29 years old, so this was about 10 years after the accident and we were married and living in Ainsworth, I had cycled to work and couldn't be bothered cycling home so she picked me up. I was in the passenger seat and we were well into the journey when Mena pulls out into traffic and this lad's car had to swerve. Before any apology can be given, he made gestures to us and gave me the v sign. I insisted that Mena chased him and we end up following him down Radcliffe New Road. On the next occasion he had to stop, I jumped out of our car and dived into his passenger side window which he had fully open. He got the shock of his life as I banged him on the nose. I always seemed to go for the nose as it shocks them. I gave him a couple more digs and walked back to our car. As soon as I got back to my car I'd already regretted it so I walked back and apologised. He accepted, probably thinking that if he didn't I'd dive in his car again .

The third incident I recollect, I was taking Mena to work. She worked at Unger Meats on Derby Street in Cheetham Hill near Manchester Town centre. I was heading down Queens Road towards Cheetham Hill and this guy suddenly overtakes me doing easily 100 miles an hour. Well that's what it appeared to be to me at the time. He roars past us and beeps his horn at me for getting in his way. I beeped my horn back and started to chase after him. It was a knee jerk reaction to go after him. I gave no thought to the consequences. I couldn't catch him at the speed he was going but then he was forced to stop at the traffic lights and I caught him up and jumped out of the car again. I don't know what this guy is like so I'm anticipating a gangster type and I'm ready for confrontation. He sees me coming along the side of the car and he panics and starts to wind his window up. That was a bad move. He really needed to lock his door first or do both at the same time because I just opened his door and pulled him out of the car. He comes out of the car with his hand still holding on to the lever that winds the window up and down and I've hit punched him before he can react. It was this incident that convinced me more than others that I needed help. I remember that the only thought going through my head at the time was that I'd noticed he didn't have his seat belt on and that was against the law. This gives you a picture of how I viewed my own behaviour. I'd chased a car down the road at high speed, I'd jumped out of my car without any regard for Mena or anyone else, I'd run up to his car and dragged him out of his car and punched him and the only thing I see wrong with all of that is that he isn't wearing his seat belt!

Mena, of course, isn't happy at all about any of this. She'd seen me doing this too much and on that occasion she not only wasn't impressed with my behaviour but what added insult to injury was that she was late for work. I still wasn't getting it. I was reacting in a way that I thought was right when someone has a go at me in some way. Philomena made it clear she thought I was over-reacting to the extreme but I guess she also knew that this had started happening since my accident.

In a fourth incident something happened that helped me see my behaviour for what it was. Mena was at her mums and I was going to pick her up. I was approaching a junction in the road and this car was coming towards me with their headlights on full beam. I stopped at the junction and got out and ran up to car with the headlamps on effing and jeffing at the driver to get out of car. When I got to the car the bloke driving was petrified and in the back of the car was two young kiddies also looking scared. I felt immediately bad. I realised that I had to stop doing this. Seeing the kids so frightened disturbed me. I had become a raging bull in these road rage incidents. I got back to my car and sat there for a few moments. It was a moment of realisation for me. I had to stop this now and control my temper.

It was a major turning point for me but I still carried around a lot subconsciously for a good while afterwards. I was trained at martial arts and this together with my disregard for pain meant that I would be a nightmare opponent for somebody so I needed to avoid confrontation. Not in the interest of self-preservation, but more in the interest of not hurting somebody badly. I remember a marshal in a race once waking me from a sleep at one of the checkpoints as I was resting before the next stage, he gave me a shove and I woke with a start and nearly broke his neck as I reacted. He was shouting 'Chris, Chris you're in an event" and suddenly I came around and was embarrassed and apologised. The marshal who woke me was not ex forces. If he had have been, he would have known how to wake me so that I didn't overreact. Luckily most of these people marshaling the events are ex forces and took things like this in their stride because they knew what to do and how to handle these things. Mena was understanding to a degree but clearly knew that this wasn't acceptable behaviour. The thing was, after every incident, I was totally in agreement that I was over reacting, so it would appear that I understood that my behavior was unacceptable, which was true but this didn't stop the red mist from descending the next time. I was always willing to stand up for myself or others before the crash. I certainly was no angel but the incidents in my life where I've had to 'bring it' to use a modern term were in incidents where you would be expected to step up. That's very different from losing it with very little provocation. For example, I mentioned earlier about working at Pips well before the crash and being sacked from there. I did a few jobs at Pips but mostly during the busy periods I would be collecting glasses from the punters. I'd lied about my age as you had to be a minimum of eighteen years old and I was only seventeen but looked older. My initial plan was to avoid too much attention and get my head down and earn some money. It used to get a little more boisterous as the night wore on and even collecting glasses became a demanding task. I accidentally bumped into a girl with a lot of glasses in my arms and she just went for me. She was drunk and was vicious so I just slapped her to one side. One of the bouncers hadn't seen the whole incident and grabbed hold of me. I shouted to him 'Woah! woah! I work here, she went for me' He backed off then and controlled the situation by pacifying the girl and her friends. She kept shouting at me and saying things like 'you are going to get it' . I found out later that she had brothers and that I'd have to watch out for myself. There was a lot of knife crime about at the time so for the next few weeks I made sure I had my wits about me. I considered carrying a knife myself just in case. In the end I decided this wasn't a sensible option but when you fear that you might be jumped by one or more vicious people and that there was every chance they would have a weapon, the truth of it is that there might be no one there to help you and my seventeen year old brain was saying to me that I had to be able to defend myself. For the next two weeks I was very wary and sods law, in the third week just when I started to think it wasn't going to happen it did happen. Just before the end of the night as I was collecting pots, I was walking back to the bar with about ten pots in either arm. To explain, when you carried say ten pint pots in one hand, your hand would be down by your waist and your arm will support the tower of glasses up towards the inside of your shoulder. As I was walking back, this lad steps out in front of me and said 'like hitting girls do you?' and punched me in the face. I calmly put the glasses down on the bar turned back around and laid into him. After a couple of punches, I had him by the throat and bent over a metal rail just as a bouncer arrives and says 'Take him outside Chris'. I frog marched him to the exit and threw him out. The bouncers on the door would then sort him out if he tried to get back in. I went back downstairs to carry on working but the manager had me called into the office and fired me. I honestly didn't know what I could have done different on the

---

137

night. He attacked me while my hands were full and I wasn't going to let him have two free shots. Both him and his sister or girlfriend or whoever she was both learnt that if they hit someone, its highly likely they will hit you back but harder! I felt it was unjust but so be it. Bollocks to them.

As the years go on, I am a much more tolerant person and far less easily agitated but I still do not like moaners or mood hooverers and negativity. All my customers understand that when they sit in my chair to have their haircut that our conversation will always be a positive one because if it isn't I tend to make it positive. For example a very good example of this is when a long standing customer come into the shop one day and sat in the chair whinging continually about a headache. He seemed to be going on and on about it so I stood behind him where he could see me in the mirror and said "See this hammer here - If I hit your big toe with it will it make your headache go?" Before I could finish my sentence he had said 'Chris it's already gone mate' Amazing the power of positive thinking isn't it?!!

I also have a big thing about bullies. I believe that a bully should get their comeuppance which is why that last Road Rage incident immediately made me feel uncomfortable because I realised that in that situation I was becoming the very thing I despised. There's a huge difference between standing up for yourself and being a bully.

Not long after I got out of hospital in 1980 when I was still 19 years old, I met a few friends in a local pub called The Belmont on Middleton Road. After a few beers in there a few of them said they were going into town to a nightclub and were egging me on to go with them. In those days last orders in the pub during the week was 10.30pm and on Saturdays that stretched to 11.00pm. If you went into town there were nightclubs that had extended serving hours to 2.00am. Every lad in Manchester knew that after 2.00am it was a bit of a free for all in the city centre known to us as Piccadilly. The streets around Piccadilly and the all night bus station in the centre after 2.00am became a volatile place and not one for the faint hearted. The lads in the Belmont convinced me to go into town with them saying that I'd not been out with them for ages. We ended up going into a club called Placemate 7 on Whitworth Street near the just outside the city centre. It was called Placemate 7 because it had seven different rooms and dance floors, some of which were dedicated to certain music. For example, they had a Bowie room or pure disco room. You weren't always guaranteed to get into these sort of places especially if you were in a group of lads already showing signs of being drunk, but we got in ok. I remember that we had a great hour or so and in that time had a few more drinks. At some point I'd needed a wee so found my way to the toilet. I don't know how long I was in there but when I came out I couldn't find the people I was with and people were starting to leave so it must have been close to or after 2.00am. I then made a bad decision to make my way home on my own instead of having a good look around for the lads. I was badly drunk and isolated in town which is not a good idea at all. This was in the very early 80's but I don't think there's been any decade in Manchester that putting yourself in that position in the early hours of the morning is a good move. I turned right out of the door of the club and started walking towards the city centre to get a bus. Although I was very drunk and unstable I became acutely aware of a bad situation developing for me. There were three lads in front of me walking in the same direction but I was gaining on them almost as if they had slowed down for me to catch them up. As I got nearer to them I got this strong feeling that I was in the wrong place at the wrong time. I saw what I thought was a brick on the floor and bent down to pick it up and it turned out to be a piece of wood. As I did that I

139

heard a voice from behind me say 'you don't want to pick that up mate' I turned around and it was another two lads who were right on top of me. As I stood up straight from picking the wood up, one of them was literally centimetres from my face staring right into my eyes. As I was staring back at him something hit me on the back of the head. I could tell it was something being held by somebody and not thrown and using my peripheral vision I could see it was the lads I was following who had turned back to get involved. As I went towards the floor from the blow to the back of my head I met this guy's foot full in the face. I also remember getting a kick in my already damaged left elbow from the back. I jumped back up instantly and put my right elbow straight through this guy's face and he's out of it straightaway. Once I saw his legs wobble I made my move and barged through the remaining lads in the direction of Placemate's doorway which was still close by. I was getting blows from all directions and blood was pouring from my nose but I kept my feet and managed to get back into the doorway of the club. The bouncers of the club were in black jackets and white shirts. One of them stepped into my path to stop me and as he did that all of a sudden I sneezed and covered his white shirt in claret. He was furious and for a moment I thought that I'd actually got myself into an even worse situation. Then directly behind the bouncer I spot two girls who I knew called Stephanie and Helen. They shouted 'we know him, we'll look after him'. I think the girls were well known in there because the bouncers amazingly then let me back into the club and the girls took me to the ladies' toilets and cleaned me up. My injured elbow from the crash was up like a balloon and had split. The girls came with me in a taxi to the hospital and then went home. They tried to stitch it up but it was a mess. I should have really waited until the swelling came down before I went. The whole incident had an effect on me. I had months of difficulty sleeping as I kept seeing the face of the guy who kicked me in the face.

Whereas some people might think of the incident and be a little frightened by it, the reason I was having difficulty sleeping was because I was so desperate to go and get him. I obsessed with it for a short time. I even had crazy thought of 'maybe I should go and just hit every fucker and eventually I'll get the right one'. This is how unstable I'd become after the crash. When I was younger, my dad used to say to me 'One day you'll come unstuck son' but I've gone through life thinking the opposite due to my determination and martial arts training. I used to say back to him 'I won't dad. The lad who picks on me is making a big mistake. He might start it but I'll finish it'. I'm the life and soul of any party. I like to have a laugh and I would never hit someone first without provocation, despite my thoughts after the Placemate incident, but I'd handle any bully anytime.

I hate bullies. I'll talk about my competition life shortly, but just after I did the 'Atlantic Challenge' which led to me being away for three days, I got the train back from St Ives. After arriving in Manchester I jumped on a tram from Piccadilly to Bowker Vale. I had two rucksacks on. One on the front and one on my back. I'm pumped up massively and feel in peak condition. I got on the tram and was stood through the journey holding on to one of the bars that you use to steady yourself. The guy stood next to me was full of tattoos and was a little smaller than me but stocky. He's in a tight tee short to show off his muscles and tattoos and his head is completely bald and here's me, a little taller than him but not stocky and with this long beard that I have. As we set off the tram wobbles and I bump into him slightly by accident. Next thing I know he's squaring up to me. His body is pumped up and tense and without him saying anything, I sense he's saying to me 'hey you prick'. I just stared right back into his eyes and without me saying anything my eyes were saying to him "yes?". After only a few seconds of this psychological duel, his

141

neck muscles give in, his head bows and it's like watching a popped balloon deflate. Sometimes just a look can do that to a bully.

Another time I remember spotting on a bus someone who I knew from my past who was a bully. I don't remember where I was going or even if the bus was going to where I needed to go but I got on the bus and went upstairs to where this guy was. As I turned from the stairs to go to a seat I see that the whole top deck is empty except for this lad who I had seen many times throwing his weight around in the local pub and stirring up trouble. I walked directly to him and sat next to him. That always worries people when all the seats are empty on a bus but the nutcase who gets on the bus sits next to you. I didn't stop at that though, while I just rigidly stayed staring forward I kept shuffling up to him so in the end I was crushing him against the window so he can't move. He didn't say a word. Eventually I decided I needed to get off and I just turned to him and said in the most menacing way I could, 'See ya!'. I loved every second of it, He was absolutely shitting himself. I wish I could have videoed the whole thing and sent it to all the people who he had pushed around in the past. Luckily, I found a way to use all the pent up energy and positivity that was inside of me and focus on channeling that eventually in a far more meaningful way going forward. I once saw an interview with a guy that I admire greatly, Sir Ranulph Fiennes. He had lost his first wife ,Ginny, through Cancer. He was saying that for a long time after Ginny's death, if he sat alone with his own thoughts for too long it became unbearable. If he got up and did something it made it much more manageable. That's exactly how I felt. If I sat along thinking about things for too long my mental health would suffer, so I decided to do something and eventually I developed my life to ensure that me sitting down with nothing to do was highly unlikely.

Chris as a thirteen year old down in Cornwall close to
where he would do his Atlantic Coast Challenge
into his mid fifies.

Duoba Family in New Zealand 2003
Back Row left to right
Jourdana, Chris, Lily, Philomena and Aaaron with Rhys
below on the right

**My 'Iron Man" Uncle Joe Ross
as a young man in the Merchant Navy**

**Me and my Mum training for the Marathon Des Sables
In Cornwall**

John (Jonas) Duoba with Chris and Arron at Arrons'
christening

Proof of the time Chris and Smithy crossed the finishing line in Karnten, Austria in 2004

Rochdale Triathlon Club
From left to right, Wendy, Anthony, Tony, Scouse & Chris
at Middleton Leisure Centre

Chapter 13 – The Claim

40 years on and I've made an amazing physical recovery from the accident even if I say so myself. I feel a very lucky man to have survived the first 24 hours after the crash, never mind the last 40 years. It's been an incredibly eventful journey from the moment that the two paramedics yanked me out of that car, to my current physical shape. I'm not perfectly healthy by any stretch of the imagination but I'm not in bad shape for a man who has just hit sixty years of age. The most recent medical I had, after some dizziness I had been experiencing when competing, reported that I had a set of test results more suited to a 25 year old man rather than someone of my age with the exception of my blood pressure which was the issue causing my dizziness and affecting my recovery rate in training. Once I was prescribed medication for this, it corrected the balance and I was raring to go again and have been fine ever since.

While I was in the hospital after the accident, I had dozens of X-rays of my elbow as initially they had done a lot of reconstruction work on the joint and put a metal plate in. One of my fellow patients at the time was a guy on the same ward as myself. Well I say ward, it was more a room with four patients in. Initially I was in a room at the end of the ward which I am told is not a good thing. Apparently in the days of our grandparents when someone was seriously ill they used to say that the person was 'at the far end'. This indicated that the person was in the bed nearest the nurses' station because they were so ill they had to be monitored around the clock. It makes sense that this still might apply in my lifetime because when I was most at risk , I was in the end bed of the ward nearest the nurses' station. Not to dwell on this too much but you think they call it the 'near end' but apparently not, it was the 'far end'

Anyway, where was I? Oh yes, I was in a room with four patients in and one of them, like me, had been in a crash but had not had the protection of being in a car, he had been in a spectacular accident on his motorbike. A car had shot across his path and he had hit the side of the car so hard that he and the bike had entered the car. The car he had hit was stolen, so the driver, somehow, had managed to do a runner. The biker had spent nearly an hour in the car fighting for his life while cars and passers by ignored getting involved and saw the car as an abandoned damaged vehicle. They had no idea that this lad was in the car with terrible injuries. Eventually a police woman went over to the car and realised he was in there and phoned for assistance and an ambulance. The fire service eventually cut him out and he'd broken both legs really badly, broken one of his arms and after surgery he also lost a testicle. He too had lost a lot of blood and spent a lot of time in intensive care but we had both survived. He was virtually the same age as myself and we spent a little time together once I'd regained consciousness as we were in same room swapping stories. I don't remember how long he'd already spent in hospital. I only remember that he was already there when I eventually woke up. I'm sure he'd agree with me when I say that we both helped each other get over those remaining weeks in hospital that could have affected our minds badly as we came to terms with our injuries. We were both told by the radiologist that if we had been in America, our x-rays alone would have cost a quarter of a million dollars because of how many we needed over the time we were both in hospital. We both considered ourselves to be lucky to have the NHS in this country. Sadly I cannot remember the lad's name which is frustrating as it would have been good to track him down and see how he was doing. I hope has come through the last 40 years and had the quality of life that I have. Perhaps someone reading this book will know him and point out to him that I've made it to sixty too. It would be great to get a photo with him. Instead of the six million dollar man, we could be the 'quarter of a million dollar lads'

Like, I've said, my memories from these days in hospital and for a while afterwards are in snippets but one day that I remember was the day I had my first proper bath in the hospital. I had not long regained consciousness and was being a pain in the backside to the nursing staff. If I wasn't being a pain giving them grief about things, I was being a pain by being inappropriate with them. About two weeks after I came around, a nurse came to me and said 'come on let's get you bathed' as it then must have been 6-8 weeks since I'd showered or bathed and they had been keeping me as clean as they could on the ward. The nurse led me down a corridor with my arm in the air and the motorbike lad and some of the other male patients were jeering and whistling. One of them shouted 'you dirty bastard'. I don't know whether he meant it literally or it was the fact that I was going to the bathroom with one of the nurses. When we got to the room with the bath, three other nurses were already in there. I said "why four of you?" There was no answer, I had to strip off in front of them and I stood there stark bollock naked with one hand in plaster in the air and the other over my privates and they tell me to get in the bath that they've run. I'm trying to work out how I can do that with one hand free and still keep my dignity and the nurse says 'here' and grabs my right arm to help me – instinct is to put my left hand over my knackers but it's up in the air – the nurses are in hysterics because I'm now stepping into the bath with one leg in the air, one arm in the air and the other being held by the nurse and my crown jewels dangling down. It was the nurses' payback time. All I can hear is giggling from the nurses and jeering from the ward from the patients. It took me ages to get in and ages to get out and to this day, I don't know whether this was their revenge for my behaviour. At the time I was a bad tempered bugger but I look back on it now and smile as I wouldn't have blamed them one bit for teaching me a lesson.

My physical recovery took time to get anywhere near back to normal. The psychological effects lasted even longer. Initially, the relief at being alive and being discharged from hospital distracted me from worrying about the serious issue of work and how this would affect the rest of my life. Once this started to sink in, I started to worry about whether I would ever do my job again given the state my left arm was in and the fact that you need two hands to cut hair, one for the comb and one for the scissors. When I got home from hospital it had been two months since the accident and myself and my family started to discuss what I would do next. I was advised that I should claim compensation for my injuries as they would be with me for the rest of my life in one way or another. Unfortunately the advice we received was that we should make a claim against Adrian, my cousin who was driving. This didn't sit right with me right from the start. I was uncomfortable about this but again lady luck played a hand in how the case went for me and it turned out that the major aspect of the claim veered away from Adrian and towards the legal firm handling the case. I cannot name the legal firm involved for reasons that will become apparent as I tell the story of what happened. For want of a better name, let's just call them the 'law firm' from here on in.

The worry was that I may not be able to hold down a Barber's job in in the future because of the injury to my arm. As it happens, with absolute determination and persistence and Henry and our customers allowing me to work a little slower than usual for the first year or so back in the job, this allowed me to develop a new way of working that catered for my injured arm and that customers wouldn't notice anything difference to my previous way of working. Eventually after many years, if I didn't tell you the accident I had been in and show you my arm, you simply wouldn't notice anything in passing other than scars. The psychological effects were different. The worst effects took years to pass and others are still with me. One of them is tiredness. Despite my physical fitness, I get mentally tired very quickly and after a day's work I am mentally exhausted. In the early years though, the mental effects on me were very even more apparent and this took over ten years after the accident to improve. It was clear when we discussed this, just after the accident, that my claim, if I had one, would be more about the brain injury than the physical injuries. It was also about the varying levels and types of support I would need across the rest of my life. Initially then, a claim was made against Adrian as the driver of the car and my case was handled by the law firm that My Uncle Cyril (mum's brother in law and Adrian's dad) had recommended to us.

Clearly there were legal hurdles to overcome to establish a claim as Adrian had my permission to drive the car but was driving without insurance. Another issue was that, despite seat belt laws not coming in until 1983, I was not wearing my seat belt and therefore the argument would be whether I had not mitigated the risk of accident by not wearing it. The initial reactions to my accident was though, that wearing a seat belt in this case may have actually been worse for me and risked further injury and potentially cost me my life. It was a difficult argument to have because it was all guess work. The debate about me giving Adrian permission to drive my car became complicated too as the 'law firm' argued on my behalf that this was very different to getting into a car with someone who I knew was drunk and who it was likely could not drive safely. There was case law on this type of thing that showed that previous cases had been upheld on the basis that, although I gave Adrian permission to drive the car, I didn't give him permission to drive it unsafely in any way. Between 1980 and 1986 I also attended several examinations and consultations. I still have the reports, or should I say my mum still has all the reports as it was her who handled most of it for me via the 'law firm'. My injuries and their seriousness were assessed several times over a few years via different and independent doctors and in addition I was eventually sent for an assessment by an established Psychiatrist about the long term effects of my brain injury.

It is difficult to describe how I feel reading those reports now. I've actually never seen some of them before, or if I have I certainly don't remember reading them. Here's me at 60 years old reading about this young man in his late teens to early 20's and it feels like I am reading about someone else. They provide a good summary of the accident and its effects on me but it is quite emotional to see some of the things said. Here are just a few excerpts:-

- *Before the accident in answer to the question 'previous health condition?' the doctor had put 'normal'* – (I think a lot of people, mainly my brothers, would challenge that.)
- *He has undergone a personality change and is suffering from Depression, Suicidal thoughts and violent towards members of his family*
- *He has memory and concentration difficulties and has to take special measures to remember to do some simple tasks like remembering to attend this examination.*
- *There is no doubt whatsoever that he has developed, as a result of his head injury, a post traumatic psychiatric disorder*
- *At times would develop violent rages becoming red faced and showing aggression, sometimes striking the wall*

- *He was aware of his personality disorder and had sufficient insight to realise the wrongdoing and in fact never struck his mother because she spent considerable periods, sometimes constantly throughout the day talking to him and working through his problems with him'*

- *He suffered with acute amnesia after the accident which has improved over the years but is still present to an extent*

- *He had three operations on his arm to improve the elbow joint which was immobilised for some time.*

- *(This one was funny). He has a lump over his left eyebrow. (They noted it as if it was caused by the accident but this was from when Simon hit me with a full milk bottle)*

What became apparent as we got into the claim was that the same 'law firm' was representing Adrian and his defence against the claim. This made sense in some way because Cyril recommended a law firm to us and it was the law firm that he'd recommend to his son too. For some reason, the law firm didn't see that as a conflict of interest and who were we to challenge this at the time? It seemed odd, but we assumed that different departments of the firm would handle our representation and Adrian's representation and that this must be okay because otherwise they would say something to us both. That didn't happen and it was sometime later that this became a serious issue for us to address. As far as what I thought about things, I didn't hold anything against Adrian and he must have known that from the way I was with him. Our cousin relationship was the same as before the accident because that's what it was, an accident. I don't even remember ever really discussing it with him and eventually when I was well enough, I continued to cut his hair. This was just a life experience for us both. It was an unfortunate one but it happened. It's was all water under the bridge (If you'll excuse the unintended pun) pretty much straightaway for me. I lost touch with Adrian over a long period of time and I have a feeling that he eventually went to live in Ireland but I'm not sure. I guess that when this book is published, a few people will say things to me about the facts that are still a bit vague for me but will be clear for them and I hope it leads to some contact from my cousins that I have not seen for some time including Adrian.

Adrian's dad Cyril always had a good word for me, he also had a good firm handshake for me every time I saw him. I had the utmost respect for him. If I didn't know any better (and that is entirely possible), I'd imagine that Cyril orchestrated the whole claim thing. He was a brilliant and intelligent man and when you look at the facts that Cyril recommended the law firm to me, if they took the case on, which they did, and they took Adrian's case on, which they did, they were always going to walk into a conflict of interest / negligence claim unless they advised us accordingly, which they didn't (advise us) and which they did (walk into a claim). If Cyril did orchestrate all of this to pan out as it did, then I am eternally grateful for what he did. He would have seen a case that could have been divisive to our family end in an amicable way that didn't see Adrian sued, which suited me, but saw a legal firm sued for their management of the case.

When it came to settlement, we were initially offered a few thousand pounds in relation to the injuries which was derogatory in terms of the injuries and their potentially lasting effects. We were so disgusted by this, we instructed a different solicitor to assess the offer and to examine how matters had been conducted. That's when it came out that the 'Law Firm' had lost my records and were struggling to continue with the case.

157

They had even failed in the basic step of serving a writ against Adrian at the very start. This turned out to be a major development as now, instead of the focus being on Adrian as the driver, the emphasis of our claim was on the conflict of interest that potentially existed between the two representatives and the mismanagement of the case. I was forced to go through the medical examinations and assessments all over again but this proved to be worthwhile as the case moved quite quickly in comparison after that. The independent firm commented on the conflict of interests in representing both parties in the case. They said; ' I must confess some surprise at the conduct of 'law firm' which is neither professional nor sound common sense. If one wants to ride two horses at once to avoid losing the race, one should be ready for some discomfort.' It was a brilliant way of putting it but it made me think of my experience with Jean Claude Van Damme years before. I think he's the only person that I can think of who could ride two horses fairly comfortably.

Eventually, on 30th August 1988, some eight and a half years after the accident, I was offered the sum that we decided to accept to settle. After legal fees, I had to pay the bank money I had borrowed on the strength of my claim. This left me with enough money to enact a plan I had to buy a neglected house near Heaton Park and do it up with some of the remainder of the money. The house was a four storey property and needed a lot of work but I had Simon and Eamonn with the skills set to sort that out and planned to turn it into four flats. This would still leave us some money to potentially put a deposit down on a move out of Cromwell Street which was part of my initial plan and also give Olwen a little money as she was about to get married. All these things were in my head and at last things were turning in our favour. I now realise that I was missing something or more to the point somebody. In my usual style I was determined to get the best result I could and I'd focused on what could be done with the money to better our lives. On the face of it, there's nothing wrong with that but there was one major thing that I'd missed out. My mum had saved me through those first few years. She had lost earnings to look after me and had dedicated her life for a period of time to ensuring I avoided Prestwich Hospital. In addition, it had been her that drove the claim too because without her I would have been sunk. What followed was that because of our similar personalities, when my mum raised this with me, this turned into a huge row and I stormed out and told her she could have it all. If it had happened now I would have been able to discuss it properly and sort it out but at that time I was still on the verge of an extreme reaction at any time and as soon as I hit an issue, I'd explode. I ended up making some bad decisions that were OK at the time but didn't resemble any part of my plan which might have created security for the future. So instead of purchasing property and doing it up, I bought windsurfing equipment and put a deposit on white Toyota Space Cruiser with bull bars on the front and back. I fell out with my mum and we didn't speak properly again for 15 years and as I've said already, it has taken me writing all of this down that has reunited me with my mum and I'm so grateful for this. If we could go back I would of course have handled it differently but I can't dwell on things like that, so I look forward to the relationship we will have going into the future and if she doesn't know it already now, my feelings for her as my mum are as strong as any son could have. She has gone much further than most mums would have been asked to go and I greatly appreciate her now for what she has done for me. It's the reason I have dedicated this book to her and I hope that when she reads the things that I have written, which she knows I would struggle to articulate in person, that she believes what I am saying. **For the record mum – I love you and appreciate everything that you have done for me.**

Chapter 14 – Moving Stories (Jonas Duoba)

I may have already mentioned a house or two while talking about my life and that's because there was a lot of them. From my childhood through to present day I have had ten places that I've called home and every one of them served its purpose, some creating more memories than others, especially as my memory has been restricted, but all of them hold a place in my heart and in the hearts of my family members. I am a proud Mancunian and I have never strayed too far from those roots in terms of my schools, work and where I have lived.

I've already talked about the houses where I grew up on Sawyer Street in Monsall and Cravenwood Road in Crumpsall. Your childhood homes should be special and mine both were. They were what shaped my life in many ways. Those two houses hold memories that will never fade for me, despite my memory problems, but are the sort of memories that young people today, in the main, will never experience. Things like having no plumbed in bath and using a sink or a tin bath in the middle of the living room for bath night. Like having an outside toilet or Lino on the floor and having no central heating are just some of the things that my generation experienced but the majority of the next generation didn't. Having those memories makes you appreciate the convenient modern equivalents and all of us who did experience those things talk about them proudly as if those were our war years. Our parents and our grandparents started a lot of stories like Uncle Albert on Only Fools and Horses with the phrase "during the war..." Whereas we started our stories with "When I was a lad..." I loved those first childhood houses. Yes they were small and yes they got a little cramped but they were our safe havens as children and I'm relieved that my memories of them have not been damaged to the extent of not being able to see them in my mind's eye and luckily I've been able to recall some of the events that happened in those houses before my memory plays tricks on me again.

Our first home as a married couple was a terraced house on Cromwell Street in Heywood. It felt good to have your own place but we knew that this was a stepping stone for the future and would want a bigger property eventually. One of my customers called Dominic, who lived in Alkrington came in and said "have a look at these. Put your name down and we'll sort something out". He was a property guy that would buy a row of terraced houses, gut them and do them up so they looked brand new inside and out and sell them. We bought this house as part of a scheme where for £12,000 you could be part of this introductory scheme for new home-owners. One of the stipulations was that you couldn't sell the house for at least three years. We wasn't living there too long when Mena went out on her works Christmas do. She worked for 'Unger Meats' which was a food company in Cheetham Hill and their works Christmas do was only for employees. To be honest I was a bit gutted that I wasn't invited and was down in the dumps about it. I was in bed and asleep later in the night when I hear this banging and shouting "let me in, let me in" I can tell its Mena and she carries on banging and shouting 'Let me in". I legged it down to the front door and opened it but she wasn't there. I could still hear her shouting "Let me in, Let me in". I popped my head out and there she was at next door's front door, who were an elderly couple, banging on it really annoyed that I wasn't letting her in. "Hey you dickhead" I shouted "You live here!"

The elderly couple had more than one experience with our nuttiness. I was right into DIY when we got that first house and used to get carried away with myself. One evening I was doing a bit of work putting a new bannister in up the stairs. There I was banging away fitting this bannister and I heard a voice from next door shouting "will you call it a day". I thought to myself how unreasonable is that? – so I shout back "Piss off". It was only when I looked at the clock I realised that it was 3.00am. I had got completely carried away and through it was mid evening. I was round there next morning with a bunch of flowers and a box of chocs and my apology of "Sorry about the language". They took to us eventually when we grew on them.

When Mena announced she was Pregnant in 1988, this meant a change of plan to accommodate our new family. I immediately arranged to get the ball rolling on selling the Cromwell Street property and my plan wasn't just to buy a bigger property so that we had room for our family to grow in going forward, it was also to buy a house near Fairfield Hospital in Bury so that Mena was as near as possible to where she needed to be when baby arrived. As it happens, we could have sold the house on Cromwell Street three times over but we ended up selling it to my mum and we had met the requirement of living there for more than three years. Everything went smoothly and quickly and we moved to Jericho, in between Bury and Bolton and in June 1988 Aran was born. (check

People used to look at me a bit strangely when I said I lived in Jericho because the only Jericho they knew was in Palestine near the River Jordan and I used to get the odd jibe of people asking me 'how Joshua was' and 'did they need any bricklayers?' This Jericho though was in Bury and was on Bury & Rochdale Old Road and It was literally on the doorstep of Fairfield Hospital and it gave me a lot of peace of mind to know that Mena was only around the corner from where she might need to go in a hurry. We bought the house for £27,000 and put £5,000 down as deposit so had a mortgage of 22K which at the time had hefty repayments and massive interest as this was the Thatcher years in Britain with high unemployment and high interest rates. Although Arron looked like a clever little bugger playing the drums in his mum's tummy (see Chapter 11) Mena had a difficult time during the birth. Thirty plus hours of labour later she was not happy with me at all. I think her exact words were "Don't you come near me ever again with that ' pointing to my manhood and I had no doubt that she meant it. Soon after bringing Mena and Arron home to Jericho it was already feeling too small so less than 12 months after moving in, we decided to sell the house to buy a bigger one. I made the sales board and put it up myself. I put up the board and put it on the market for £29,000 on a Sunday and I could have sold it two days later on the Tuesday. I said to the guy who offered me the asking price that we hadn't even started looking yet so didn't have a house to go to. He didn't seem to be perturbed at all about this and it alerted me to the fact that it might be worth more than I'd put it up for and we were going to end up with a quicker sale that we needed. So I apologized for wasting his time and put it back on the market immediately on the same day (Tuesday) for £34,000 thinking it would give me more time but two days later on the Thursday, somebody offered us the asking price so I put it up again to £37,000 and sold it on the Saturday one week after making the For Sale sign.

Each offer was from a different person and the latest offer of the asking price of £37,000 made me think that I couldn't keep putting the asking price up. The latest offer was from a single bloke and it just wasn't in my nature to keep doing this. I only kept putting the price up to buy time but it was getting ridiculous. I said to the guy making this latest offer that I had to apologise as this was the third time this week we'd been offered the asking price and we were nowhere near getting another house yet. He said that there was no problem with this as he was living in London and his firm was relocating him all expenses paid with all his furniture in storage and hotels would be paid for. He simply said to let him know when we were ready and had found somewhere we were happy with and we would do the deal then at the price agreed. We shook hands on this. That's when we found and fell in love with the house on Bury and Bolton Road in Ainsworth, another suburb of Bury

This house had a back garden that backed on to farmland which was just our cup of tea. The couple in it were quite elderly and had lived in the house for a long time. They had asked for £40,000 and we had organised paying a deposit of £15,000 and having a new higher mortgage of £25,000. I was positive about the move and we loved the house and I knew this was right for our family but I felt the burden of the size of the mortgage which was hefty for those days. For the first time the interest rates and the size of the debt made me feel like I was putting my head on the chopping block and I felt the pressure.

Next thing we knew, we received a phone call from the couple we were buying the house off. They invited us to the house on the Sunday to have a chat. We wondered what they were going to tell us. So up we go to their house on the Sunday and they've made scones and cup of tea and I'm already looking around the house thinking of what I will do to it to improve it when we move in. The couple then tell us that they've had a chap around at the house and he's offered £10,000 more making the total price £50,000. You could physically see the disappointment in both Mena and myself. Our hearts sank. I immediately thought that this was Karma on myself as I had put the price up of our property and now I was getting a taste of my own medicine. All I could hear in my head was 'what goes around comes around'. I had not haggled one bit about their asking price of £40K and now here we were being offered the mortgage for £50,000. I thought that this was it and was thinking that the situation wasn't recoverable. Then totally unexpectedly the couple say to us "We have brought our family up in this home and from meeting you we think it's nice to be able to offer you the opportunity to do the same so we are letting you have it for £40,000. I can't tell you how emotional I was. I cried. They were prepared to honour our agreement because they wanted us to have the house. We couldn't believe the gesture they were making and we couldn't believe our luck that we'd come across such a decent couple. It was yet another sign that we were doing the right thing and how lucky I was. I'll never forget the pleasure that the elderly couple seemed to get out of telling this news. They knew how important it would be to us and the fact that we got so emotional substantiated this for them. Whenever I hear the phrase that 'it is better to give than to receive' I think of that couple and how that gesture changed our lives at that time. This is where my brain injury kicks in though because despite the fact I can see their faces and they were so important to us, I cannot for the life of me remember their names. While living in Ainsworth, Mena got the doctor's message (see chapter 11) that we had no time to waste if we wanted more children so Jourdana and Rhys were born while we lived in Ainsworth. It was around this time that I felt the pressure on me became overpowering at times. I was trying to do the house up to cater for our growing family and of course through the issue with her arm, Mena was being treated for cancer and this had an effect her work and her pay and I felt like our world was crumbling around us a little financially as my work was up and down too. I was being very self-critical in my thoughts and in my mind I was talking to myself and saying how disgusted I was in myself being so materialistic. I had been investing money in a vehicle (campervan?) equipment and my hobbies and we had started to look financially unstable with an ever increasing interest rate and less money coming in. I started to look at smaller houses and leaving our dream house that we had created. I had become irritable with it too and was bad tempered. One night I was in my mum's kitchen feeling like the weight of the world was on my shoulders and my brother Simon and I got into an argument which grew into a scuffle and then developed into a major wrestling bout that, in truth, I'd started. So here are two grown men seriously wrestling in their mother's kitchen and I'm the cause of it. After a lot of grunting and physical effort from both of us we were eventually in a stalemate situation – we were on the floor and both had each gripped around our waist and we were locked there. We both wanted to save face especially me after being the cause of the whole thing and then all of a sudden I felt an excruciating pain. Benson, the Rottweiler that we had all grown up with but had a stronger bond and affinity with Simon, had sunk his fangs into my calf. Because he knew me too, he hadn't savaged me, he'd just buried his fangs gently into my leg. If I had been a stranger he would have happily launched a full scale attack on me but he had gently applied the bite so that it was enough to hurt like mad but he seemed to be trying to judge it to not cause too damage. I'm not kidding, it was a measured and intelligent bite. The dog was a genius. Pain doesn't affect me like it does others so I spoke calmly as close to Simons ear as I could get and said 'Simon, Bensons got his jaws around me calf'. We agreed to end the situation and then there was this strange kitchen ceasefire as I slowly let go of Simon, Simon slowly let go of me and Benson slowly let go of my leg. My calf muscle was like a piece of wood for days after. Despite Benson holding back, It was still a dog bite and it got infected and I ended up needing a tetanus shot in my bum. I should add that I didn't blame Benson one bit, or hold anything against him. I loved his loyalty to Simon and his loyalty to the family as a whole. If I had been fighting against a stranger then God help them. As it was he had more loyalty to Simon and that was right. While I am talking about Benson, a story I love to tell people about him was from when I was about 16. Mam did shifts and couldn't sleep so she would go for a long walk in the early hours through Cheetham Hill, which didn't have the best reputation for safety, but she used to take Benson with her. He would walk up to ten metres behind her looking like he was unfit but being a Rottweiler he was as solid as a rock. Eventually they ended up on crescent road near where Tesco is now. There, parked close to the traffic lights was a black Mariah with a handful of police officers in having a break. This was a hot summers evening so they had all their windows down and doors open. As she passed them, one police officer says to her "Should you be out here at this time Mrs? It's a bit late for you to be out alone". Mam's reply to him was immediate "I've got him behind me". The police officer looks a bit confused as Benson's not in full view yet but suddenly as if on cue, Benson catches up and jumps through the open doors into the back of the black maria and all these coppers come immediately spilling out into the road to get away from him. Mam just shouts "Come on Benson" and he just jumped out and caught her up as if nothing had happened. The coppers obviously saw the funny side of it so left it at that.

The episode with Simon and Benson didn't help me at all with the way I was thinking at the time. In fact it made it worse. I was still condemning myself as a materialistic piece of shit putting the house and the windsurfing gear before my wife and her health. I was repeating in my head how I could have let anything come before Mena and then when Simon was trying to help me I ended up fighting with him. We struggled through for a few years at Ainsworth and my mental health was up and down to say the least and I knew it was the pressure of the mortgage we had taken on was worrying me and this was manifesting itself in me becoming bad tempered and falling over mentally. We went into arrears with the mortgage and things were getting worse. I went in to the

Bradford & Bingley Building Society in Middleton to put a proposal to them. Instead of us falling further behind with our arrears, I proposed that we stretched the current mortgage over twenty five years. We had already made six years of payments so effectively I was proposing spreading the last nineteen years of payments over twenty five years to reduce the payments which meant we could catch up and afford the next twenty five years of payments. The manager turned me down flat. I said to him "So you'd rather repossess our house than us pay you money over a further twenty five year period with you getting more interest? He just said it wasn't something within his control to do. I called him Dick Turpin in a suit as I stormed out. I left the shop disgusted and angry but worse still worried about what we would do to catch up with the arrears before they took the house off us. In the midst of all that I was travelling home from work one night in the car listening to Piccadilly Radio. A guy called Steve Penk used to have a show that played pranks on people all the time but at the same time had news items and conversations that were serious so it was difficult sometimes to know the difference. I had the radio on out of habit in the car and I was on autopilot driving home with my mind racing about lots of things and there was a newsflash which sort of woke me from my autopilot state. Penk announces that the Bank of England have doubled the interest rate. It hit me so hard that I pulled over so that I didn't crash the car. I was there for about 15 minutes thinking that this would ruin us. It was the longest 15 minutes of my life. I didn't see a way out and after 5 minutes I started to have some depressing thoughts about whether my family would be better off if I wasn't here anymore. After 10 minutes I was sinking to rock bottom and after 15 minutes, mentally, I was right back there on the edge of the pavement on the side of Cheetham Hill Road when I was 19 deciding whether to step out or not. The radio was still on but its music coming through. I couldn't tell you what music was being played because I was just sat staring through the windscreen. Then I hear Penk laughing and I'm thinking how could he possibly find something funny in this and no sooner do I think that, he announces that it was only a joke and that interest rates were actually the same as they had been at the start of the month. I should have felt relief really and I suppose somewhere in my rage there was an element of relief but the rage was overpowering. I'd gone from thinking about what would happen to me and the family to very quickly feeling hate for Steve Penk. If I had got hold of Steve Penk at the very moment when he said he was joking then at the very least they would have been removing the studio microphone from very deep into his rectum. Whether these things should effect you so much or not I don't know but the hatred for Steve Penk didn't actually subside for many years as I often remembered just what I felt like in that 5 minute pocket of my life while he played a track and then. came back and said it was a joke. At the very least now if I saw him, there might be a swear word or two involved. He has no idea what he did to me that day and I wonder how many others were affected like that. People in debt commit suicide so why would you run a prank that just wasn't funny but risked pushing people to the edge? Steve Penk - you're a knobhead.

We realised that we either needed to move again to gain space or we needed to extend the house in some way and make it a bit bigger. It was a semi attached house with a bit of land at the side leading to garage at the back. We decided to extend the house at the side and the back towards to the garage and extend the garage back further again. We'd bought some land at the back of the house and they'd let us have the same width of my garden and further back about the same size as the footprint of the house. I got this guy to draw up plans and it was looking fantastic. It was a double storey extension and the plans looked great. The thing we were worried about was that the extension pressed the border of the land between us and our next door neighbour Frank. In fact the foundations had to go onto his land by a foot. We needed to discuss it with him so invited him around for a meal one night to show him our plans. Frank was a single guy and a photographer. We had got on well with him and when we showed him the plans and that we were planning all ivy along the garage to make it look better than just concrete, he was really nice about it. We went further and committed to putting in a new block driveway for him because of the inconvenience it would cause him. His reaction was 'Chris it's going to look fantastic' 'No problem at all". Mena and I were well chuffed that he'd been so nice about it so it was all systems go.

We submitted the plans and a couple of weeks went by and we got a letter from the planning office and it confirmed that we had been knocked back. We were told that our plans would have to come in by half a metre at the side and two metres at the back and also come down a metre in height at the back. I got on to the phone to them and asked them what this was all about., I told them that it wasn't worth building if we did everything they wanted us to do. They confirmed that they had received a complaint and when I asked them from who they said that they couldn't divulge that but that the objection was that the person was experiencing stressful times and can't work. Our other next door neighbour was Edith and she didn't work so now I'm thinking someone else must have done this, not thinking for one moment about Frank. I used to walk home and look at everybody and think about which one had it in for us like that. It took a while but the penny dropped eventually that it was Frank who had gone against everything he had said to our faces. I thought about confronting him but he avoided me and in the end that was probably for the best. I did eventually find out what he had said on the complaint form and he had put that the extension would give a 'terraced house effect' We never spoke about it in fact we never spoke again.

The Ainsworth house did hold a lot of good memories for us but the reasons to move were now stacking up. I don't know whether this next incident contributed to our desire to move or not but I do know that it was one that I'd like to forget but can't. I arrived home one day with our Jourdana and as we go in the house, my wife meets me and says "Chris - go and get Geoff out of that tree' I repeat what she's saying because it sounds ridiculous. "Go and get Geoff out of that tree?" Then I realise something is terribly wrong as Arron and Rhys are not in the garden and they are in the house. I say 'How come the kids are not in the garden?' She says 'I've got them in the house now go and get Geoff out of the tree." I go around the back of Geoff's house and there he is, hanging from a tree in his garden. He'd committed suicide. He was only a few feet off the ground but it was clear that his neck was broken. Another neighbour, who was luckily an ex policewoman, had seen what was happening and had come out so that as I grabbed Geoff and lifted him she started to try and undo the knot in the rope. As we are doing this I am saying to poor Geoff who is clearly dead "Sorry mate." As we let him down we hear a sound as the air is pressed out of his lungs that freaks us both out a little. Next thing we know we see a car pull up and its Geoff's wife. I am so grateful that the neighbour helping me is a policewoman because there is no way I am breaking the news to his wife. My neighbour sees my reaction and just says "I'll do it'

Eric Clapton proved the point to me that the least important thing in life was money. When he lost his little boy, I remember thinking how unimportant it must be to him to have all that fame and money and that he'd give it all to have him back. Once we had decided to move we put the house on the market and I started to relax a little about the money pressures.

It was only a few weeks after we had made the decision that I was round at my mum and dad's house in Littler Lever helping mum prepare for a surprise birthday party for dad who was to be seventy the following Sunday. I vividly remember it was a Wednesday, which is amazing for me to have such a detailed memory of the day of the week but there is a reason for me remembering it more than most other days. Dad was sat there having eggs and bacon and fried bread and putting salt all over his breakfast. I shouted at him, "Dad what are you doing? You've got high blood pressure, you shouldn't be putting salt on your breakfast like that". He was a proud man though and a bit stubborn. "I'll be alright" he said. Unbeknownst to me, he wasn't taking his medication either. This was a typical male and macho approach, burying his head in sand. Won't go to the doctor and won't take the medicine either and anyone says anything about it, he makes light of it "I'll be fine". I'm healthy and pretty stubborn myself. I think I'm invincible at times but I know what's good for me and I take a tablet every day that my Doc prescribed because of my high blood pressure which ties in genetically with my family history of high blood pressure. Even my Grandad died of a stroke and had high blood pressure. Anyway, I went home and around 5'o clock the same day there was a call from my mum to Mena and she said "Your dad's getting pains across his chest. He's in bed". 'Right mam" I said "Phone an ambulance immediately and I'm on my way". I didn't have far to go from Ainsworth to Little Lever, about 2 miles. I arrived at the house and headed straight for the bedroom. He's there lay in the bed holding his chest. He told me that he had pains up his arms and he looked white. I said "Dad I think you're having a heart attack, try and keep still and calm as much as possible. The ambulance arrives and as it pulls on to the driveway, he swings his legs out of the bed and starts to stand up. He is such a proud and tough man he doesn't want to be carried to the ambulance. As he does this I moved towards him and said 'Dad what are you doing?" and as he tried to stand, he collapsed on to me and his weight took us both to the floor. He was lay on top of me with our weight against the bedroom door. The ambulance crew by this time were up the bedroom door and they struggled to get in because we were blocking the doorway. Eventually we managed to move him into a position where they could get to him and start to try and resuscitate him and I tried to stop them and say "woah woah. If he has died I know he doesn't want this" As I had got closer to my dad over the years, he had always said to me "promise me something son. If anything ever happens to me I don't want to go in a nursing home. If I'm dead, just make sure I'm dead. I don't want none of that kiss of life stuff, just make sure I'm dead". I always joked with him by saying "with pleasure"

I don't know how long they were trying but they didn't pay much attention to me because they tried to resuscitate him all the way to the hospital in the ambulance but he wasn't coming back. I remember feeling privileged that I'd been with him in the room when it happened. My brothers and sister were heartbroken as I was too but I felt lucky to have been with him for his last few conscious moments and to see him try and stand as a proud man. The next day, one of the ambulance guys came to see me. He said "I had to come and tell you this. Your dad was a very strong man – we brought him back twice in the ambulance. We had to by law but as strong as his body was to come back twice it was as if he was determined not to'

I've since thought about my dad's passing a lot as I've reflected on my life and I've made it clear to Jourdana that I don't want a funeral. If and when my moment comes I've told her to just go to undertaker and tell them to come and take me away and don't tell anyone. Just get on with what needs to happen legally but that's it. Jourdana's response was "It's already sorted Dad. We are going to bury you and plant a tree there" "That's great" I said . "Well what kind of tree do you want?" she asked. "Oak" I said. "Strong as anything. Don't forget to put a bottle of Erdinger in there eh?" "No Problem" she said. "Sorted"

Arron knew my dad well and probably felt it worse than the others as Rhys and Jourdana didn't know him that well because they were so young and Lily never met him. When I got home that day I needed air so I said to Philomena 'I'm going for a walk' and I picked up a stalkers hat. It was just something that was there, I don't actually know why I did it but I did. I walked in the dark down Ainsworth Road and did a left at a crossroads and I didn't know where I was going or what I was doing. I was just walking. I walked up Starling road and about half way up there I did a left and saw this house with a for sale sign outside. I didn't even know it was on the market and from there you could virtually look across towards the back of my house. I instinctively said 'Dad I need to be closer to work'. I went off into some bushes and had a pee and started to walk back making the same turns that I had made and eventually on to the Bury / Bolton Road and I looked down at my shadow and on the floor I see the silhouette of my dad. As I'm wearing this hat the shadow looks like him a lot. I tried to move and to step over the shadow but I still got the same effect. I just said to him "Why don't you come and see me properly?" I walked the rest of the way home and I suddenly felt like the weight had been lifted from me. I'd been existing for a while now with the weight of the world on my shoulders but this simple experience I felt I had shared with my dad, whether in my mind or not, had lifted me out of it and I felt strangely optimistic for the first time in a long time. It was as if something good was around the corner and I'd convinced myself that my dad had said 'stop worrying, it's going to be ok'.

A few days later a customer of mine called Brian who had a skip business comes in and says 'Chris have you not viewed that house yet ?" He knew I was looking for a house. "Which one" I said. "The one facing our Kate's on Highfield Drive. It's right up your street". "Right then " I said "I'll have a look at it" He knew the woman who owned it. I think her husband had passed away and house was too big for her. He arranged for Mena and I to go and meet her and we went to view the house, which we found out was on the market for £120,000. She was a lovely lady this woman and as were looking around, Mena and I were going up the stairs and I said to Mena "there's no way I'd pay 120K for this". As I walked into the first bedroom, I realised it was the woman who owned the house behind me and not Mena and so must have heard what I said. I was a little embarrassed as she said "I think it's a bit dear as well". It was being sold through an estate agent and she had obviously gone with their recommended price. She had lived there from day one raising her family so had probably bought the house in the 60's or 70's. We went downstairs and there were two living rooms. The second of them was in desperate need of modernisation and as I walked over to the window in that room to look at the garden, I realised the back of the house was very much elevated from the ground and I could see steam coming out from the wall underneath us. "What's that?" I said. "Oh that's the boiler replied the owner. "Boiler?" I said and she replied "yes the boiler. I'll show it you, it's in the cellar". My eyes must have bulged out of my head and Mena knows exactly what I'm thinking. I'd always wanted a cellar. So we went to the kitchen and then into the back garden and down some steps and then double back and down some more steps to a lower level at the side of the house and where there is a door and window. She opened the door and we stepped in and all I can think of in my head is 'Fucking wow' It was just what I'd always wanted. The cellar is the whole footprint of the house and is huge and all I can see is a gym, a sports room, a cinema room and a music room. I can see that Mena is also looking at it and then looking at my face and I can see that she is thinking "All he can see is a gym, a sports room, a cinema room and a music room". In fact it was a house under the house. I can see the girders holding the house up and the thoughts are racing through my mind. I'm also thinking £120,000? I'd pay that for the cellar alone! We put a bid in straightaway and there was no haggling so that we didn't lose it to somebody else offering the asking price. It was well worth it. Mena was happy for me to get my cellar and Gym. You've got to remember that after the crash I became obsessed with getting fit and meeting challenges and Mena got that completely. In fact before we were married, rightly or wrongly, I had said to Mena that I loved her to bits and I really did but that she mustn't make me choose between pursuing my fitness and her because as much as I loved her, I couldn't never give up the pursuit of complete fitness. I owed my life to not accepting that my injuries could hold me back and I just could not accept not doing that anymore as I felt it would drag me back into a poor mental health state. I needed to maintain my efforts and pursue achievements no matter how big or small they were. Mena understood that from day one and she supported me wholeheartedly. Everything went through and when we got the keys and moved in. The only thing was we didn't change our address and contact details in some of the most important places, one of which was Mena's medical records which we found out when Mena had Lily. I planned to be at the birth as I had been for the others and when Mena went into labour and taken to St Marys Hospital, the hospital had our details wrong on their records. We had not updated them when we moved from Ainsworth which meant that they were trying to ring me at the wrong address. Subsequently I got there late and missed the birth and was gutted but Lily was beautiful and both her and Mena were okay so I was very lucky. We developed the house over the next few years. We converted the loft into another room and I immediately put internal wooden stairs down to the cellar and put a three piece chesterfield suite in there with a big 40 inch tv screen all wired up to the hi fi system so that it was a cinema room and blacked out the window near the door so it really was like being in a cinema as it was pitch black. We put Punch Bag weights and big mirror so it became a gym as well. We put a fridge with beer in and the dream was well and truly a reality for three years until one day I returned home from work to be greeted by Mena who said. "I want to move". I said "OK where to? " "Abroad!" she said.

Chapter 15 – New Zealand

In 2003, I had been working in the shop for just under twenty eight years and I had owned it for three of those years. Coming home from work and living in Highfield Drive near Middleton, was an absolute pleasure, We had been in the house for about three years. I had the cellar I'd always wanted and turned it into a cinema room and I had converted the loft so it was now a four story property. One Saturday I came home and there was Mena sat in the front garden in a bit of a mood. I said to her 'what's wrong?' She said 'I don't like it here. I want to move'. I just said 'OK we'll move then' She said 'What about the house and the Cellar and all that?' 'We can get another house with a cellar you know -it's just bricks and mortar' I said. She was obviously thinking of a bigger move. 'I mean move abroad' she said. The idea of emigrating had developed for a while following a brilliant family trip we'd had to see Olwen and her family in Dubai. Mena and the kids had travelled along with my mum to go and see Olwen and spend 4 weeks or so in Dubai across Christmas 2003. I had stayed behind to carry on working because it was a busy period. Not long after they had left, I was reading one of my running magazines and by amazing coincidence there in front of me being advertised was the Dubai Marathon starting in two weeks in January 2004. This was no coincidence in my mind so I acted upon it and booked a flight to Dubai. Olwen and my family were all excited and glad to see me (I think) and it wasn't long before Olwen found out that I was not only there to see her and the family but compete in the Dubai Marathon. She was hopping mad. I couldn't convince her that it was just as important to me to see her and her family as it was to compete in a great Marathon. My comment of "killing two birds with one stone" probably sealed my fate, she was not happy. In the end I ran in the marathon but pulled out after 10 Kilometres with a calf injury. It wasn't a tear but as I

178

had already booked to do the Austrian Ironman with Smithy later in the year I feared making the injury worse and dropping out of this race later anyway and ruining my preparation for the Ironman. It was a wise decision as you will read in Chapter 21.

We had all loved the experience of Dubai and saw how Olwen and her family were enjoying life in a different environment. Mena had mentioned Australia as our ideal move at the time but I'd said that I'd much prefer New Zealand because I liked my four seasons. The way we had been discussing it previously was a 'if we ever did emigrate' sort of discussion but now Mena was seriously considering it. We discussed it further and we both agreed that it was the right time to do it so I talked her into New Zealand as our best option. We looked into it and we had more than enough points on their system to emigrate there. We then enquired through an agency and very quickly I had two possible jobs to go to. One was in Auckland and the other one was in Rotowaro which was famous for its mines.

We are not the sort of people that, once we had made a decision, would dilly dally. Within months, we had sold the family house to a buyer who completed quickly and we sold the shop building on Middleton Road but not the business to my brother Simon. Steve could run the business while I was away permanently or otherwise and Simon would be his landlord. So just a few months after first discussing the possibility of emigrating, our family landed in New Zealand .

Before we left home we had organised the rental of a mobile home so were not too worried about not having anywhere to live. When we picked it up, it was nowhere near as big as we thought it would be. There was very little storage space for things like my bike so we were a bit cramped to say the least with four kids and all my gear. Mena was seething and what made it worse was that on the first day there it was raining. I could see that Mena was thinking we are in a mobile home that's too small, it's raining and her preference beforehand was Australia which was warmer. I'm thinking 'this is great'. She was thinking 'this is a mistake'.

Our plan was to have a recce mission not a holiday when we got there. We went to look at the first job I'd been offered at a shopping centre which was like a small Trafford Centre back in Manchester. I was in my element. Where we first camped, we had the sea right next to us and I am thinking 'I can swim in the morning and it's crying out for a barbers here'. I can ride to work on my bike and set up a barbers with sports memorabilia all over the walls.' They love their rugby and sports here. I'm in heaven. In New Zealand they love their rugby team the 'All Blacks' and they hate Australia with a vengeance and here I am watching the trailers on TV in the build up for the Rugby World Cup in the Barbers shop where I am going to work and I am bouncing off the owner. She is telling me that I can get work with her two or three days a week and what my hours will be. She also asks if I can do women's hair. I said 'Yes if I have to' as I realise that there are not enough men so I will have to adapt to women's hair too. To be honest all I am thinking about is swimming in the morning, there are great roads for cycling and this is all right up my street. Mena is trying to get me to see the reality of our situation. She asks me 'How are we going to earn enough money to buy a house? You are going to earn money but it won't be enough to survive and build a life here' As we go on I realise that everybody has two jobs here to survive. I would have to cut hair during the day and try and get five or six days work every week and then drive a taxi at night or something. Mena has already clocked all this and I've been so in love with the lifestyle that I've been blinkered to the financial side of it. It would be like going back to square one and spare time would be rare for a while at least.

We are only one week in and it all started to sink in. We also learned that we were not allowed to have our own property because I didn't have a formal qualification. Basically I would have to go back to college for two years get an NVQ level 3 and then apply for residency but in the meantime we would have to rent. What money we have would then go on rent and not saving to buy a property. We had arrived here thinking that we could quickly settle as I had an offer of two jobs and had not dug down deep enough into the reality of things.

We had sold the house on Highfield road and paid our mortgage off and couldn't risk the rest of our money going down the rental drain. We went to see the second job in Rototowa. There was another awaking for us there. It was how remote these places were and also much less commercial than at home. Little things like getting a curry was thirty miles away in Christchurch. At home we were far too used to having things on our doorstop. The penny finally dropped. This was not going to happen. Mena knew this from day one. I think she had handled it all really well. If we had argued about whether to do this and we had not tried it, Mena would have been faced with a permanent reminders from me that we hadn't followed our dream and all the 'what ifs'. As it happened, it was a clear and practical way of showing us that this was just not realistic for us at that time.

The kids were having the time of their life on one big holiday. I think Mena enjoyed it too. It was an incredible experience for a young family like ours. I loved it out there but I knew we would have to go home. I'd met this guy who was the manager of a shop as big as half an average football pitch. I remember walking into his shop and thinking 'wow - this is how it should be'. There were tables and chairs, long sofas, Cabinets full of sports gear, camping gear, fishing rods, Surf boards, canoes. I was in my element. I thought to myself 'Now this is a proper shop'. I loved their attitude to the outdoor life. I wanted that sailing boat and canoe and the kids are exactly the same but the Mrs knows that we need more than that. We need to earn enough money to do that for a start. In England it's making a living then sport in that order. In New Zealand and Australia it seems that it's sport first and then making a living and I loved that about those places.

Once I knew this wasn't going to happen for us, I immediately started to turn our venture into a proper family holiday. It started with an excursion on a boat out into Russell Bay to swim with wild dolphins. I say it was a boat but it was more like a small ship. When we had got out to sea, somebody shouted 'captain there's a shoal of dolphins over there' and the Captain had responded 'No babies about?'. I wondered what that meant. We all had wet suits on and we were instructed to get into a huge square net that keeps it shape by being tied to the sides of the boat and then lowered in to the water and we swim out of it. They spotted dolphins and we swam over to them. When we started swimming I spot this girl who is close to me in the water. The rest of those in the water think they can swim but I can see as clear as anything that this girl is trained like me and we can both swim properly. We stop and she says to me 'You're a swimmer aren't you?' I say 'yes' and she laughs and says 'so am I'' All of a sudden something moves underneath me. I look down and it's about 2 metres wide. It was huge and I said 'fucking hell, I'm a sardine in the food chain here". What the fuck am I doing out here?' I'm already on my way back to the ship and she must have had the same thought as she also swam back to the boat. I thought we were out of our depth. These were wild dolphins and not tamed. 'Flipper' they were not!!! The captain had checked for 'babies' as the mothers tend to attack people going near them so they avoid babies.

We also went to Taupo where the iron man was held in New Zealand. I wanted to see it as I wanted to compete there one day. I was in my Rochdale gear and went for a ride on my bike. In my head I was still approaching things as if I was emigrating. I went into a shop for a coffee. A guy served me and I said "coffee please". He started to converse with me and he noticed all my gear and asked me about my holiday. I talked about the Iron Man event. He took the money off me for the coffee and turned his back on me and goes to the till. As he came back, I say that actually I am going to emigrate here. He does no more than throws my change on to the table and turns his back on me and walks off. What have I just said ? One minute I had this great rapport going with him and then all of sudden the shutter come down on the chat. I went outside and sat with my coffee for a little but I was puzzled. One of my customers, Daz , who I call Daz the builder to differentiate from my good friend Daz McGuire, had given me a telephone number of his brother, Lee, who had emigrated to New Zealand and I was close to where he lived in Auckland. Both Daz and his brother Lee had played water polo at Plant Hill and had represented Great Britain. I contacted Lee and arranged to meet up with him with the family where he lived. We were on the way to his house and I was really tired as we pulled in to a garage to get fuel and I put petrol in instead of diesel. A full tank! I went back into the garage and told him what I'd done. He told us we couldn't go anywhere in that vehicle as it would ruin the engine so he went out and put cones around it. He then explained that he wouldn't be able to get somebody to drain the vehicle until the next day. As I said, I was already tired and this was really pissing me off. Then when they said that the earliest that that they could come out was the next day, I couldn't get my head around this. Back home the AA was out to you within the hour. The guy behind the counter suggested that we sleep in the motor home but Mena and I decided that we can't do that as we felt it was dangerous . So we decided to get a taxi to the nearest B&B and then come back tomorrow. As we were about to leave the garage, a guy turns into the petrol station and he's only got one of the pumps that can drain a tank. After a short conversation he drains the tank for us. You couldn't make this up could you? How lucky is that? After he drained it we filled up the tank before leaving. Because I had now had two full tanks of petrol and diesel, I did a deal with the owner for £100 for both.

We eventually met Lee at his house in Auckland. I parked up on his driveway and was having a meal overlooking the bay and then we went out the next day for breakfast. I told him about the guy at Tarpua and he starts laughing. "What are you laughing at" I say. "Chris" he says " I could have a fight here every day". "What do you mean" I ask him. Lee says " You come out here and do you know what we are classed as?" "No what?" I say. "Immigrants" he says. Just like some people at home don't like our Asian communities because they see them as immigrants, then that is how we are seen here. There is not enough work for the locals and they see us as a threat". Mena and I just thought that this was another nail in the emigration coffin.

We left Lee's house and took a ferry to South Island. That's when we made the definite decision that this was to be a holiday and not a continued emigration recce. The next event validates that decision. I'm in a car lot looking at cars on the North Island. I'm not sure about the name of the place but it was after Tarpua and was on the way to the

South Island but still on North Island. I was in a car showroom looking at 4 x 4 cars and there are no English cars there. They were all station wagons and the prices are quite expensive. I thought it would be cheaper out there. The owner came right up to me "alright mate? Can I help you?" I said that I was just looking at prices and thought they were all a bit steep. The owner says "yeah mate you've to rip these pommie bastards off haven't you mate?" I just stood there for while with 'pommie' in my head and thinking isn't that the English? Surely he has realised that I am English but he's just said that directly to me. I'm looking at him a little confused and he says "Where you from mate?" He must have thought I was from somewhere other than England. "I'm a fucking Pommie bastard" I said right into his face and he went beetroot. He scooted off like I'd just passed wind. This was further evidence that had we emigrated we may be faced with this challenge on top of the financials. It was something that I'd not anticipated at all and possibly our experiences were not that typical but we had to be take them into account.

We got a ferry to South Island and drove down to Queenstown which was the Mecca for outdoor adventure and sports. We had a fantastic experience white water rafting which the whole family did and bungee jumping which Arron did. Arron was around fifteen and jumped at the chance to do the bungee jump and then started to rib me, calling me a shithouse because he was the only one doing it. He did the jump which was from a platform about 130 metres high and it was amazing. He continued to wind me up all the way back to the caravan park. When we got back my response was "why would I want to pay £50 to put my back out when we can do this?" I pointed to a poster advertising doing a sky dive' We walked straight into the camp office and I booked the highest sky dive we could possibly do which was 12,000 feet and a vertical dive.

This basically meant that we would jump out of the plain head first and experience maximum velocity. I said 'two of us please' and I turned to Arron and said 'we'll see who's a shithouse'. I could see that he was thinking about what it would be like but I had really cut my nose off to spite my face as I was the one who suffered with heights!! Next morning we got to the Airfield and went through the drill with the organisers regarding all the gear and the safety elements and they got us rigged to go up. We boarded the plane, which as you might imagine is a small plane which we were stuffed into to suit the order coming out of the side door. As we climbed, our instructors attached us to themselves and made their final checks and I was to be the first out with my partner. I was pushing all my nerves and issue with heights to the back of my mind and both Arron and I were showing a lot of bravado to each other but we were both nervous and at the same time, tremendously excited. The plane took off and immediately starts the climb to 12,000 feet. The plane was having to zig zag in order to climb quickly but stay above the landing area for those jumping out. What a view. We could see the mountain range (Cooke mountain). I said to the pilot 'wow this is high, what altitude are we at now?' He told us 'two thousand feet'. 'Oh right' I said. In my head I was thinking 'Shit, this is only 2,000 feet and we've got another 10,000 feet to go!'. I looked over at Arron and he's as white as a ghost. It took us a while but we eventually got to 12,000 feet and the guy I am attached to opens the sliding side door and we swings our legs around so that we are sat down in the plane with our legs dangling over the side. I didn't want Arron to see that I was nervous as he was next so I tried to look enthusiastic and excited, which I definitely was but that wasn't all I was feeling as I'm looking straight at the ground below. Before I know it, we are falling forward out of the plane and into a vertical dive. At that precise moment, you realise that you've just jumped out of a plane attached to a man who you are trusting with your life and you are dropping like a stone. The instructors are trying to make this as much an experience for us as possible. After a while in the vertical position, we are instructed to put our arms out like wings and that slows you down a little, then he is moving his arms and maneuvering yours to change direction. Just as you start to get used to it and take it all in, he has opened the parachute and we jerk back and it feels like an emergency stop in your driving test. The parachute was only open for a short time and all off a sudden it felt like he had dropped me and I went to grab his legs because I absolutely shit myself. What he was doing was deliberately loosening the attachment between us for when we landed. I don't remember him saying anything about that in the briefing. He continued to have a bit of a joke with me when he realised I thought that he had dropped me. When I landed the adrenalin was pumping in me and Arron was just behind me. After we had both landed, Jourdana and Rhys who at the time were 9 and 8 respectively, came running to us. I just said to them 'You've got to do that. It's unbelievable' and I turned to the instructor and said 'can my kids do it ? he said 'yes' and off they went and did it. The instructor came and had a word with me after they had landed and he said to me ' I've been doing this for fifteen years and I have never met a parent like you. Most parents discourage their kids from doing this but not you!' I just said to him 'We've all got to die sometime mate. When your number's up, your number's up. It shouldn't stop you living"

Queensland was fantastic, there was always something to do for everyone. The family went on a wander around the shops and got myself a coffee and sat chilling on the veranda decking of a coffee shop/ cafe above Lake Wakatipu, watching paragliders and people on the water. I began to realise how boring some aspects of it was. There was not much diversity going on. It reminded me of the television series 'The Prisoner' where it's an idyllic setting but everyone was robotic in their manner and everybody looked similar. It's not like that here in the UK where there are so many differences between us and there's always something going on. I began to see that they are all a little similar. That also applied to the food. They didn't have the diverse choices we have in Manchester because of our multiculture. What I did like though was their overall approach which was that your health is your wealth and not cars and possessions.

We arrived home and Simon was a bit gutted that I'd come back because he'd started to make plans for himself as a property owner. That said he was also overwhelmed that I'd come back because he missed me. Amazingly the deal hadn't gone through our banks yet anyway. The usual reasons, solicitors fucking about with no urgency. So the transaction hadn't happened yet even though we were all signed up. The building was still mine. I made the gesture of paying all the legal fees so that Simon wasn't out of pocket and we both said 'what's meant to be is meant to be'. Another five or six days and he would have been my landlord. Thankfully things had moved slowly while we were away and it was my brother we were dealing with and not someone who might say to me that a deals a deal. I appreciated the way that Simon dealt with it without any hesitation.

When I came back unexpectedly, Steve had to deal with that. He'd been telling people that he owned the business but me coming back put a spanner in the works for him. I started to realise how he was ruining the business because we were losing customers hand over fist. One time a guy came into the shop and said to Steve 'you're the boss aren't you?' and Steve went quiet and uncomfortable looking. He'd obviously told this guy he owned the Barbers. Around that time a friend called Paul who ran for Salford Harriers and was a GB runner came in to the shop looking in incredible shape. He has a little banter with us and then he sits in my chair for a haircut. As soon as he gets in the chair he says to me 'I don't really need a haircut' I should have guessed really as he was completely bald. There wasn't a hair on his head. I laughed and said 'So what do you want?' He said that he had just come in to say goodbye. I asked him where he was going and he said "I've got a few weeks to live mate' He told me that he had cancer of the esophagus. He'd been treated before but unfortunately it had come back with a vengeance. That's one of the reasons he had no hair too but he did look really well. We had a short conversation and we bear hugged and he left. I went back to cutting hair and couldn't stop thinking about what Paul had just told me. Steve was whinging on about having a cold. I'd had enough. I turned to Steve and said 'just cut this guy's hair and shut the fuck up or I'll throw you through that fucking door'. He didn't say anything. There was a massive atmosphere as the next two customers for each of us go through the chairs and had their haircuts so I decided to close the shop early that day. We closed up, he went home and he never came back again. It was the right outcome. It was never going to work once I'd returned from New Zealand. We were exact opposites when it came to the glass being half empty (him) or half full (me) and I can't mix with people like that never mind work next to them all day.

We moved in temporarily with Mena's mum for few months until we got ourselves sorted. I was cutting one of my regular customers' hair one day and he said have you looked at the semi on Mainway? I couldn't think of any semi-detached properties on Mainway. I thought they were all detached properties and out of our league price wise. Mainway was in Alkrington. Middleton and was an unusual type of dual carriageway and had some fantastic detached houses on it. It was known in the area for having some of the bigger and more expensive properties in the north of Manchester, one of which had been famous for belonging to the comedian Bernard Manning. I immediately arranged to go and view the property with Mena and we both fell in love with it. The woman who owned the house was elderly and had left it up to her brother and sister to sell the house as she was going in to a nursing home. The asking price was £200,000 so we went back to the estate agent and offered £180,000 for a quick sale. We heard nothing for two weeks so I called into the estate agents to ask what was happening. They informed me that a couple had offered the asking price of £200,000. I was furious that they had not got back to me as we were first to view the house. I told them that we would pay the £200,000 and that there was no chain behind us as we were ready to move immediately. The estate agent picked up the phone to the owner and said "I've got Mr Duoba here and he was the first to view your house and is willing to offer the £200,000 and has no chain behind him". The owner said that if I was willing to complete within the month it was ours. I think the way I behaved in the estate agents that day may have also had something to do with the speed of the deal too. They may have been keen to get rid of me. I did the same with the Solicitor. I think I may have mentioned what I'd do with the rolled up deeds to the house if it didn't complete before the deadline of one month. This was the right move for us and we couldn't lose it. We did the house up as we went along after we moved in. I just remember sitting in the bath one day looking straight on to Mainway as we had no blinds and the windowsill was low in the wall and I waved at people as they passed. This was my ninth home and my own family's seventh if you count the motorhome in New Zealand and Mena's mum's house (which I am doing).

Chapter 16 - The End of Martial Arts for PC Duoba?

To most people that know me, it may have appeared that I eventually got back to 'normal' after the accident, if I ever was 'normal' in the first place but there were several things that were never the same for me and that I still experience today. The main thing about me is that mentally, I tire across the day and my ability for processing things in my brain weakens the later the day gets. After the accident my brain was like a mobile phone battery and as the day goes on it starts to drain on power and I start to run out of memory. It was explained to me medically that when I get tired my memory doesn't have the same capacity as it should have and later in the day I only have half of the brain and memory capacity that would normally have been available to me. It's why I find the end of the day far more difficult than the start and also meant that when intense concentration is required my brain seems to put in for annual leave.

Since having children, both Mena and I had thought it was a good idea to put our kids into martial arts classes for the positive discipline that it demands and Arron was of course the first to do so. It was as good a reason as any for me to get back involved too as I thought it might help Arron settle into it. If I am honest, I struggled. Not with the physical side of things but with my memory and co-ordination but I battled on as I was never one to give up on anything if it was up to me. When you attend a martial arts class for a while, you eventually end up getting involved in meetings or exhibitions and we ended up at a Martial arts exhibition of Shaolin Kung Fu at Abraham Moss and I was to perform a routine discipline called a 'Kata'. If you carry out the discipline correctly it merits the next belt. I found myself having to perform this routine in front of the Master. The master is called Master Ang who is a guy I was introduced to by Pat and Anthony who are Philomena's brother and sister who were already black belts. By coincidence Master Ang also lives in Alkrington and also has a wife called Philomena. I got ready to perform the discipline in front of Master Ang and almost immediately after starting my mind went blank. I literally didn't know what to do next and the master's face was like thunder and he did not look happy at all. All of a sudden I spot Philomena stood just behind the Master. Just to explain, this Philomena is not my wife, she is the Master's wife. She is trying to get my attention and showing me the next move. Philomena is a Master and black belt too and of course knows the routine well. What follows is this comical situation where I am facing the Master looking like I know what I am doing but I'm looking right past him at Philomena who is carrying out the next move and I am copying her and then. it clicks again. We got through it and I'm not sure what the Master made of it but I made a point of apologising to him at the end of the meeting and explaining that I had a head injury that impaired me by shutting me down when it felt like it. He seemed to accept this but must have wondered why everybody in the small audience found it a little comical. I'm not certain if Philomena ever told him either. My knowledge of martial arts got me in a fair bit of trouble one evening when I was younger. I had been in the Belmont Pub on Middleton Road for a few drinks with a couple of mates who I can't for the life of me remember the names of and we were walking home pretty drunk. I'd be either sixteen or seventeen at the time. The two mates started to wind me up a bit and challenging me to show them some of my Karate moves. One of them said 'Come on Chris. Show us what you can do'. I eventually got riled enough to show them. We were outside a big old house with stone posts forming a gateway and the two lads were pushing against the wall attached to the post and continued to goad me to do something so I aimed a powerful kick at this stone gatepost. I got the shock of my life when not only did the concrete post go over but part of the wall they were leaning against with their hands also collapsed. The three of us just stood there staring at the debris on the floor. Then I looked up and noticed this guy looking right at me from the bay window of the house so we legged it. We didn't get very far before a black Mariah pulled up. A black Mariah for anyone out there not around in the 70's was an infamous police vehicle especially made to give rides to people who would be helping the Police with their enquiries! A copper jumps out and said to us all 'Show me your hands' We showed him our hands and he immediately saw the colour of their hands which still had brick dust on and threw the two of them into the back of the Black Mariah. I didn't have any brick dust on my hands so he told me to 'Fuck off home''. The thing was the brick dust was on my feet. They were taken into Collyhurst Police Station and then this sergeant major of a copper starts to work on them and they spill the beans and give him my name. Meanwhile I'm tucked in bed at Cravenwood thinking, have I got away with this or not? It wasn't long before there was a knock on the door and there's the copper to arrest me. My mum and dad weren't best pleased to say the least. I get to Collyhurst cop shop and I get escorted to a room where the sergeant is sat behind a desk and I go in and sit down in front of him and he immediately he smacks me across the face and says "Did I say sit down?" So I stood up and he gives me a smack across the face again and says "Did I say stand up?" and he says "Now sit down". I'm waiting for another smack but it doesn't arrive. He tells me that I'm heading for court and I'll pay for the damage that I've done. He was right too. I eventually got done in court and ordered to pay for the damages. It remains the only thing I ever got in official trouble for. Before he let me leave the courts that day though he pulled me to one side and said that he wanted me to apply to the police force to be a copper. He said that I was just the sort of person that the force is looking for. I'm guessing that he meant because I am tall and didn't appear to be intimidated. I told him that I'd just signed apprenticeship documents to be a barber. He seemed to accept this as my answer and asked where I worked. It wasn't long before he paid me a visit in the shop and I ended up cutting his hair that day and for the next thirty years and we became good friends. I knew him only as Les. He stopped coming in about seven or 8 years ago so I had to assume that he'd passed away. It was the most unlikely start to a long friendship and I'm certain that if `I hadn't already agreed my apprenticeship that he might have convinced me to be a copper.

My martial arts days ended though when I started to attend a session in a hall in St Annes, Crumpsall ran by John Boyle, who I knew well and who was qualified to a high level in Karate and also competed at full contact Karate. I had got up to a high standard of Karate before my accident but hadn't progressed through the belts due to the fact that they used to carry out all assessments on a Saturday and I was always working on a Saturday. My ambitions had always been high though and before the accident I had big ideas about qualifying for the GB team to go to the Olympics. This is the way I thought about things. I had to aim for the very best standards in everything I did and after I'd met 'John Lennon' at that martial arts meeting in Ardwick, I'd reflected on the high standards he had demonstrated and his effortless style and thought that's where I wanted to be and set my sights on being a GB team member. After the crash, the very best ambitions for me now just meant attending Shotokan Karate sessions and eventually aiming to progress through the belts but I was ignoring the fact that my brain was holding me back.

John had been observing me at a session as I went through some routines and he came over to me and just said 'Chris, you need to call it a day and find something else to get into because it's just not happening mate'.

What he could see and what I might have been blind to until that point, was that my co-ordination had gone. I knew what I should be doing but the messages from my brain to my limbs were all over the place. It was a sensible move to stop the martial arts from a safety point of view too as my head injury always meant that it was an ongoing risk to subject myself to potential kicks to the head. My mum tells me that I was due to do my black belt on the day after the accident but now the frustration was that I would never do that and rather than think about that negatively, it was time for me to focus on other things that could fulfil the ambition that was left within me. John Boyle himself went on to run a very popular gym in Blackley Village called Blackley Health Studio who a lot of people in the area will know well.

They say that when one door closes another one opens. I believe that is absolutely true but you have to be willing to look for that door and willing to push it open and then go through it. Michael Jordan, the basketball giant, is one of the world's greatest sports stars ever. When he had to face failure, he simply used it as his motivation to work hard to achieve his eventual supremacy. When my martial arts ambitions ended it meant that I had to focus elsewhere to do something that I enjoyed but that I could push the boundaries on and be constantly challenged. What I didn't know at the time was where that would eventually lead me and that I wouldn't have to look very far as I was already very much into cycling and getting fit. It was just a question of learning how to swim properly so that I could become a triathlete. More excitingly, even that achievement would turn out to be the start of the real athletic achievements in my life and explore my real capabilities.

Chapter 17 Weekends Duoba Style

As I said earlier, it was on our second honeymoon that I realised I had the bug for windsurfing. Living in Heywood wasn't ideal for that kind of hobby but Mena, seeing how much I liked it, booked lessons for me with a guy called Martin Ashby who had a windsurfing shop in Bury on Wash Lane Road. He took us to a place called Clowbridge Reservoir, past Rossendale and on the way to Burnley, where he gave me lessons. Mena had lessons too and on our first visit she fell off and cracked her knee on the rocks and fractured her knee cap. Not realizing how badly she had been hurt, I'd said to her to stop being so soft and to get back out there and to her credit she went back out. I don't know about Mena but Martin never forgive me for that and even for many years afterwards if I saw him he still would say 'I'll never forget that day when you said to your wife to get back out and she had that bloody injury'. I honestly thought she just banged her knee and it was the sort of thing that eventually it stops hurting. Mena is made of toucher stuff than that and she wouldn't give up on the day.

Most people would need months of lessons with something like windsurfing before they would enter an event or race. With me, I've always been very lucky and if you just show me how to do something and let me have a go, I'll generally be able to do it. It's a mixture of no fear and some ambition. I am not frightened of failure or getting hurt and I want to do things to the best standard I can. So when Martin showed me what to do, by later that afternoon I wanted to enter a race. Don't get me wrong. I've still got loads to learn but I'm ready to compete and happy to get thrown in at the deep end. Once you know how to get out and back and how to use the wind and tread water if necessary then that gives you a lot of the skills required. Its then a case of perfecting things like adding beach starts. A beach start is when you have so much wind that you just get yourself to the water's edge and step on to the board because the wind will then take you out. A Deep Water start is when you have fallen or jumped off the board in the sea and you have to get back on and get going again. You can't just stand up. You need to position yourself with your feet and legs in the right place to the board and then use the sail and the wind to bring you into an upright position. One of the most dangerous moves whether on a windsurfer or a boat is the Jybe. This where you change the position of the sail to get the best out of the wind or to go in a different direction and you have to duck under the Boom as it swings around at pace. The faster the wind is the quicker that the Boom will swing across. My teeth found out about this one time when he hit me full in the mouth. That cost me some teeth that day. When you watch a schooner and the crew change the direction of the sail, if anyone gets hit by the Boom, then they're in the sea. When you are windsurfing it's a smaller scale but still has that same power . The main difference is though, if you end up in the sea then there's normally no one there to help you get back on. I'd hit it off with Martin. We were the same sort of person. I bought a load of gear off him and we became good friends. He was a professional windsurfer.

Eventually, we'd reached a point where we had a space cruiser with the boards on the roof and all the gear inside. I would take it to work and if the weather was great I headed straight up the M66 to get some windsurfing in. We had different boards, long and short, and chose them dependent on the wind. The more the wind, the smaller the board. This created speed. The less the wind the bigger the board and the sail. They stayed on the car permanently. If I entered a race I always used the large board and got the most out of the wind.

I used to go windsurfing with my cousin Roy, who is the brother of Adrian who I had the crash with. I'm going back about twenty years or longer here to just before the millennium. He was the only person I would train with at that time because he was the only person that was naturally on the same wavelength as me and believe me that was a crazy wavelength at times.

Roy comes from my mother's side of the family and was and is a big part of my life. I don't want to go into detail but he'd been through some very real ups and downs in life but since then had delivered talks so that others would benefit from his experience. At the time, he saw what I was doing and he wanted to get involved and be part of it. I enjoyed being with him and our styles of doing things in training and enjoying sport were very similar. We were going to a gym at the time and then he got involved with a girl called Maxine, who was ahead of her time in terms of personal training and who owned a gym in Prestwich behind the Grapes well before Gyms became popular again.

One day we were at Elton reservoir to do some windsurfing and I said to him 'We are not going home until you've windsurfed across this lake without falling off' We were there for ages but in the end he did it. We were sat on the grass banking afterwards as it was a nice day and he turned around to me and said 'where were you when I was 16? I've just experienced one of the best adrenaline hits that I've ever had without taking a drug'. I knew what he meant of course because the rush of achieving something in sport is pretty special.

The following week, we went windsurfing at Fleetwood together at the estuary. It wasn't a particularly windy day and we were windsurfing out to the open sea and it looked a bit choppy. All of sudden I see a huge

Cargo ship with the name 'Pandora' on the side coming down the estuary. Now an average person might think that they need to steer clear of that but I'm a lad from Blackley and my natural instinct is to windsurf towards it and get up close to it and surf off the wave created by the ship. The ship sounds its foghorn and it's as loud as fuck and the vibration alone is incredible and shakes me and my sail. I'm going up the estuary on this wave and what I didn't realise was that it was so big it's pushing me up the beach. So I ride the surf and end up stranded about 200 yards up the beach. I'm thinking 'how awesome was that?' and Roy is watching this. I'm shouting to Roy 'Did you see that twenty foot wave' and then I spot this guy who looks like captain Birdseye running towards me on the sand. I can see him coming from quite a distance away and he's aiming right for me. I'm thinking he can't be the captain of that ship so who is he? He gets up right into my face and says 'Are you a fucking dickhead? Where are you from?' 'Blackley Manchester' I said " I fucking thought so' he said "You're all dickheads from that part of the world' I ask him what his problem is and he says ' He can't fucking see you know. He hasn't got brakes you know. That's why he sounded his foghorn' His parting shot was "get out there' as he pointed to the open seas. I said 'wind your neck in mate' and off he goes. Roy is absolutely loving this and is pissing himself laughing. Eventually he says ' come on then let's get out there'.

We start to windsurf out to sea. We've got a head wind now so it's tough. We need to get 2 miles out and so are zig zagging against the wind. Roy is in front of me and says 'Chris that Buoy keeps moving'. I said to him that it was impossible as it is a landmark of something like a sand bank or something like that. Roy says again 'That bastard is moving'. I maintain that it can't be but as I look at it I think it is moving and it's getting bigger as It gets nearer. As it gets very close I can hear what sounds like a motor. I move away but it follows me only this time it knocks me off my board. I've now got it into in my head that there is a propeller underneath this thing and it might chew my legs off on. I was trying to swim away and Roy is roaring laughing again and then I realised that captain Birdseye is controlling it from the shore. It's a remote controlled Buoy. This was of course well before Drones became a big development I went straight to coast guard's office where this guy was controlling this buoy - he had been using binoculars to see how to put this thing right on me. I banged on the windows shouting 'Hey Birdseye get your arse out here now'. He didn't come out and I don't blame him because I saw my reflection in the window and I wouldn't have come out to a guy that looked that angry either!!

Around the same time of year, we went back to Fleetwood. This time there was me, my wife Mena, the three kids (Lily hadn't been born yet) and Simon Mac. I call him by this name so that it distinguishes him from my brother Simon. Simon McAlister was my brother in law, my sister's husband. It was a beautiful day and windy as fuck which makes for a cracking windsurfing day. Even though this sport was a thing for me, we wanted to make a family day out of things where we could. Simon Mac had come out with us especially to do some windsurfing. The Kids were too young then to get involved but were there to enjoy the day out at the coast and watch the windsurfing.

When we got there we were really excited at the conditions. There was an off-shore wind, a wind blowing out to sea, so we would have to tack back. Tacking is a way of windsurfing against the wind by turning the sail into the wind. Because the wind was blowing out to sea we would have no such problem getting out there. We would be travelling out there from 0 to 25 miles an hour in a few seconds. I helped Simon Mac put his rig together. The board we use has a rubber bung that you tighten on to the board with a unique type of spanner and then put the mast in which then clicks in and is maneuverable and you're all set to go. We are both just excited to get out there so Simon went first and he literally just whizzed off at a pace. I made a school boy error. I got my board and my mast set up and I've rigged things up and my mast had clicked in and off I went. It's hard to describe the level of exhilaration you get. The only way I can describe it is that you feel at one with the wind. You are accelerating at 25 miles per hour but it feels like 100 miles per hour.

The power that you feel through the wind is incredible and your board is skimming across the water like the stones you used to throw to skim across water as a kid. You are skipping across some waves and then the next thing you know you are airborne. You have your feet strapped in to the board and a harness on so that you have full steering on the arms like power steering and all the force is in the board. I get to about a mile out and I had to turn around so I turned the sail and all of a sudden the mast come out of the board and it's in my hands not connected. 'Shit', I shout 'what's happened here? I realised that I'd inserted the mast into the rubber housing on the board but I had made the terrible error of not tightening the nut that fastens the rubber housing onto the board itself and as I'm sailing out the nut has worked its way undone and I've seen it bounce across the board and into the sea and I'm left holding the mast. It's windy and choppy and the waves are about six foot high. I'm now sat on the board because the sale is no longer connected to it and I'm still a mile out at sea and drifting. What do I do now? Should I wait here until the Coast Guard comes to get me on a day where a lot of people might be getting in trouble through the wind or do I try and do something?

I unraveled my sail and put everything across the board and lay on top of it and started swimming back to the land using the board as surfers do as a surf board. I have to Swim along the coast to try and get on dry land again. I'm pumped up and swimming hard but don't seem to be getting very far through the choppy waters and stop a few times as I'm getting exhausted. In fact it wasn't long before I was absolutely shattered. As I stopped to rest I felt the board going backwards and I realised that I was stopping every 15 yards and it was floating back out every time and I was in a rip tide. I was so exhausted that my eyes were closing and I wanted to sleep. I had to shake my head and shout at myself 'what are you doing'. I had my wife and three kids on the beach. That's when I realised what I needed to do. Because I was in a riptide I needed to let the rig go. It was a grands worth of equipment but it was the only thing I could do to get me back to dryland before I drifted out further. So then it was just me and the board but the swell in the sea was so big I can now no longer see which way is dry land and which way is out to sea which was alarming in itself. Then I saw a familiar sight. It was the top of Blackpool Tower. Now I don't know an awful lot about Blackpool but I do know that Blackpool Tower is not in the sea, so I now have my bearings back. I start the long swim on the board along the coast towards the tower and gradually finding my way back towards dryland. Eventually I get to a point between where I'd started and Blackpool Tower and I am able to get out of the sea with the board and I start the walk back up the coast towards Fleetwood. I know that people are prone to exaggeration but from the time it took me to walk back the distance I had travelled along the coast on the board seemed to me to be seven or eight miles. I am just happy to be back on dry land again though so the walk doesn't bother me one bit even if I am dressed as a surfer walking along the coastal road. As I reach the family again I don't realise how long I've been gone for. Mena greets me with 'where the hell have you been?' I say "Where the hell have I been? You're lucky I'm back at all'. She just thinks I've left her with the three kids and I'm having the time of my life. Simon just thought that, as I am the most experienced windsurfer, I was making the most of the wind. When I explained what happened to him he couldn't believe it but I don't think they both really understood the situation I have been in. Having said that I don't think I fully realised the battle I'd had as they said to me that I have been gone for over five hours.

This wasn't the first time I'd been close to disaster in the sea. I was once in Anglesey at Tregele bay. Something happened to me while I was there that I will never forget. I was out windsurfing in the bay and found myself out in the sea with a twelve foot swell but no wind. I was trying to tack my way back to shore with the sail down and I fell off. As I couldn't mount the board again from the water, I decided to hang on to the board and let the swell take me into the beach like a bit of drift wood. I wasn't that far away but there were rocks at the side that I needed to avoid. That's when I felt someone below me grab both my ankles and pull me down. I absolutely shit myself. I stopped concentrating on avoiding the rocks and damaging the board, I needed to get to dry land and get out of the sea and away from this person trying to kill me. After a mad scramble, I sat on the rocks relieved and looking out to sea and shaking, trying to work out what had happened and this local guy walks on to the rocks and sits down next to me and says 'Are you ok son?' He has obviously just witnessed what's happened to me. 'Yes' I say . "you were lucky there wasn't you?' he said. I look at him and ask him what he means. He then tells me that two experienced swimmers died a couple of weeks ago on the same spot. For a moment I'm thinking that a ghost of one of the swimmers has tried to drown me, a bit like the opposite of a mermaid but then he says 'you know what has happened don't you? The swell in the water is about 12 feet high and millions of gallons of water are going up against the rocks and going back down and creating a whirlpool which goes fast under the sea to the seabed. What happens then is your legs get caught up in that whirlpool and it starts to drag you down. The two swimmers didn't have a board to hold onto so it took them out to sea' I did have a board which saved my life.

I raced at many reservoirs. I did one at Southport that was a twenty four hour event with Roy. He also eventually had lessons with Martin Ashby but at the time I am talking about here, he'd only had lessons from me. I just reiterated the lessons I received from Martin on to Roy. We were at Cowbridge one day and Roy was out on my board sharing my equipment. I was on the water's edge with Martin Ashby and Roy is out there flying around on the board and Martin says to me 'Is he strapped in?' I said to him 'No. He can't do that yet'. So we are just watching him holding on to the Boom and after about twenty minutes Martin says "How can he do that without being strapped in for that length of time?' Not being strapped in and holding on to the boom to stop you being flung in the air is the equivalent to doing nonstop chin ups at an exceptionally fast pace for the whole time you are out on the water. Instead of being harnessed in, Roy had to use his body weight to hold down the boom and his arms were also steering and maneuvering the board.

When Roy comes back in I just act normal and say 'my turn now you fucker before the wind disappears' Martin sees the proof that he is not harnessed in and his face is a picture of disbelief. Roy looks at him and says 'Are you alright mate?' Roy is the only person I ever trained with who trained to exhaustion. We were both on exactly the same wavelength and it was great fun.

A neighbour of mine in Ainsworth, Martin and his wife Janice, used to spend their weekends with their two girls at a static caravan in Anglesey where they also had a speedboat and were able to have fantastic days away, windsurfing, water skiing, scuba diving and all sorts of activities. He had kindly invited myself, Philomena and the kids to spend time down there with them and It inspired me months later to do something similar. Simon Mac (my brother in law) and I put £10,000 each into a kitty and bought a static caravan, a speedboat and all the equipment including water skis etc. Then, every weekend we would go somewhere with the kids and wind surf and water ski. After a while we wanted to add to the thrills so we bought an inflatable doughnut. We would get in the donut and the other one would drive the speedboat and try to dislodge the other one from it. The one driving would speed along and try and create a huge wave that would then toss the person into the air and they had to hang on for dear life to stay in it. One day I was in the doughnut and Simon hit the wave perfectly and put me about ten to fifteen feet into the air. I held on to the doughnut stubbornly and flipped over a full 360 degrees in the air and landed with such force that the doughnut acted like a trampoline and I was fired into the air and off it. I was never able to reproduce that for Simon no matter how hard I tried. I did create my own killer challenge though.

So Roy has got to hear about everything Simon Mac and I were are doing and he's having some of that. By the way, just to remind you, I have to refer to him as Simon Mac because when I just say Simon that's my brother Simon. Me and Simon Mac and Roy go to Holyhead one day and we take the doughnut out with us. Simon Mac and I are in the speedboat and Roy is in the doughnut. Simon and I just look at each other and we both know that we are going to try something a little different. Roy thinks he is mega strong and of course he is but we decide to really test that. We are literally flying around Holyhead in the boat and being a harbour there are not many waves so we are a bit gutted to say the least. So we are going around in figure of eights and Roy is just laughing at us. So here we are working around trying to get him out and somehow we find ourselves in a position where he is travelling at high speed in a whip action and he's heading straight for the harbour wall. We were only trying to take him close to it but we misjudged the length of the rope and he's heading right for it. All we can see is his white teeth. He is neither grimacing or smiling, he is just hold on for dear life. He can't let go because he's travelling at such speed, he will just carry in without the doughnut towards the wall and hit it with great force. It's like a Blackley version of 'Jackass' before it even came out. Simon Mac and I are still laughing and saying 'ooh this is going to be close. have we judged this right?' All the veins in his neck and head are now visible. The moment of truth arrives and holding tight to the doughnut he misses the harbour wall by inches. We are laughing even more and he's still in the donut. What strength he had. Of course looking back he was close to possibly being killed. All he said when he got out was 'Good one wasn't it?'

I was once at a place called West Kirby on the Wirral doing a bit of windsurfing. There's a mile long stretch in the open sea and the challenge is about how fast you can do the mile on a board. I think that the world record is about 34 kilometres an hour. I've decided that on this day that's what I am doing. I'm getting out the short board and I am going to go at this full pelt. I harnessed myself into the board and I am going at some speed., I've built up to about twenty mile per hour and as I am just about to try and increase my speed even faster, for some reason I took my foot out of the trap that holds your feet to the board and slipped.

I hit the mast straight on with my crown jewels. The sail comes up and I end up in the water. My first thought is 'oh fuck I've lost one of me mates'. It had disappeared up into me but it came back a few hours later. I had no kids at that time, so for a few hours I was panicking thinking that this was the end of my ambitions to become to a father. Thankfully that wasn't the case.

I have always maintained a willingness to have a go and see what I can do. Although it was a lot later in my life, in fact only a few years ago a couple of smashing local guy called Gary Hollingsworth and John Ingman approached me regarding getting involved and joining a much younger team of lads from the Blackley area who were competing in the very competitive world of Box Car Racing representing The Co-op Academy. Generally they would travel various distances to participate in events that took place on go kart tracks mostly. Some events were at army barracks and certain events were annual. Every year they entered the English Championships. I was able to add value to the team, not just by being a participating member of the team because the team was already extremely capable, but I was able to add to doing my bit on the track by advising them on nutrition as some of the events involved great distances and ran throughout the night. My experience in endurance sports was something that added value to their team. Petra, who was preparing food to run through the night was thinking spaghetti Bolognese and pasta. I told her that was great but they needed something more substantial and containing fats rather than carbs just before the difficult session through the early hours so I told Petra to stock up on cheese pizzas with veg to build up energy again. When the time came for the food to be eaten Petra shouted them in to get their food. When she said pasta nobody budged but when she said that they had cheesy pizzas there was a stampede. Petra looked at me and I just shrugged as if to say 'no surprises there then'. In the early hours we'd spotted the Dutch Pro Team in their tent eating Mackerels and sardines thinking they were doing the right thing. We were in our tent eating Jaffa cakes and honeycombe and broken biscuits. One of the Dutch team scowls at me when he walks back to the living quarters. They think we are a bunch of no hopers eating all the wrong things and they don't realise its exactly the opposite. They've got all the gear and a really smart looking Go kart full of sponsorship but we've got the knowledge and the determination to get the best out of each other. We made sure we had the sugars in our body to be out there and awake, ready to go through the night and the following morning we introduced some fats through bacon butties, sausage barm cakes and cheese to get us up to the next gear for the morning session. Gary and John were over the moon with our performance and as it happened the Dutch Pro team finished below our respectable position of 8th out of 30 teams. There was also a girls' team from the local co-op academy competing too and they also did well. You should never rule out the Mancs in anything. Gary knew what he was doing when he recruited me. I think I added a little edge to an already brilliant team including Gary and his Mrs, Karen and John Ingman and Petra who prepared all the food. They were surprised, as I think some of you maybe, that I was recommending food like Bacon butties, Sausage Barms and Pizza for a sporting event that requires stamina and a level of fitness. People who know me and see me wouldn't guess for one minute that I would entertain that kind of food myself under any circumstances but the facts are that there is a time and a place for even the wrong things to get the right result. If you are thinking about getting yourself fit, or becoming athletic or competitive in any way, you need to study the subject of food and what each type of food does to your body and your performance at the appropriate times. This will help you get fit or get in shape or compete.

Chapter 18 – Lifeblood

I have been a barber for 45 years this year (2020) albeit for the first year or so I was a trainee. My training had to end very abruptly when Henry hurt his back and had to have many months off and I took over not only as the main barber but running the shop. I knew that one day I would own it and of course I've already told you how that came about in September 1996. All across those 45 years the lifeblood of the shop has been the customers. I must have met literally thousands of people all in all but there has been a core of customers that have been with me for a long time. I owe my living to the skills that Henry gave me and those loyal customers, most of which are still with me today regular as clockwork having their haircuts until of course COVID 19 came along and interrupted that regular contact I had with them.

Being a barber opens up a whole new skill set for you. It's actually a multi role and you acquire the abilities to operate at a lower level as a psychological counsellor, a nutritionist, a triage medical advisor, a legal advisor, a mentor, a networker that links up people and just a plain good old listener. I can't even begin to guess at how many times I have helped people with both minor issues and even serious problems. The main thing though is the contact that you have with people and the relationships you build up over many years. Meeting people from all walks of life has been hugely interesting . Every one of them has taught me something and I'd like to think that they have got something out of me more than just a haircut. I dedicate this chapter to them, my customers, the lifeblood of my work. I couldn't talk about them all but here are just a few samples of my experiences across the last forty five years. Names have been changed or left out in certain stories to protect their confidentiality. If I have used their real name, it's because they wanted me to. I love to give each story a title of what I have learned from it or what the customer got out of it.

Little things can cause a big issue

Sometimes customers will say something to me and if I think they just want to get it off their chest I'll let it go in one ear and out the other. Now and again though, I'll push them on it and ask them what they meant. One of my regular customers is a building site manager and was on a huge job to build a retail outlet on a local site. He came in for a haircut one day and was muttering ' If only I'd stepped on it'. I asked him 'stepped on what?' he told me that he'd spotted a Newt on the floor near his site office and instead of stepping on it, he'd mentioned it to someone. Unfortunately, Newts are protected and the whole site had to shut while they sorted things out. It meant several months of delays to the job and effected dozens of people and cost thousands of pounds. Hence his comment ' if only I'd stepped on it'' I love these stories where I've learned a few things and also had a bit of a giggle at how serious he was about this little newt.

Getting bigger doesn't mean getting better

A guy call Eddie who had a big haulage company once gave me some invaluable advice while I was cutting his hair. He said to me 'Do yourself a favour Chris - stay a sole trader. I made good money with two trucks - now I've created a fucking monster" He did eventually sell it to his brother. I had enough pressure running one shop, I couldn't imagine running multiple sites. If I ever did venture to dream about opening another shop. Eddies advice soon stopped me and I'm glad that I never did.

Have belief in yourself

Having belief in yourself is massively important. Sometimes the only barrier to achievement is yourself and your own negative thoughts. One of my customers, Mike was a guitar player. He's played guitar for many years and was at the top of his game. He was also in a Jam Tribute band and they are just about to play a gig and the person on before him is Toyah Wilcox. There's a problem and the organiser comes to Mike and tells him that something is wrong and would he mind going on and playing a couple of songs to keep the audience going. Mike says no problem and without even a second thought, went on. Then he froze in front of a few thousand people. He just stood there and stared into the audience.. He ended up coming off the stage having played nothing. Later he went on with his band and played their set. Sometimes it's not the skill set you have, it's you that makes the difference. You have to believe in yourself and have confidence in what you are doing and absolutely most of all, Crack on!! Sometimes in times of trouble you simply have to crack on. With Mike I believe if he had have played the first note it would have all been plain sailing after that as his knowledge would have done the rest. That's how it is with anything. There will be times of doubt or wanting to give up and what you have to do is simply take that next step and crack on.

It's a small world but I wouldn't like to clean it

I wrote in chapter ten about meeting Mena, that a police officer called Frank, who was one of my customers, had radioed ahead and told the patrol cars to pay us a visit every five minutes. I thought it coincidental at the time that we'd bumped into Frank that night but I didn't have to be in Manchester to bump into my customers. I've come across them in many places all over the world. I was having a coffee in Italy and a customer come up to me and asked if I had my scissors with me. I told him jokingly to 'fuck off'. I bumped into two customers on the other side of the world in New Zealand albeit that those meetings were planned. I was once on the way home from training in Portugal and was sat on the plane ready to taxi on to the runway for take-off and the Captain announced "Ladies and Gents we just need to delay by ten minutes while we take on another passenger who's a little late. Some of the passengers are annoyed and there's a few exchanging comments of dissatisfaction about the delay and the 'idiot' that's late and I'll admit I was joining in a bit and I remember thinking that this poor fellah is going to get on the plane and every single passenger will be looking at him and giving him grief in their heads. The door is opened again and on gets the passenger. I take one look at him and realise its one on my customers. All he has in his hands is a pair of shoes. He spotted me and says "Alright Chris?". "Alright Steve?" I say. After we take off he comes over to me for a chat. Turns out he's a professional golf caddy and his pro got knocked out of the tournament he was in earlier than expected so he booked a last minute flight home and raced down to the airport. It was a good enough reason to be ten minutes late to be fair.

Of course there's the daily contact with customers when I'm not at work and I'll go cycling or walking or running in Heaton Park and if I hear 'Hi Chris' once, I'll hear it between ten and fifteen times every day, and I absolutely love it.

I love the contact with people. I bounce off them and I always feel the better for stopping and having a chat with people. My appearance doesn't really fit with that and some people give me a wide berth or even walk the other way but my customers know me and what I'm about and would never let me pass without saying hello. It's one of my main motivators across the day.

212

Double Decker

Everyone of a certain age has a story about the old double decker buses. People, especially those abroad, associate that type of bus with London but all our major cities had them. Those were the days when you could run for a double decker bus and jump on at the back where the corner doorway where the safety rail was with no door. Of course when getting off as a young lad you would show off and jump off while the bus was still going so you would hit the ground running. One day one of my customers told me a story of when he had done just that. He jumped off while the bus was still doing probably about 5-10 miles per hour and instead of hitting the ground running and eventually stopping in a cool and unflustered manner, as soon as he hit the ground he ran into a lamppost! Ouch!!! Painful or what? Many of my customers will reminisce about their childhood while I am cutting their hair and tell me about the things they got up to as teenagers. If I had £1 for every time that happened I'd be a rich man. One of my customers, who will remain nameless, was doing just that when they told me that they used to be a couple of mice from Tib Street pet shop on a Saturday and cause havoc in Manchester city centre with these mice. If you're reading this from Manchester and you are above the age of 50 you will know about the pet shop on Tib Street which was like an Aladdin's cave to a young child, full of animals and creatures for sale. The guy who ran it looked cross-eyed and was a bit intimidating but was ok actually. Anyway, back the story of the lad and his mate buying the mice. They would take them in to Lewis's store near Piccadilly and let them go in lifts or even in the restaurant and then watch the carnage it created. You have to laugh but I'm guessing that they would get strung up for it now. Can you imagine if camera phones existed back then? What's this got to do with double deckers? Well my customer told me that they would wait until just after 5pm and the queues for the buses out of town would be huge. The double decker buses would be heaving with people and just as it pulled away from the stop this customer of mine just lent forward and carefully tossed a mouse on to the bus at the open corner where people get on so that it landed on the lap of people sat at the back on the long seat near the conductor. He told me that as the bus then pulled away all you could hear were the shrieks and screams. Very immature but very funny. Kids needed to do something to pass the time on a Saturday afternoon outside of the football season I suppose.

Tense Experience

Not every customer gave me a laugh. One evening I was in the shop on my own. It was a Friday and it had been our busiest day of the week so the takings were very good. I was just about to lock the door for the end of the day but as I reached it, it opened. Three men walked in. All three of them were big lads and I immediately got a bad feeling about the situation I now found myself in. I don't scare easy. In fact I don't really scare at all but I realised that this situation made me very vulnerable.

It became apparent that one of the guys was the father and the other two were his sons. I'd already closed the blinds before I was going to lock the door so that wasn't going in my favour either. I locked the door behind them for three reasons. The first was the business one, I didn't need any more customers as I was closed. The second reason was that I didn't want them to feel that they were easily intimidating me so locking the door made it seem like I wasn't worried. Finally I had already made my mind up that if this did go down the way that I feared it might, I was determined that one of them would go down with me. The youngest man sits in a chair to have his haircut and the father sits down at the back. The other guy is walking up and down behind me and I'm thinking any minute now I am going to get a punch to the kidneys or worse a knife. I am trying to cut his hair and watch his brother at the same time. I finish the young brother's haircut and he gets up and the other brother sits in the chair. The father is still sat at the back saying nothing at all. The young brother gets in one of the two empty chairs that are left and says 'I'm just going to wash my hair'. So that it is clear that I'm not frightened I say 'that'll be self-service prices then" "Do you want yours washing too?" I say to the other brother. He says "No – I'm happy". Then the father gets in the chair and as I'm cutting his hair he asks 'Have you been busy today?' "Yes" I say "fairly steady for most of the day today". I can't remember much of the rest of the conversation because I was that focused on keeping both of the brothers in my peripheral vision and in the mirrors as they were sat near to the till. I finished cutting the father's hair and I walk to the till. At this point I am still expecting the worst and we are now at a point where it is most likely to happen. I say to them 'That's £17. £5 per haircut and £2 for the self-service wash. The father pulled out one of the biggest wads of cash I'd ever seen. It was all £20 and £50 notes and I'm guessing it was about five grand. He gives me £20 and he said "Keep the change and sorry for keeping you late" I nod at him and as I make my way to the door to unlock it I'm still waiting for something to happen and I'm thinking 'Here it comes now' I open the door and let them out and he says 'Good evening sir' and I close the door and sat down. I didn't realise it at first but I was shaking like a leaf which wasn't like me at all.

Business Advisor

As I have got older, although eyesight can deteriorate a little, you are able to see things in the bigger picture much clearer. One of my customers, John, was a neighbour of mine and had a big and beautiful house and had his own engineering firm. One day he came into the shop all stressed out. He'd bought this fantastic machine for half a million quid. So I ask him 'What's the problem?' 'The 'machine is great' he says 'but it's sitting there dormant at weekends losing me money. 'Right' I said 'so Saturday and Sunday nobody works. Why don't you open up at weekends?' He goes on to tell me in that in the engineering industry doesn't by tradition work weekends and finding people who will just work weekends don't exist so he can't recruit anybody. 'oh right' I say ' Well what I would do is put an advert in the paper or an engineering journal and say I've got this job on working on just a Saturday and Sunday working on a brand new machine and paying an amount the same as the staff you've got working Monday to Friday.' He looks at me and says 'Fucking hell. I never thought of that'. 'It's your place isn't it?' I ask him 'Yeah' he says. 'Well then' I say. 'You can do anything you want". Sure enough he got applicants and he got some people who would work just Saturdays and Sundays and kept his machine running seven days a week. Sure enough, his current employees spat their dummy out. They say to him 'We would have done it for that' Sometimes you can't see the wood for the trees and the answer is so simple. Providing its profitable then it's worth finding a way forward even if it costs a few bob.

The Christmas Dinner Affair

About three years ago, one of my customers, Lee Skarratt, invited me to join their family for Christmas dinner at The Ocean Treasure Chinese restaurant. I cut Lee's hair and a further three generations of his family and this is the kind of relationship I strike up with some of my customers. They become friends and we know about each other's families and what's going on in their lives. It was a lovely gesture and I gratefully accepted and enjoyed it. He picked me up and we had a few drinks and then my family joined us. Separate tables but all introduced. I also cut Lee's father in law, John's hair. Sometimes even customers like John will really surprise me with how they see our relationship. Fairly recently John was going to a wedding and his Mrs told him he needed to have it cut before the day. John came down to our shop and found that I was abroad racing. So he drove to another Barber's shop and stood outside. He told me he stood there for a good while but he just couldn't go in. He said it felt like he was cheating on his wife so he didn't go in and drove home. He went without the haircut and I'm guessing his Mrs went mad.

Rambo VI – No Bull

One of my customers is ex special forces. He is around late 30's or early 40s and has left the forces to go back to civvy street. He's not married but has nephews and nieces. He told me that after six months of doing normal things it was doing his head in. He said to me 'Chris, I've had enough of school runs and buying cooked chickens from Tesco. What I need to be doing is hunting the chicken first. He told me he was off to Cumbria for the foreseeable future and after I've cut his hair we bear hug and off he goes. About twelve months later, another ex-marine came in to the shop and said to me "Have you heard about ********* " "No. What? I say. He told me that all of these farmers in a specific area up in Cumbria have been reported to have got together as they have an unexplained phenomena happening on their farms. Usually they have real problems with poaching of expensive animals like prize bulls but unexplainably, no bulls or any other expensive livestock have gone missing in recent months but a small amount of chickens have gone missing on a fairly regular basis. Eventually they worked out that they had a local Rambo type figure looking after their major livestock and actively dealing with and deterring poachers for them. The price they have to pay for this unpaid premium service is to turn a blind eye to an occasional chicken going missing. I giggled for the rest of the day as I pictured Sylvester Stallone appearing from nowhere in the dead of night saying "Put that fucking Bull down!!"

The Killer Question

I had another customer who is sadly no longer with us whose wife was in a very good job that meant that they regularly attended dinner parties as an add on to her role. He went to a dinner party one evening with his good lady wife and the venue was full of barristers and solicitors and some well to do people. He could easily have blended in but wasn't in the mood for small talk that night so he thought bollocks to it. As he got embroiled in conversation with different guests and they asked him what he did for a living, he replied "I kill people'. Without fail, he told me, the person would come back with "Sorry?" as they thought that they had misheard him and he would say louder "I kill people". After a while people stopped bothering him and he sat on his own in peace.   Now, here's the thing. I also didn't know whether he was joking or he was being serious because I never really got to the bottom of what he did for a living.

Mind Control

I once had a customer in who, after a long chat while cutting his hair, paid for his haircut, said goodbye and left, I felt that I had told him everything about me but I knew nothing about him. In the next week or so another customer was telling me about his brother who was in the forces but had a very secretive job. He also said that I might have seen him because he'd been in for his haircut the previous week. I said to the customer "I knew it. He had to be some kind of special forces or M15 or something because he controlled the conversation from start to finish and yet I didn't notice it until after he'd left. He must have been your brother.

218

Outside Looking In

One day I noticed a tramp outside the shop who was walking around in small circles and kept looking into the shop. I eventually went outside to him and said "Excuse me sir – do you want your haircut ?" His clothes seemed nice and expensive but old and dirty. He responded in a very posh accent and spoke beautifully "I've got money. I'm not short". Eventually I got talking with him and found out that he was a banker and that one day he came home and he had a nervous breakdown and ended up wandering streets. He could afford to stay in any of the hotels but he didn't want the hassle and pressure of booking in. I happily gave him a free haircut and we parted on good terms.

Lawman.

One day I was in work at the Barbers and who was sat next door in the Parkside Cafe but Denis Law. He was a very approachable guy and once he'd eaten his bacon butty he was happy to have a chat with me. The guy who owned the café was called Alf and he often had the occasional celeb having a brew. 'The Lawman' was something special. It was that normal a conversation I couldn't tell you what we spoke about. It was just two blokes chatting.

The Barber Goes Nuclear

One Friday afternoon I can see one of my customers is stressed out as I cut his hair. I can spot these things a mile off because I cut their hair every few weeks and I can see the change. Cut a long story short, he told me he'd just come back from china. No names are shared but he is extremely concerned about some valves that have been signed off for purchase from there for a Nuclear plant and they are substandard in his view.

He looks worried sick and eventually I am too. It's a few years ago now so I think it turned out ok. Don't worry this was well after Chernobyl and I think he was over-reacting if you'll excuse the pun!

Something For The Weekend Sir?

When Henry was in charge back in the day, he stocked condoms. The classic phrase a barber used to use when showing the customer the back of their head when checking the cut was ok for them was to finish with 'something for the weekend sir?' which of course meant "do you need any condoms?' I'll always remember being stood in the shop one day and there were three lads outside all around 15 or 16 years old and looking very conspicuous and looking at the condoms. Eventually one plucked up the courage to come in. I knew what he had come in for but I was going to have some fun with this. I said to him "Yeah?" He said quietly "Can I have one of them please ?" "of course" I said, my voice getting louder and louder. Eventually I was verging on shouting **"WHICH ONES DO YOU WANT? DOUBLE FOR EXTRA SECURITY OR EXTRA FEATHERLITE FOR PENETRATION?'** He was trying to stop me saying the words by just saying "Yes Yes – that one yes". He hadn't gone red he went purple. It was a bit cruel but it's part of growing up isn't it to buy your first condoms. He should have gone to Boots!!

Like Pulling Teeth

I'm told that the original barbers were in Ancient Egypt around 5000BC and were the first people providing a skilled trade of male grooming. Nearer home our original barbers in England were called Tonsorial Artists. Tonsorial is from the Latin for cutting / shearing.

A Tonsorial Artist would provide not just services of cutting hair but also shaves and dentistry and minor surgical procedures like blood letting. The red and white barber's pole outside (which we haven't had on Middleton road for many years) in the old days stood for blood and bandages. When I first joined Henry at the Barbers in the mid 70's, he used to have magazines like 'Mayfair' and Playboy' for the gents in the corner of the shop which I referred to as the dirty corner. I rather liked the idea that Barbers operated as dentists too and took teeth out. I wish we'd brought that back for just a few of my customers over the years. I could have had a good go at that alright!!

Proud of His Dad

One priceless memory from my first few years working with Henry was of a dad and his son coming into the shop to have their haircuts. Henry sat the dad down and the little kid sat in my chair which I had put a booster seat in for him. He was about 8 or 9 years old. Henry was right into horse racing and gambling henry into horse racing and gambling. In fact some of the old fashioned barbers used to run a book in the old days before the big betting shops took over. Some might have carried it on for their customers too. Henry is talking to his customer, the dad, about horse racing and the word riding is mentioned and the young lad, who is sat in my chair, as innocent as anything turns to his dad and shouts "You were riding mummy last night daddy wasn't you?" There was a silence of a few seconds and I can see the customers behind waiting to have their haircuts hiding behind newspapers and looking at the floor but all their shoulders are going and you can tell that they are pissing themselves laughing.

The dad has just gone blood red and gestured for the lad to face front "be quiet while Chris cuts your hair". The little lad carried on though "Mummy was shouting all the time, she shouted ..." "That's enough son" shouted dad. "That's enough now". Be nice and quiet while Chris does your hair". We all got the picture though.

Records are there to be broken – so are legs?

I have a customer who is on my kind of wavelength called Tim. He holds the record for the lowest ever altitude for a parachute jump. Don't ask me what height it was because I don't know. All I do know is that he told me he broke both his legs and he holds the record to this day. I'm pretty sure that no one will beat it and live to tell the tail.

The Customer isn't always right though!

A customer said to me recently 'Chris. You need another woman' I said to him 'No. I need another set of running shoes. The bonus with running shoes is that when I get a beer out of the fridge it doesn't say "' what are you doing?" '

The Barbers has been an incredible place to own and to work in and to live in above. The building itself represents a major part of my life second only to my family. From the day I moved in with Henry after I was recruited to the 'Modern' to now it's been a hub of laughs, advice, debates, football rivalry, politics and just about every subject going but most of all for me it's about positivity and inspiring conversations that created a buzz certainly for me and I hope for others. My customers tend to be loyal to me because that's the way I am. Negativity is a no no in my shop and always has been. I have many customers who have only ever had two people cut their hair for years and years and that's Henry and me. They've seen the different iterations of the shop and the changes that took place under Henry and then the dramatic changes I put in place. If the truth be known if I had a major choice in it, I'd have completed the journey with The barbers and took it towards the New Zealand model that I so admired. Being able to have a few barber's chairs going with multiple TV screens showing various live sports with seating all around for a coffee and a chat while waiting to either have your haircut or have a sports massage or physio in the same building. I would have loved that together with sporting clubs being born out of the shop and its customers being a place for like-minded people to gather but it's someone else's turn now to take the mantle as I decide that it's time for a change for me.

Things change as you get older and you have to move with the times and you have to move mentally too. I'm mentally burned out now in the shop. Customers change, atmospheres change. Sometimes, I even feel burnt out listening to the daily noises in the shop. For example, back in the day there would generally be around 100 cars pass the shop in day now its 100 cars in minutes. It's come to a stage where mentally it's not right for me. As I leave the shop that I have loved and worked in for 45 years I take with me lots of memories, good and bad but I'll not be leaving my loyal customers. As I pursue other different ventures, one of them will be to carry on that contact with my lifeblood. All I need is a bike, a pair of scissors, a comb and my clippers and guards and I'll be travelling to them.

As my Grandad Walter said to me when I was 15 and just starting "you'll be in a trade that can take you anywhere in the world Chris" He was right. Here I am at 60 and I'm only just taking advantage of that as I consider going mobile for the first time to allow me to do other additional things.

223

Chapter 19 – The Triathlete

From the moment I got home from Hospital after the crash in 1980 and from the time my mum describes as me excessively lifting weights in the family kitchen, I was determined to remain active one way or another. I was never going to accept the prognosis that the surgeons had given me leaving the hospital but I knew that I would face some serious challenges along the way and I didn't even know what I meant by 'remaining active'. At that time, I had no idea what I really wanted to do or to aim for. I just knew that I wanted to get fit and prove the doctors wrong. When you hurt an arm or a leg and you can see and understand the damage, you can also see and understand the limitations that the damage might have and find workarounds or just use your determination to work through the pain and physical challenge. Even people losing multiple limbs have shown through the Paralympics or the Invictus games that human beings and their attitudes to devastating life changing events, can be incredibly inspirational to others. When you have a brain injury things are not so clear. Firstly you cannot see or accurately measure the damage and its effects and what's worse is the fact that you cannot predict how this might change or affect you going forward. So if you cannot predict how it will affect you, it's difficult to then plan what you can do to combat it. My method of dealing with all of this was to adopt an attitude that this was not going to hold me back. I decided that if I couldn't give 110% to what I was doing then I shouldn't be doing it. It was a given with me that I would never feel sorry for myself. This was in my genes. If I were to allow myself to feel sorry for myself or think that I was unlucky then this could only lead to disappointment and failure. I formed a pact with myself that I was never going to let these things stop me doing something that I wanted to do and I would crack on with absolute determination until I found my potential limit, if indeed I had one. I had to be realistic of course but when it came to the sports I wanted to get involved in, I couldn't see any reason why I couldn't compete at a very high level. The two sports that fell by the wayside early on were Martial Arts and Football. The reason being, that it was obvious to me that a blow to my head whether accidental or not could put me right back to square one and although I had enjoyed both and was not frightened by the risk one bit, I quickly decided that someone else would interfere at some stage and stop me progressing because of my medical history and therefore I shouldn't waste time on those things. Others might say that they were not my forte anyway and I'd pretty much accept that. I had other fish to fry. I just didn't know what type of fish yet but I was confident that I would happen. I had great faith in myself and a belief that I was destined for great things somewhere along the line. I knew my determination and lack of fear would eventually help me with something down the line. Lack of fear? What does that mean? A friend of mine asked me once "on a scale of zero to ten with zero being no pain and ten being excruciating painful to the point of even the toughest of people screaming with pain, where is your pain threshold? I was not trying to be clever when I answered. I just answered with all honesty when I said "death"

I had always had an interest in cycle racing since I was three years old when my dad took the stabilisers off my bike. I had also always run and cycled to work and back to keep fit so the first sport that seemed to meet my aspirations to excel in something was Cyclocross. Simon Mac and I had heard about this through a friend of mine called Mike Cookson who owned a bike shop and we got involved in it as soon as we could. Just to give you an idea of what Cyclocross is, it is mountain bike type racing that happens most of the time in autumn and winter due to the conditions that are required of the circuits (muddy and wet) and the race itself involves the competitors doing as many of the circuits as quickly as they can within the hour. The circuits comprise of varying terrains like pavement, wooded trails, grass, hills, some of which could be steep. A combination of those would also contain an obstacle, that you had to dismount your bike and carry it on your shoulder until you hit a terrain suitable to put the bike down again. It was hugely competitive and great fun but for me it was the enjoyment of pushing myself in competition against the others. I was just like my Uncle Joe in that I certainly didn't compete for medals or reward. I'd much prefer to disappear after the race whether I'd done well or not. I didn't care for any of that. Simon Mac and I entered whatever events we could and we were in our element. The bigger the challenge the better for us. It gave me a taste for competing again properly. We travelled all over the North West with Cyclocross and it was to be a huge stepping-stone for me. Even though I was enjoying it, something in my mind was saying 'you've done that. Now what else can you do?' I had no idea but this was all leading on the next level for me. I already considered myself a decent swimmer from my days windsurfing, or should I say from my days falling off windsurfing and sometimes having to swim challenging distances to recover from disasters. I was also regularly running and competing in Cyclocross. Around July 1998, I was having a conversation with a guy (I wish I could remember his name) who was also involved in Cyclocross and I asked him whether he was going out for a bike ride that weekend. He said "No I can't do it this weekend. I'm competing in a triathlon". I asked him what a triathlon was and he explained to me that it was a three part endurance event of varying distances but essentially it was a race that involved a swim, a bike ride and a run. He told me that the event that he was going to that weekend was a one mile swim, 25 mile cycle and a 6 mile run but other events might vary those distances. I fancied a bit of that. I couldn't enter the event that he was in that weekend so I researched where the next one was that I could enter, which turned out to be in London. I mentioned it to my pal Anthony Lowe and he said "Yeah I'm up for that" so we entered it. I knew Anthony through my cousin, Roy Brown, who he shared a house with. We had weight trained at Maxine's Gym in Prestwich together. We only had a couple of months to get ready for the event so I suggested that we should get into a triathlon club which had also come up in my research. I found out that Rochdale Triathlon club were based out of Rochdale baths so headed up there with our gear to try and get further information and perhaps do a bit of training. When we got there we walked into the pool area and were immediately confronted with the sight of what appeared to be a load of dolphins in the pool. I say Dolphins but of course I mean humans that can swim like dolphins. We spend just a few seconds watching and both Anthony and I, in unison, say "shit" The reason we have reacted in that way is because we both thought we could swim but now we were watching people who could really swim. We realised, that at best, what we were doing was drowning in style to badly quote Buzz Lightyear. It all happened in a few seconds and in total sync with one another. We walked into the pool area by a few yards, saw the swimmers, said "Shit" and both immediately turned to leave and walked sheepishly towards the exit. Just as we were about to get to the exit, a voice shouted "Can I help you lads?" The voice was from a guy called Brian Silk- Parkinson. A man who was to be a very positive influence on me and essentially, changed my life forever. If we had kept walking or he hadn't seen us or shouted us back, the things that I have achieved in my life as an athlete may never have happened and some of the most wonderful friendships possibly never formed. It was another pivotal moment in my life. We froze and turned around and went back telling him that we were thinking about joining a Triathlon club. We didn't mention at that time that we had already entered one in 2 months' time. Brian said "Get changed and get in the pool in the slow lane and swim because we've only got a few minutes left before the pool's needed. I looked at the lane he had just pointed to as the "slow lane" and thought where the fucking hell is the slow lane? Anthony and I exchanged looks of raised eyebrows and we both knew exactly what each other was thinking **"That's their slow lane? Shit! That's our fast lane!"**. I was being strategic when I told Anthony to take his time getting changed. I thought we might make it to the end of the session without Brian seeing us swim but unfortunately we still made it to the water and did a couple of lengths. That was all Brian needed to see where we were up to. We got changed and went to the Café and met Brian and talked about joining. We told him that we had entered the London Triathlon in September which was about 6 or 7 weeks off and he just said "Are you serious? You both can't swim!" We then told him it was an Olympic standard event of a 1.5K Swim, a 40K Bike Ride and a 10K run and said "Well we've entered so we are going it do it anyway" Brian's reaction to that was one of someone being confused " Where are you lads from?" I told him "Blackley" and he said "That'll explain it then!"

The event followed my 38th Birthday in that September 1998 and Anthony and I travelled down to London together. I felt confident that I had trained hard enough to compete in this event at the level that was required. The London Triathlon was prestigious and my thoughts were to do it for a charity called 'whizz kids'. I had children of my own and had always wanted to do something for under privileged children who perhaps hadn't had the same opportunities as myself or my own kids. When we arrived we got ourselves sorted in terms of where we were staying and headed out to get some breakfast. We ended up near the famous Billingsgate Fish Market before we sat down to eat. It was my first time in London and so I was amazed to hear all these cockney accents around me like we were in an episode of 'Only Fools and

Horses'. Even though I was in London I couldn't believe that everybody sounded like 'Delboy'. We eventually head over to the Dockside where the Triathlon was to be held as we really wanted to suss the Swim out. The event details had the swim down as a distance of one mile. We were sat on the dock trying to take in the swim that we were going to have to negotiate when all of a sudden this Land Rover turns up towing a speedboat. It looks official and we immediately work out that the guy getting out of the Land Rover has something to do with the race. We speak to him and ask him directly if he's a Marshall. He explains that he is and he is going to mark out the swim course for tomorrow morning. What great luck, we were going to be able to see the swim circuit ahead of anyone else and get ourselves psyched up for it. The guy gets in the speedboat and goes out and out and out and out and we are both staring thinking ' where the fuck is he going?' He then takes a big yellow buoy out and puts it in the water. Anthony says to me 'he's got to be fucking joking - I'll not make that buoy never mind the rest of the race. The guy then travels a distance parallel to the dock and puts another buoy out and then comes back. I'm thinking that I know what a mile looks like and this isn't it. I've swam a mile many times in the pool but this looks an enormous distance in an open water race for the first time and I am getting proper worried. I'm trying to reassure myself by repeating in my head, surely that it more than a mile. The guy heads back over to us in the boat and gets out near the Land Rover. I take the opportunity to say 'Excuse me mate, that's not a mile is it' and he says 'No. Is it Bollocks mate!" Both Anthony and I start smiling and I'm thinking thank God for that when the guy adds "It's half a mile mate. You swim twice round!'. My jaw hit the floor and I looked at Anthony who was a worse swimmer than me and he's gone white and is looking like he is going to faint or something. We both later agreed our first objective for the race – Don't drown!!!

The next day we are there at the start of the race. I'm thinking positively apart from the fact that the swim looks enormous and in my mind I'm talking to myself and saying 'if I can avoid drowning and complete the swim in 45 minutes I'll be very happy'. They started the race at 11.00am. There were approximately 300 men and women competing and of them there were about 30 elite athletes who were in the first wave and are going to start first, so we don't get in their way. After that there are groups sorted in terms of age groups. I'm in the last wave as I'm 38 at the time. The klaxon sounds and off we go and I'm swimming towards that first buoy. It's an amazing sight when hundreds of triathletes are swimming at the start of their race as they are relatively close together and it feels like you are in a washing machine. To spectators, it looks like a shoal of fish with water splashing all over the place and people hitting each other accidentally as they swim towards the same first target. As I round the first buoy things spread out a little. Those with good starts are getting ahead and those that are slow swimmers are dropping back. I'm happy right in the middle and in the thick of the race but with room around me. I am so pleased that I've reached the first buoy without drowning I have a real adrenaline rush and push on. Amazingly I've completed the swim before I know it but I've gone at it so hard I can't feel my arms and I can't lift myself out of the water. It feels ridiculous because I suspect that I may have made my target time but I can't get out of the water as my arms are like jelly. Thankfully, a marshal gives me a hand and pulls me out of the water. As I get out I try and get a look at my watch but the Marshal pushes me on because there are others trying to get out of the water behind me and so I move along to the next transition on to the bike quickly and can't focus on the time. As I was getting out of the water though I was sure that I heard a Marshall shout '32 minutes'. I'm thinking that I can't have done the mile swim in 32 minutes can I?. I get to the bike and as I'm climbing on I can see an official clock and it's got 11-34am on it. Wow, he was talking to me !! I've done the swim in 32 mins. I am buzzing. That's me I've really done that. I look back at the water and there is still a huge shoal of human fish thrashing in the water still on the swim stage. I'm momentarily really proud of myself but now I need to crack on.

So now on to the 25 mile bike ride (40K) which is four loops of six and a quarter mile stages (10K) of out and back to the start point at the docklands. It's a beautiful road surface so this is right up my street and I'm racing along. I've been on a bike since the age of three. This is my strength and once I'm on the bike I feel confident and on top of my game. I complete the first lap of 10K and then my thoughts turn to Anthony. I've done a loop of out and back on the bike circuit already and I've not seen him. I start to fear he has drowned. I start the second loop 10K miles and I see him across the road on his bike. Great. I know he's survived the swim and I know he's on the circuit but I don't know what lap he is on.

Now you'd think that counting to four is easy. Just counting there and back four times is easy isn't it? Not when your adrenaline is pumping and fatigue is trying to get the better of you. I can't believe that simply counting to four that day eluded me not once but fucking twice. I didn't see Anthony again so it threw me. When I had completed the 40K on the bike I got confused. I hadn't seen Anthony again. In my mind that meant that I can't have completed the whole cycle stage as I surely would have seen him at least twice as we looped around the circuit. I stopped and a marshal came over to me and said are you alright son? I said 'I'm not sure whether I've done three loops or four' and he said 'What time did you start?' '11am' I said and he said 'well only the elite would do to this point in that time so you must have another loop to do' So I carried on and did another loop which unbelievably added another 10K to my cycle stage of the race . It sounds ridiculous I know but at the time I thought my logic was sound.

I eventually got off the bike and head to the start of the 10K run stage. The run is set out so that from the start line you head out to a turning point beyond Canary wharf and then run back to the start. That was 5K. So when you did that twice you had completed the 10K run stage. I'm up for the run but I am already cheesed off about the bike stage as I am unsure at that point just how much extra I have done or not. I set off on the run overthinking it and confusing myself further. Instead of treating the run as a there and back twice, I treated it as four stages: 1 there, 2 back, 3 there and 4 back. I've only just had a problem counting to four, so well into the run I started doubting myself again especially when I catch side of Anthony again. I'd finished what I classed as the first leg and turned to tackle the second leg back to the start and I'm only running for a short time and I see Anthony again across the road. We high five as we pass each other and I set off on the second leg coaching myself in my head saying to myself 'Come on now. You can count to four now can't you dickhead?' I crack on and eventually I'm on my way back to the finish line. I'm now on the home stretch almost and I am sure that I have counted correctly this time and who do I see going back out? Yes, Anthony. The voice in my head says 'You've got to be fucking joking - I've done it again'. I am convinced that I can't count to four and that I've miscounted again. It's messing with my head. So I go out again and run there and back again, another 5K!. I finally finish my first Olympic style Triathlon consisting of a 1 mile swim, a 40K bike ride and a 10K run but I have actually done a one Mile swim, a 50K bike ride and a 15K run. I didn't know this as I crossed the line. I started to get an inkling of the errors I had made when I looked at my final time. I'd expected to try and get inside 3 hours and yet I'd finished in 3 hours and 38 minutes and 1 Second. As I'm walking on the Docklands after the race, I see Anthony sat in the lotus position with his head down. I say 'What's wrong with you". He looked up at me and said "I've done a lap less on the bike". All of a sudden it dawns on me what's happened. He's only done three laps and that's why I've not seen him that much. I realise now I've done five laps on the bike because he's only done three. I say to him 'Fucking hell, no wonder I didn't see you. Then to add insult to injury he says 'So I thought I'd do an extra lap on the run to make up for it" I burst out laughing and he looks at me as if I'm laughing at him but I've just realised that I can indeed count to four and I've done another 5K run too. Fucking hell - no wonder my time was three hours and thirty eight minutes. I'd have smashed three hours if I'd have got my stages right. This taught me a lot. Go with your gut and believe in yourself and if you think it's right then do it. Despite the misunderstandings that meant I had completed extra distances on two of the disciplines, the feeling I got from this first triathlon and the fact that I felt I had hit my objectives showed me I was ready for even more. I felt that just like Cyclecross, I had to consolidate my achievement and take on more triathlons and with increased distances. Both Anthony and I went into that race questioning whether we were good enough when we should have had faith in our own abilities. We'd done well and it was already time to step it up. Over the course of the last 22 years since then I've completed well over twenty five triathlons of varying distances in very different locations all over the UK and abroad. They were all very individual in their own right and were fantastic events.

Chapter 20 – Training, Racing or Just Plain Jollies?

I joined Rochdale Triathlon Club in 1998 which got me into the Triathlon world but it also introduced me to some very special friends that I ended up travelling with, competing with and training with. Sometimes our training would tie in with a trip abroad to take on some fantastic cycle routes and take in some of the local surroundings and culture. People, and I include my family in that, may have thought that it was just a jolly but it wasn't. Yes we did enjoy it very much and yes we would have a drink during the evenings but during the day we would be cycling long distances and it would be great preparation for competing in an event. The people I trained and travelled with might not have been a super crank like I was but they were cranks in their own right as they were also about pushing themselves to limits too.

They are also great friends and I can't imagine that I'd have had half the fantastic memories that I do have from our weekends on water or our 'training' trips without them being involved Simon Mac, Roy Winstanley, Dave Smith (Smithy), Graham Richards (Scouse), Anthony Lowe, Tony Maddocks(Mad Dog), Wendy Grundy and Andy Pilling. They will all feature in some way in some of the following racing and training stories. I've given them all their own headings to give you a clue what they are about.

Full English

Before I talk about these friends and what we got up to while training and keeping fit, just while it is in my mind, here is a great bit of advice. Never ask for a Full English breakfast when you are in Wales. We did just that. Myself and Simon Mac were passing through Holywell in North Wales on the way back from competing in the 'Denbigh Tri' which was a triathlon consisting of a 400 Metre swim, a 15 mile bike ride and a 5K grueling run up to Denbigh castle. We had stopped to refuel with an all-day breakfast in a large café en route back to Manchester. We ordered a full English and 40 minutes later everybody had been served bar us. Then our breakfast arrived. They put it on the table and said 'enjoy'. It was ice cold! It looked like they had cooked the breakfast but then stuck it in the fridge for half an hour before serving it to two English wind up merchants.

There was no way we were going to let them see we were disappointed so we got stuck in and enjoyed every bit of it, 'mmmmmmmmmm', exaggerating our enjoyment with every mouthful. Sorry, I just had to tell you about that. It was genuinely funny.

He Ain't Heavy, He's His Brother

I was in Karnten in Austria doing an Iron Man in 2004 and I was with Dave Smith, who was also competing. Dave had lost his brother in law Mark earlier that year very suddenly after having a heart attack and it had really shook Dave. Mark was only in his mid-forties and it had made Dave think about doing the things that he really wanted to do in life and facing the mental and physical challenge of competing in an Iron Man race for the first time in memory of Mark.

Dave had got it into his head that he wanted to complete the course in less than 12 hours 30 minutes. It was an ambitious goal bearing in mind that it was his first iron man and he had nothing to compare it to. I knew his first target should have been just to finish it, which would have been a great achievement in itself. Then you can start looking at times because you have your personal best and the experience to measure against. With all that in mind you can't say what a good time is for someone without those stats. You can say what kind of time will be good enough to win it but that's just detracting from what a novice, if they really are a novice, should be thinking about. Well into the event I spotted Dave at one of the checkpoints with only five kilometres to go of the marathon section. He was on track for a good time but he'd hit one of many mental barriers that we all face and needed motivation badly. I gave him a massive bear hug and said 'Come on Smithy - you're going to do this". It worked instantly and in a rush of adrenaline he set off again and raced off ahead of me.

About halfway from there towards the finish line, so only about two and half kilometres from the finish, I spotted him again. This time he had stopped and was bent over hands on knees and looked beaten. He had hit that point where your head is telling you that it's over and you can do no more. At this point of your thinking 2.5K might as well be 250K because that's how you feel physically and mentally. There is a fuel wall that is difficult to beat as it means that your body has simply run out of fuel and it's difficult to still keep the effort up. Then there is the Psychological wall where your mind plays tricks on you and It convinces you that you are possibly dying and that to go on is suicide. I had learned all about this in my first iron man in Roth in Bavaria from a group of special forces guys. Dave had hit the Psychological wall. He was in absolute bits. He said to me 'I'm dying". I said to him 'No mate, Mark's dead - you're alive and kicking and you're going to finish this fucking race'. It worked, he stood upright and set off again with me and for the next two and a half kilometres

I ran by his side saying 'come on you can still beat 12:30 (his target time). Right to the finish line I was glancing at my watch and he was just about going to do it so I roared him on the last few hundred metres shouting "you're fucking doing it - you're going to beat 12:30" Just as we crossed the line together, I stopped my watch - it said 12 hours 29 minutes and 59 seconds. He had done it by one second and I'd helped him do it. The feeling of elation was fantastic. He was beside himself with the achievement and elated until we both looked up at the official timing device and it said 12 hours 31 minutes and 1 second. 'Bastard' I said. I then realised that I'd started my watch as I entered the water but the main clock had already started by just over one minute before I pressed mine and set off so I was out of sync with the race timer. It meant that his official race time was 12 hours 31 minutes and 1 second but his personal time from hitting the water to finishing was probably quicker than mine so he'd done it. This is what I mean by achievement. It's all relative. An Olympic Gold medal hopeful athlete will feel like a failure with silver but for some, picking up any medal would feel like an ecstatic victory. Just finishing an Iron man within the allotted overall time of 16/17 hours, dependent on where it is, and the set cut off time for the swim and the bike of 10 hours should make you stand like fucking Batman or Wonder woman after crossing the line because you've just achieved an amazing physical and mental feat.

Sofa So ~~Good~~ Bad

In 2004, I was away with Dave Smith, Anthony Lowe, Tony Maddocks, Scouse and Wendy and we were going to cycle from Venice to Rome. Dave was not happy staying in digs for £30 per night when we got to Italy. I'm not sure if 'Digs' is a commonly known term up and down the UK but just in case, for us in Manchester it means lodgings or a paid room to stay in away from home like a bed and breakfast for example. So on the second night there Dave was put in charge of choosing digs to stay in. It was also Anthony Lowe's birthday so we wanted to be able to have a drink that night. Dave found somewhere for £10 per night which is a great price but we were all suspicious regarding the quality of the rooms. It was a three story building that looked alright from outside . We pay and go upstairs into the rooms. We all had our cycling gear on and we wanted to get ready to go out for a bite to eat and a drink. The shower in the room was disgusting. It was basically a pipe that came out of the wall and I certainly didn't feel cleaner after I had been in it. I got dressed and I sat on a chair in the room which was fairly big with other furniture in.

My eyes were drawn to a sofa, also in the room. I had to blink a few times as I thought I was seeing things. The sofa was moving and as I stared at it, it seemed it was alive and moving in waves. I hadn't a drink yet so I couldn't have been seeing things. I go over to the sofa and it is absolutely full of lice. 'Fucking hell' I shout "if my Mrs gets wind of this she won't come near me again with a barge pole. Smithy have you seen this?" Amazingly we didn't pack our bags again and leave, we just took the piss out of Smithy and what he had booked us in to. I was already planning ahead in my mind. I wasn't going to be taking my clothes off that night that's for sure. Anthony was tee total and that night we've all started to egg him on to have a few drinks. I think most of us had made our mind up that if we had to stay in those rooms that we needed to be shitfaced to sleep there. Anthony refused point blank to sleep in his room, he decided to sleep on the staircase.

It was a three story building and Anthony was on the middle floor. Half way through the night I woke feeling something wasn't right and it wasn't that the room was full of creatures. I got a very powerful sense to go and check on Anthony as something was wrong. I went out to the stairs and found Anthony who'd been sick was sleeping on his back and had started to choke. I quickly turned him on to his side and helped him as he coughed up and cleared his airways. Using some pillows, I propped him on his side against the wall so he couldn't slip on to his back again. I got a towel and cleaned up around him as best I could and then didn't know what to do with the towel. Don't ask me why I did it but I just threw the towel down the stairwell. Unfortunately the towel ended up draping off a light fitting. It was too late to start climbing to get it back so I left it and went to sleep in a chair in my room. I was still very drunk myself. In the morning I walked down the stairs past Anthony, who was still alive thank God and awake but not looking too great and then further down the stairs I see the towel, which is now burnt a little from the heat of the light bulb. Smithy asks us all are we going down for some breakfast and I said "you have to be joking. Can you imagine what the kitchen is like here ? Bollocks to that!" So I went out for breakfast and they all followed me.

Baggage Handlers or Wind Up Merchants?

We'd flown to Venice for this bike ride. People ask me about how we get bikes abroad and its very straightforward really. They are cargo luggage and go in the hold of the plane so we have to protect them in some way from any damage in transit. We take the wheels off and deflate the tyres, as they would burst as a result of the pressure in the hold of the plane. From Manchester to Venice, it is clear that we are way behind some of the processes that have been developed on the continent. For example, if we were flying from Rome to Manchester, which we would be doing on the way back, the bikes would be bubble wrapped and put on the plane so that they wouldn't get damaged or do any damage to other luggage. Here in Manchester we simply take apart what we can and then it's all taped together to stop it separating on the plane. Unfortunately this still left them accessible to the baggage handlers. The panniers become your hand luggage. Panniers for people who haven't come across them are bags that go across your bike to store your gear. I believe the word comes from the French for bread-basket. We arrived in Venice and went to pick our bikes up from the carousel and start to put them together again and we soon realised that our cycle pumps and lights had all gone missing on every bike. So we all now have got flat tyres and no pump. Bastard baggage handlers are having a laugh. No bike pumps and nothing to improvise with in the middle of an airport.

We get outside the Airport and are scratching our heads for ideas on what to do next and Maddocks starts laughing. He opens his panniers and gets out his pump and his lights. "Don't know about you lot but I'm alright' he says. Just as he says that, he looks down at his bike and says "Bastards". They've took his bike chain! It's a funny moment because of his "I'm alright" comment but we are all pissed off and much worse than that is that we can't go anywhere just yet. We discuss it as a group and decide that it is a waste of valuable time complaining as we will not get the gear back immediately. Whoever has done this has gone to nick every light and bike pump, probably for a laugh and then when they've looked at Maddock's because they can't find his lights or pump, they've nicked his chain.   Maddocks is an ex superbiker, Barry Sheen / Carl Foggarty style and standard. One of his party tricks on his road bike (not motorcycle) was coming down a steep hill that was a one in four decline with bends to negotiate. He would come down that hill and not used his brakes at all . He would take the brakes off the bike to prove it to you before He did it. He'd been on bends in the past on a superbike doing ridiculous high speeds with his knee out touching the floor so doing 30 and 40 miles per hour on a pedal bike around bends on a hill similar to Factory Brew in Blackley was nothing to him.   Back to Venice and Maddocks has a mischievous but workable plan. In his panniers he has small toolkit that's for maintenance on the road on the bike. Part of that kit is a chain splitter in case of chain damage. He gets the cutter out and while we shield him from prying eyes he works on a bike that we've spotted outside the airport chained to fence. He takes the chain off the bike and adjusts it accordingly and fits it to his chainless bike. Being the great guy he is, Maddocks leaves a note for the bike owner that we will leave it in Rome when we've finished and it can pick up from there outside the Coliseum. How decent is that of him? We all used Maddocks' pump to get the air back into our tyres and get to a bike shop and get sorted with some of the gear we were missing. Amazingly we found one reasonably quickly. It was nothing like we have at home though. Over in Italy they have lots of Vespas but not as many cycle enthusiasts. We were three to four miles away from the Airport in a small town centre. We didn't buy anything else, just made sure that our tyres were at the right pressure and set off to find digs in Venice as we planned to spend the next 24 hours there.

Watching The World Go By in Venice with a Beer in My Hand – Where did it all go wrong?

We found somewhere decent to stay and went out and had something to eat and then we headed back to Venice and had a boat ride on the waterways on a tourist boat not a gondolier. They call them buses because the water is their streets. We found a decent bar on the water's edge selling some of our favourite beer, Franziskaner. So there we are , sat on the water's edge in Venice with a bottle of beer in our hands and Anthony Lowe, who as I said, was teetotal says to me "I can't believe that you've just spent a fiver on a bottle of beer" Want he was referring to was that a similar bottle of beer back in Manchester would have been about £1.20. I turned to Anthony and said "Anthony, look where we are". As we sat with a beer in our hands on a beautifully sunny day, all we could see were the venetian buildings, the waterways, the gondoliers and the romantic couples of all ages in the boats. The setting was amazing. I just said to Anthony "I'm getting another one of these in a minute".

Next day we were packed up and off on our bikes heading for Rome. We weren't planning to just cover a route directly to Rome but were Planning to do it in stages through other cities. Our flight out was to Venice but our flight home was from Rome and we planned to take in a number of cities in Italy along the way. We did this trip twice which doesn't help with my memory because I may well mix the two trips together but I remember specific events of note while we were on those trips so I've written about the memorable stories along the way

Giving St Trinians A Chance

It's a little difficult to remember all the details but the good bits stand out for me. When we landed in Venice we had 5 days to get to the Airport in Rome for a 10pm flight back to Manchester, so our only deadline was to be in that airport with our gear for say 7or 8pm on that night to check in. We didn't have a strict itinerary so had the freedom to ride to wherever we wanted. So the next day after riding for 80 miles with a break or two, we were in the area of Bologna and found a youth hostel to stay in. I am not happy at all because it's a bit shitty to say the least. It was like an old St Trinians with rooms that resembled dungeons with rusty metal beds in. The feel of the place was damp and cold. I was less than impressed and my face give it away. There were actually blood stains on the bedsheets and I said " We can't be staying here, look at the state of that bed" We hadn't paid anything yet so I said "Let's move on and find somewhere better than this" The showers were crap, they were communal showers with ten showers in a changing room and I pulled a face about that too. The others were finding it funny that I was getting all worked up about it and I wasn't happy at all. We have a wander to the café area and look at the food and I'm now firmly for moving on. Then I spot the bar and there's a Franziskaner pump and I immediately say to them all "Its only for one night isn't it? Let's give it a chance". They all piss themselves laughing saying "you've changed your tune haven't you?' We hadn't even took our cycling gear off, they'd stopped serving food but soon enough I had a beer in my hand and was now promoting the place as a great place to stay. We asked if there was anywhere nearby to eat and was told that there was a great restaurant up the road. We all got a shower, in the now perfectly acceptable communal shower, and get changed. We dive into the restaurant and the manager / main man comes up to us. He is the double of Leonard Rossiter out of Rising Damp. He had a very smart jacket on which I can only describe as multi coloured tweed that looked like high quality. Dave smith once said to me "what is with you? Its either nothing or the best". He was right, I'll either do without or get the best quality going and I can spot quality a mile off. Back to Leonard Rossiter and I'm weighing him up. His teeth are all a bit skew whiff and not pearly white to say the least but it is a very smart jacket and I can't make my mind up about the guy which is not like me. He came over to our table and said hello and gets this menu out. Again they have some nice German beers and the menu looks great. He's really on the ball this guy and suggests he gets us our beers and drinks and then taker our order for food. In what appeared to be seconds, the beer was on the table. I'm taking to this guy now. Our food comes soon after ordering and we are getting more and more chilled out. The food is delicious and we had a great evening. When we made our way back to the hotel the bar was still open and we had a couple more before waking up in the morning in the dorm of this hotel. There were about 40 to 50 beds to choose from and only six of us staying there but what bed am I in ? The only one with the blood stains on it. Brilliant. They took the piss out of me something rotten. "Thought you weren't staying here Chris?" "Now you are actually deliberately sleeping in the blood stained bed as your bed of choice" I just said "please don't tell me Mrs"

We got up and had breakfast in God knows where. I don't even know what town we were in. Judith Chalmers would have been so impressed with me. "Today we are in .. I haven't got the foggiest!!" Scouse was in charge of the route and as a result had put together where we needed to get to each day to make Rome in five days which was about as near to a plan as we were going to get. I was happy generally taking directions off Scouse or one of the others.

Don't Be Mardi (Gras)

We arrived in a place called Viareggio on the third day which was famous for its Mardi Gras carnival and has it all set up for the next day which means that the next day is Shrove Tuesday, Pancake Tuesday back home, the day before Ash Wednesday and the start of Lent. The Italians, being a very catholic country really celebrate these feast days much more than we do. I didn't know or remember the name of the town when we got there but looking it up later re the distance we'd travelled and the Mardi Gras celebrations, I think it was Viareggio one of three places in Italy that were famous for the Carnival of Mardi Gras. We'd done about 90 miles cycling that day and don't forget we've had all our lights pinched except Maddocks so as it's getting dark, we are all following him. We are working our way through the town and there's not a room to be had because of the celebrations. We go to a place that looks like a premier lodge and the woman inside tells us that everywhere has been booked up for the Mardi Gras. She tried ringing around for us but no chance - our next closest town was 30 miles away and its now pitch black dark and we have no lights and we are tired too. Then we see this copper in a cop car. Scouse can speak Italian so explained the situation to him that we don't want to move on without lights etc. and can you help us out sort of thing. I remember thinking even cells at the cop shop would do us. Scouse says to us that he has told us to follow him as he knows somewhere so we do. He does no more than get in his car and puts the blue lights on and indicates to us to follow him -So there's this Italian cop car being followed by six bikes, five without lights and he's leading us out of town. This isn't your normal setting is it? He takes us well beyond the town centre and then out on to a country road for what seemed like ages. I'm winding the others up half concerned about what's going to happen and half giggling as we are all cycling along behind this car. I shouted "You do realise lads what's going to happen to us – look at us all in lycra. He's taking us out of town to a field where he's radioed ahead and a lot of other coppers are waiting at a certain point and we are all going to get molested" We were all giggling and laughing and the others were shouting 'Fuck off Duoba' but the longer the journey went on , the more we thought it might happen. We are going further and further away from the town centre and I have no confidence that this is leading to something and we are going to have a long ride back to the beer once we found this place.

We must have travelled a few miles and he pulled up outside this place a bit like the Three Arrows Pub at Heaton Park in Manchester (apologies for those that don't know it but it is a typically decent pub that can be found in most cities). It's a little more tree lined around the pub which had big thick wooden doors in the centre. When we pulled up, it was all in darkness. I'm still winding everyone up saying "Told you. They are all behind that fucking door" "Fuck off Duoba" is still the reaction. The doors open as the copper knocks on them and he says "This is my

245

brother". Turns out his brother has a guest house just out of town and he's got no one staying there. As I'm looking around, to the left of me is a bar with Franziskaner. I need no more convincing. "Right this is perfect lads". Wendy, Maddocks, Scouse and Smithy follow suit. We haven't seen a single room yet and we are committed and booked in. We say a huge thank you to the copper and we are all sat at the bar with a beer in our hand. Anthony and Wendy being far more sensible went and had a look at the rooms. We have another beer and I take in the surroundings. We are in a beautiful old country pub type bar. The whole appearance of the wood and the surroundings are tremendous and the atmosphere was as good as we could have ever hoped for and there's not a soul in there but us. We have fallen on our feet again.

Our mate 'Scouse'

As there are six of us, we want three double rooms to keep the cost down but that means Wendy sharing with someone. There of us are married (myself, Maddocks and Smithy) and Anthony, Scouse and Wendy are either single or divorced. Wendy is in training for an Iron Man. I know that Scouse is getting closer and closer to Wendy and, for me, he is falling in love with her. Wendy has picked up on this and has approached me about it. She didn't want to say anything to Scouse because she doesn't want to risk falling out with him or making it awkward for everyone. We devise a scheme to protect our mate from upset but also to look after Wendy and make things more comfortable. We all agree to draw straws on who is sharing with who. Wendy was happy with that. We draw the straws, which of course are fixed only in way that makes sure that Scouse and Wendy are not sharing and we all crack on, shower and get ready. We have a few more beers downstairs and then get menu for the evening. This was a really nice pub, really smart and the menu was all home cooking. We couldn't have asked for more. Things were great and it gets to about 11pm ish and we are proper chilled out after a long day , so chilled out it was unreal, more so than the two previous nights and even better. The owner comes up and says 'right lads, we are off the bed now' and of course we are just looking at him and thinking that we are only just getting into this and really enjoying it and want to continue and he's said 'we are off to bed'. I remember thinking oh no, our night is over here and we are right in the middle of a great chilled session . To be fair they are not a young couple, they are an older couple and 11pm to them is ready for bed and they run a guest house so I suppose they have to be up to prepare breakfasts if we want it early. We are sat there in these beautiful armchairs and the owner says to us "There's the bar, there are bottles in the fridge. Help yourself, sort yourself out, we are off the bed" We are just staring at him as he walks off. Next thing you know his Mrs comes into the room with a tray in her arms full of Tapas snacks and bits and bobs of food. She sets the tray down in front of us and leans in and in a soft voice says 'have a great evening - goodnight'. We are all waiting for the catch as they leave the lounge and go to bed and leave us with the place to ourselves. We are all staring at each other. Are we in heaven or what? From having nowhere to stay we've gone to the best place ever. I can't even remember whether they charged us or not or what the cost was the next morning because it didn't matter. All I remember is what a great welcome and what a great evening we had in this place. If I could remember the actual name of the place I would be an even happier man.

Airport Dash

The next day, the Friday, Smithy went on ahead. He was flying back a day earlier than us on the Saturday, due to his work, so he cycled to Rome which was going to take him about 4 hours plus breaks and he would have a night in Rome. We all bear hugged and off he goes. We finally set off for Rome on the Saturday, as our flight was Sunday home. We arrived in Rome on the Saturday afternoon and were looking for digs to stay in. We found somewhere pretty quickly just as Scouse gets a text message off Smithy saying that he is home and well and saying to Scouse in a cryptic message 'but there are two of them' None of us know what this means so thought it was just a misspelt text or something. We get up the next morning for an early breakfast as our flight is at 10 o'clock. We set off nice and early to cycle to the Airport and pick up the signs easily. We are cycling for about an hour and don't seem to be making good time. It doesn't feel right at all as we knew we had picked our digs to be nearby to the Airport for this morning. It then dawned on us what Scouse had said "But there's two of them'. The crafty bastard was taking the piss. Turns out that there are two airports in Rome (Fiumicino, also known as the Da Vinci Airport and the other one is called Ciampino) There's no doubt he's made the same mistake but instead of tipping us off, he's probably giggling away at the thought of us cycling the wrong way when we are on a tight deadline. We stop and get our bearings for the right Airport which is Ciampino. Its now 8am and our flight is 10am. The problem is that if we carry on using the A road we are on it is 30 miles but if we jump on the motorway it is only 25 miles away . We get the map out and can see the only way we can make it is to get on the motorway and do a time trial. We can cover 25 miles in less than one hour if we work hard. A time trial keeps up a high pace because the back rider takes over the front man and then this repeats and ensures that the team is all going at their fastest pace. We are working our socks off and the whole way we have cars signaling to us and sounding their horns thinking we are lunatics. We just ignore them and are cracking on in the hard shoulder. Luckily their road surfaces are beautiful and there was no wind so we were flying. As we are coming down the motorway to the right of us we see this other motorway merging into it and we think shit. We are going to end up in the middle having to cross traffic to get to the hard shoulder on the next section. We are doing well over 30 miles per hour by this point and as we merge and cars clock us they start to back off and slow down enough for us to hit the hard shoulder. Scouse shouts "Come on they are letting us go" We are on that motorway for a short time and we arrive at the Airport and head into the main foyer. Amazingly we are still in time to get our bags and bikes checked in as they are not very busy. The sweat is pumping out of all of us. We've just done 25 miles in 40 minutes in heavy motorway traffic which is some going. We all head to the toilets to get washed down and I remember saying "I can't be arsed with that" I tell the others that I'll stay as I am. Humming!! I've probably had these bike clothes on and off for a week and at best have given them a rinse every two days and now I just can't be arsed. We board the plane and it's a four seater across – two seats either side of the aisle. Maddocks is next to Scouse, and Anthony is next to Wendy. Then there's my seat and I look to the right and there's this woman sitting in the window seat next to where I should be sitting. She is stunning and I'm guessing in her late 50s or even early 60's. Before I sit down. I thought, as embarrassing as it is, I'd better prepare her for what she is going to work out for herself very soon. I say to her 'You'll have to excuse me madam. We have just completed a time trial on bikes and I haven't managed to get cleaned up so I am humming a bit" She just turns and says as sharp as anything "Don't worry, I like a bit of rough!". The other four set off laughing. "It could only happen to you Duoba" says Maddocks ' I had a short talk with her and she was an ex model and had been all over the world. She'd done cat walks in New York etc. and we were swapping stories about travelling and that. She related to our living out of a suitcase approach and we had a decent chat. She didn't let on whether I 'pen and inked' or not and what looked to be a difficult situation at first had ended up that I was next to a person who understood at least what I did and why I did it. When we get back home, we checked with Smithy and he confirmed that he had played a bit of a wind up on us as he had done exactly the same. He explained that he had also hit the same point where the Motorways merged but as a single cyclist he was really at risk of being hit. A cop car then pulled him over. Once they knew where he was heading they had helped him. They didn't have a rack for the bike so they got him behind them and then blue lighted it and he followed them to the Airport. The cop car was travelling at 30 miles an hour and they had Smithy in the rear view telling them to up the speed. He was a strong rider Smithy but he was also in their slipstream so had plenty more speed in his locker. This could only have happened in Italy due to the culture there. Back home he'd have got a rollicking and possibly arrested. Over there you get an escort and cars getting out of the way.

Live, Enjoy and Repeat but Don't Push Your Luck
We enjoyed the trip so much that we decided to repeat it the following year. The main thing of note on that trip was that something happened that threatened the group dynamic and we thought that this might break us up but in fact it bonded us further. We carried on the straw charade for who was bunking with who. We just couldn't think of anything better to do to address Wendy's concerns other than being straight with Scouse. He was our mate though and we just dreaded him being upset about it so straws it had to be. That is until he found out. On the second or third night there he must have suspected or I may have got careless I don't know but suddenly he grabbed my hand and snatched the straws out. He could see that I was fixing it but that wasn't the main problem. He thought I was fixing it so that I shared a room with Wendy which was worse than the real reason. Wendy of course thought a lot of Scouse as we all did and was desperate not to upset him. We've all got showered

that night in the digs that we were in and headed out to a restaurant for a meal. You could have cut the atmosphere with a knife. We were so used to banter and laughing. This wasn't us. This was a disaster for all of us but Wendy and Scouse were in the thick of it. I remember thinking, Shit is this it? Is this the end of our group? We enjoyed our training together, we knew each other well and it was like another sort of family to us but I was already thinking we might not be able to fix this. Scouse got up from the meal and walked off. I can't remember whether it was Smithy and Maddocks went after him. They had obviously known for a while what was happening and could also see that not only was this trip in jeopardy but our future as a group was too. They came back and said - 'He feels like shit'. We had a beer together and the talk started to move to getting flights home. I said that I hadn't enough money to do that. I'd have to borrow some to get the flight home earlier. We headed back to the hotel and when we got up in the following morning it was absolutely lashing it down. Nobody had made any decisions yet as we wanted to sleep on it. Scouse was there but the atmosphere was still terrible. We have realised that the trip was probably over so we decided as a group to get the train to the next destination. It was raining and none of us were in the mood for a tough physical day cycling. We headed to the station at a place called Santolino, purchased tickets and got on the train. Scouse was at the back of the carriage on his own and seemed to be stewing over the situation. He looked proper down. He's still obviously not got used to the idea of what has actually happened and how long it had been going on for. He seemed really low. We'd had almost silence for about half an hour and then Smithy and Maddocks start singing quietly at first but then building up in volume to the famous tune of 'I Left My Heart in San Francisco' but changed the words to "I LEFT MY HEART –--- IN SANTOLINOOOO" – There was an awkward couple of seconds and then we all, including Scouse, burst out laughing and he says "you

251

fucking dickheads". Scouse had a massive crush on Wendy but on that trip he realised that was all it could be and put it behind him. Me, Maddocks, Anthony and Wendy were his mates and we thought nothing less of him because of it. It was just one of those things and we were just grateful that it sorted itself out as it could have ended worse. The group's cruel sense of humour was what fixed it and that was right too because that cruel sense of humour got us through most of our challenging times.

Scouse died later that year in October 2005. He had been out on his bike and was involved in an accident where he ended up in a ditch at this side of the road. He was taken to hospital and treated for a leg injury that may have led to the end of his triathlon career. He didn't get a chance to find out because after spending some time inactive while resting from the injury he developed a blood clot and had a massive heart attack and died. There can be much speculation when somebody who is very fit and athletic like Scouse suddenly dies like that. We believe that when he had his initial accident that the treatment he should have received was as a very fit athlete and is very different to somebody of the same age but not fit or athletic. That is because if the doctors don't know how fit you are and you are told to rest then there is always the chance of a blood clot because of the inactivity. We have seen and heard of doctors and hospitals treating patients who are athletic very differently because of the dangers of a thrombosis / clot.

We were all there at his funeral in our Rochdale triathlon kit and we all rode behind the hearse. It was a terribly sad day for everyone but a fitting tribute to a great lad who was part of our Tri' family and will never be forgotten. To make sure of that Rochdale Triathlon Club had five stars added to the back of their cycling tops to commemorate the five club members that had passed on. They were Paul Taylor (who I will write about later in the story), Scouse (Graham Richards), Mark Hannon (who was Smithy's brother in law) and two guys I knew only as Big AL and Aussie Andy. Wendy had been a proper mate through those times for Scouse and it's nice to know that there was a romance that did blossom out of those memorable trips as her and Anthony Lowe are still together today many years later. I'd love to be able to end the story by saying that what we didn't know was that Anthony and Wendy were the ones rigging the straws on those trips but you'd have to ask them that. I'm just glad that they found each other. When I publish this book I'll be cracking open a bottle and toasting all of our lost family and friends and Scouse will be right up there.

Cosa Stai Guardando? (Italian for 'What Are You Looking At?')
On one of our Italy trips, Myself, Scouse, Smithy, Maddocks, Wendy and Anthony Lowe were out there training on our bikes. We had completed a day of cycling through Florence and had found a restaurant in a place called Montevarchi and were having something to eat and a few drinks. It was coming to the end of the evening and the rest of the place was almost empty. We were just getting ready to leave when out of the blue , five drinks were delivered to our table that we hadn't ordered. These weren't ordinary drinks either. I think they were called Lemoncinos. Shorts of yellow liquor in a fancy glass. The waitress pointed over to a table of three Italian army guys all in full uniform and she said 'These are for you from them'. We shouted over 'Thank you' and 'Cheers' and after downing the drinks we returned the compliment and sent drinks over to their table. Next thing we know, they came over and sat with us and before we knew it we were in a drinking competition. One of these guys was a Sergeant Major and the other two were squaddies or equivalent to that rank. After a while the staff are making it obvious that they want to go home and have put the closed sign on the

253

door. They really should be kicking us out but the drinks are still flowing for a while. Eventually one of our gang says "we need to get going" and the Sergeant Major reacts by saying "We go when I go as I have the keys". Apparently the military are the bosses and he can keep this place open as long as he wants. We are all shifting a little uncomfortably now as we always have an early start on these trips and it had started to feel like we were being held prisoner rather than out for a drink with mates. He is clearly abusing his authority now without considering anyone else in the group and he thinks he is controlling us. We arrange to get one more round of drinks in and as we down them I stand up and I say "right we are going" Now we all stand up and he goes to shake everybody's hand and when he gets to me I very quickly realise that he's trying to get the better of me and he squeezes my hand firmly. Me being me, I squeeze it right back and he increased his grip and so did I. In the end we were staring at each other and squeezing to the point of breaking each other's hand. He let go and so did I and we all walked outside. I am ready for this guy and I am not even considering the fact that I am in his court and he is a sergeant major so has some clout. As we walk outside we are all a little drunk and scouse is more worse for wear. Whether drunk or not I react in the same way I always would. I will always deal with a situation as it arises no matter what condition I'm in. We get outside and this Sergeant Major flips Scouse in a sort of judo role on to the floor. He grabs his arms and forces him into the floor. Scouse is smaller than anyone else and he's more drunk than anyone. I just went "Woah" and he turns towards me and tries to do the same to me. I went with the move and used my momentum to come around the back of him. I am now behind the Sergeant Major with the two squaddies staring at me. All of a sudden he is trying to flip me again. Scouse is still on the floor and the other three are partly down the road. This has happened so quickly that Anthony, Maddocks and Smithy haven't even picked up that it's going on. They still think we are walking behind them. That's when the situation started to dawn on me. I have now got a firm grip of this fellah and he is in a position where I could have really hurt him. I have him in a hold where I could have easily snapped his neck. It's all just got a bit serious but there's no backing out now. I am staring at the Squaddies trying to make it look like I am asking them 'what do you want me to do?' All of a sudden one of the squaddies says what sounds like " Mario, Mario, your bambino's" and they jump in and grab him from me. He lets go and I let him go and the word Bambino's is still in the air so I say to him "you got bambinos?'. He indicates two and I say to him "I've got 4 bambinos". He just repeats the word Bambinos and dives in for the man hugs. This is very much like your typical North Manchester middle aged drunk in the local pub that latches on to you somehow and one minute it's 'who the fuck are you looking at?" and within a heartbeat it changes to "I love you mate!" and then just as quick back to "who the f......" and again and again.

Training For Ironman with Scouse and Anthony Lowe

In March 2000 I was training one weekend here for the Roth Ironman event. I had just completed a long bike ride with Scouse and Anthony of around 80 miles. We had cycled from Boarshaw to Rochdale to Littleborough, around and up Blackstone Edge and down Crag Vale and back into Hebden Bridge before heading for Todmorden and then home, or so I thought. Scouse was leading us out front then Anthony and then me. It had been a grueling ride and as we arrive in Todmorden I expected us to go straight on to home. Scouse inexplicably turns right and starts climbing the hill to Bacup which will put another loop on the ride and start with a hill with a gradient of about one in four or five and not a nice surface either. As Scouse turns right, within about 2 seconds I hear Anthony shout "You can Fuck that" and goes straight on and I initially I happily follow him thinking bugger that, myself. It lasted about 60 seconds because I knew we were out here training for the Ironman not for just any old event. "Fuck it" I say and turn around and chase the fucker. I'm shouting him to slow down so that I can get on his back wheel and but he keeps going up this hill. I work my arse off to catch him and as I draw near him he shouts "Don't leave my back wheel" so I embed my eyes into his gears / cassette and I stick with him. I am blowing out of my arse big time due to the fact that I've had to try and catch him and when we get to the top, he stops. I unclip my feet and I am physically sick on top of my bike as I had not time to get to the side of road. I get a tap on the back "Well done mate" and we rode into Bacup and then back home to Scouse's house for a bite to eat. He was training me mentally as well as physically. He said to me "just when you think your safe and on your way home you cannot take your eye off the ball. That last leg will be the toughest so you have to be mentally on the ball big time.

Heaton Park Run

The Park Run idea was one of the best and most successful attempts to get people to start running and exercising every week up and down the country. Heaton Park Run was started in 2009 by 'Sweatshop' which was a running shop based in Manchester. The first event only had about 30 people in it. Now they attract hundreds of people at the event. On the particular day I am going to talk about, you could enter a 5K run or a 10K run.

The usual suspects, Scouse, Anthony etc. entered us all   What they neglected to tell me was that they had only entered us all in the 5K. They told me we were in the 10K. As I ran on for the second half of the race, I thought I hadn't seen the bastards much. The race used to start at the

Commonwealth pavilion built for the 2002 commonwealth games and also ended back there. The cheeky bastards were hid behind trees pissing themselves laughing as I passed still looking for them. They had set me up good and proper. I realised what was happening and I stopped to prevent further embarrassment and we had a good laugh as always. I had the last laugh though because the race organisers congratulated me on winning the 5K. At that time I was probably at my quickest for the Olympic Standard Triathlons. I remember seeing the times that the athlete competing at the Commonwealth Games representing the Cook Islands had set and I was quicker. I toyed with the idea of emigrating to the Cook Islands so that I could qualify for the next Olympics.

King of The Mountains (All Downhill From Here?)

In July 2009 a few of us travelled over to Tourmalet which is in the Pyrenees mountains between France and Spain. We were heading over there to watch a famous stage of the Tour de France. There was myself, Andy Pilling, Anthony Lowe, Dave Smith and a doctor called Ralph who we simply referred to as Doc. The stage of the race is The Col Du Tourmalet and is one of the most famous climbs in the Tour De France and has produced some incidents over the years. We went over primarily to watch the stage but we took our bikes with us and couldn't resist planning to try out some of the climb ourselves. If as a cyclist spectator you visit a stage of the Tour, you need to be clear of the route a good two to three hours before the Tour participants arrive to do the leg. We were at the base of the mountain on the morning of the race and the place was buzzin'. There is a great atmosphere at most key stages of the race but this is great.

We were enjoying having coffee and watching the crowds when the guys collectively say that they are making a move to do the climb on their bikes and watch the race from a high vantage point. I say to Smithy "I'm staying here for a little longer, soaking up this incredible atmosphere". Doc says "are you sure you'll get to the top on time to be clear for the race. Smithy says " yeah course he will. Don't worry about him". We are all good cyclists and know our capabilities' Doc looked a bit puzzled by this at first. Off they went and I got myself another coffee and a croissant and soaked it all up.

We had arranged to meet up at the top at a ski station. I finished my drink and grabbed my bike and started cycling up the hill which was tough to say the least but manageable. After 20 minutes of climbing I arrived at the Ski Station and started looking for them. After a few minutes of looking I'm thinking 'where are they?' I walked over the road and I can see the cable cars and chairs. "Shit" I say out loud because I've just realised that I'm at the Ski Station alright but I'm at the Ski Station at the fucking foot of the mountain not the top!!! What had given it away was the cables cars and chairs going up and not down. What a crank I am, I thought. I get on my bike and I start cycling up the mountain. After I have been cycling for a good while and at a decent pace too so that I can get to the top as quick as I can, I come to a bend in the road and I'm keen to see around this bend to gauge what I've got left to tackle. I get there and looked up ahead of me and this little voice in my head says "For fucks sake you're only half way!" As I cycled onwards and upwards at a much slower pace now I realised that people on the route were sat down with their bikes as they had decided not to go on for the moment and watch the race from there.

I'm starting to panic a little. I've got to get to the top before the motorbikes arrive to clear the route for the race, which by now is not far away in terms of time so at any point now the Police might freeze you exactly where you are and turn you into a spectator.

I increased my speed and continued with the climb. I was strangely starting to enjoy the challenge now because I was getting a slight taste of what it was like in the race itself. Some people refer to it as getting in the zone when you settle into a pattern of effort and focus that enables you to sustain a performance that might actually be out of your reach in normal circumstances.

I went into a sort of autopilot for the remainder of the climb and the only thought that passed through my mind that I could consciously remember was a feeling of elation as I imagined speaking to the doctors who told me just under thirty years ago that I had life limiting injuries and yet here I was literally only a few minutes away from actually competing with the world's elite cyclists in one of the toughest climbing stages of the Tour de France. It was stretching the truth of course but I was here nevertheless. The next thing I knew, I'd arrived at the top and there they all were sat down at a table in a cafeteria having a beer, including the Doc. I pointed to the pint in front of him and said "Are you for fucking real? We've got another 70 mile back after this" The Doc just laughed and responded "Do you not realise that the quickest method of hydrating yourself is a pint of beer?" I've never been one to not follow doctor's orders so I went and got myself a pint and a huge plate of paella to go with it. We drank, we laughed and we watch the stage of the race when it arrived. It was a good day to be alive and another one I would never have had if something hadn't have pulled me back on to the pavement on Cheetham Hill Road that day.

This year 2020, the stage of the race that I cycled is measured at 19 Kilometres. I gave myself a minor pat on the back but didn't get giddy about it. Good job really because the ride down was far more dangerous. If you just freewheel you'll reach ridiculous speeds of up to 40 miles per hour. If you used your brakes all thew way down you'd have an accident by damaging the tyres through overheating and possibly other components so you must only apply the brakes when absolutely necessary. An accident much spoken about in the area when talking about downhill safety is when an Italian, Fabio Casartelli, lost control of his bike and was killed colliding with a wall on the descent of Col De Portet.

On a separate ride we did that descent in tribute to Fabio to sample the dangers he was facing . Coming down at those speeds on those bends was a trial in itself. Get on you tube and look for descents in the Tour De France. There's a fantastic one starring our own Chris Froome.

Jollies?

I'd just been to Villamora in Portugal training. When I got back Mena said to me, we are coming with you next year. I just said that was no problem as long as she didn't mind that I would be training a lot. Mena said she didn't mind and so we planned for her to come with us next time with the three kids, as it was then. Arron was about eleven, Jourdana was six and Rhys was five. When the time came, It was difficult to ensure that everybody enjoyed the experience. I would get up early and do a swim then we'd have breakfast together and I would shoot off on a 80/90 mile bike ride. By the time I got back I'd meet the family on the beach and Mena would say quite rightly that this was time for me to play with the kids but of course I desperately needed rest.

The guys I had been training with, Neil Shankley, Scouse and Anthony Lowe were all back at the hotel having a siesta because in an hour or so we were supposed to be going for a run. Mena never said about coming again. I think at least Mena saw examples of what we did on these trips. We did enjoy them and have some great laughs but during the day generally we would be putting the hours in where we could to train so that we could participate in Triathlons and Ironmen events.

The emphasis was on the training and instead of this trip being a bonding exercise with the family it ended up the opposite. If I was going to compete in these races I had to train with people of like mind and at home the conditions were just not right.

The Fisherman's Retreat

I did try and incorporate my training to ensure that we had plenty of family events. One day I cycled 90 miles on a bike in the morning so that we could head as a family to the fantastic Fisherman's retreat for early evening with the children. The evening we did this and the owner Herve, had a cask ale event with different beers on. I got completely shitfaced. I'd been on a massive bike ride and had no food in me and started drinking. Philomena was not impressed. Having had the kids all day and out to relax she now had another kid to look after as I was no used to anybody. I can hear both my daughters saying now "what's changed?" I suppose the only thing that has changed from that night is that it isn't every night that you can get a mixed grill like The Fisherman's served

Chapter 21 – Ironman

I did my first Triathlon in London in 1998 and all in all I've completed more than 25 Triathlons in the last 22 years. It was only after my second triathlon though in in 1999 that I decided that I wanted to test myself further. I felt I had more in my locker and wanted to push myself harder. It was Scouse that first put in my head about the Roth Iron Man event held in Bavaria, Germany in July every year. We were swimming at Rochdale baths and then went upstairs in the café for something to eat before a bike ride and Scouse said that he had just completed the Roth Ironman. The way he described it and the mental energy that oozed out of him after doing it sounded right up my street. I loved the sound of the title and that it was only for those who could face up to three tough endurance legs of an overall hugely challenging event. It was a triathlon consisting of a 2.5 Mile Swim, 112 miles cycling stage and a marathon to finish off. This was the kind of challenge I was now after and I genuinely had no idea whether I would complete it or whether this was to find my breaking point or not. I started attending Oldham baths as part of my training for Roth. The pool was about 30 yards in length and I was being coached by this big guy called Byron. He was a high standard swimmer who had tried in vain to qualify for the Olympics but had not made it and so had focused on being a coach. He was doing some one to one training with me and was looking closely at my swimming style and stroke. Now normally, when you were being coached, you would swim and the coach would walk at the side of the pool carefully watching the stroke. So off I go swimming as quickly and as efficiently as I can. Next thing you know there is a body underneath me in the pool looking up at me. He doesn't seem to be moving his arms and has them crossed across his chest but he is keeping up with me easily. What I don't realise is that he is kicking his legs like a dolphin with no upper body movement at all.

I'm freaking out as he glides below me effortlessly staring up at me concentrating on my swimming stroke. My next couple of strokes are all over the place as I try to breathe and concentrate on what I am doing. He doesn't seem to need to breathe as he is swimming underwater for so long facing upwards at me. He stayed there for the whole length of the pool. We both got out and I'm out of breath and a little freaked out and he is talking as if he has not done anything. I'm now staring at him thinking 'what have I just witnessed – who is this? The Man from Atlantis?' Now there are glass bottom pools and cameras under water but not in those days twenty odd years ago. He taught me some valuable lessons about swimming that held me and will hold me in good stead for the rest of my competition life. The main thing he taught me was the very first thing he told me. He taught me that the speed of a swimmer is assisted by your pull in the water not out of the water. Once I developed my style to get the best out of that, I was becoming a very capable swimmer and that was all I needed to add to my skill set to enter the Ironman. Three months before the event in Roth, in the midst of my preparation, my participation in the event was under threat. It was a beautiful summers day before work and I was out training on the bike nice and early and I passed the fire station on Rochdale Road on a downhill section of the road doing about 35 mph. Before I could react, a car had backed out of the driveway of a house at speed into my path and I hit the bumper of the car and somersaulted over the top of the car bouncing on his bonnet and ending up landing on the road on my right arm, which of course is my good arm. I immediately jumped up and run to the driver's window to remonstrate with him and as I do that, my right arm just collapses. I didn't know it at the time but I'd torn my rotator cuff in my shoulder. My anger with the driver was quickly replaced by an understanding that I needed to get to A&E. The driver (I can't remember his name) was horrified at what had happened and took me to the A&E at Crumpsall hospital which luckily was only a few minutes away by car. They confirmed the injury and said that a month off work and 100% rest would see it right and I was eventually sent home. Although I was very unhappy that this was to interfere with my training, there was never any doubt in my mind that I would be on the starting line at Roth in three months' time. Nothing, not even this set back, was going to stand in my way. At the time I was being coached by a guy called Graham Stevens, who was part of Rochdale Tri Club . He was particularly educating me on how to get body fat down and he was also a physio and connected to Laurie Brown, the former Manchester United physio. He booked me in for a session to see Lawrie and told him exactly what I was planning. Lawrie thought I was a crank straightaway but seeing and hearing about my determination to make it to that start line at Roth he told me the only thing that I could do. His exact words were "You're mad son planning to do all that but if you want to compete in this iron man event in three months' time, you have to listen to what I am telling you. You need to stop doing everything you don't have to do. No biking, no swimming etc. The only thing you can do is walk and work and at work if you can use your left hand rather than your right then do it. That's it. That's the only way you will make it" The thing is when you get advice from someone who knows their stuff, you listen. I was also impressed at his acceptance that I was going to do this no matter what anyone said. Most physios and doctors would have told me not to do it but Lawrie confirmed that he thought I was crazy but advised me on the best chance I had of doing it. The only thing I knew about Laurie before meeting him was what I had read in the press about his situation at Man Utd when Tommy Docherty got the sack, at Matt Busby's insistence, for having an affair with Laurie's wife. You can sense decency in people and Laurie came across as a really good guy. It was no wonder that, faced with the choice of sacking Tommy Docherty or letting

Laurie go, that Matt Busby insisted that the board sack Docherty. Those were back in the days where standards were high even at a cost to the club as Docherty had a good record and was liked by most Man Utd fans. Back to my situation, I could barely lift the clippers at work with my right hand and working left handed was ridiculously difficult but improved greatly in time as I started to do everyday things that I could with my left hand like brushing my teeth and making a drink and lifting my mug of coffee to my mouth. Brian Silk told me flat out not to do the Iron Man. He was worried that in addition to worsening the injury, it could mentally destroy me. I respected Brian's views and saw the sense in them but simply said to him "Brian. I've entered it and I'm doing it. I've got seventeen hours to complete it to get the tee shirt. It will be a nice training day" Brian's response was pretty straightforward. He looked me straight in the eye and said "You're a fucking lunatic". I flew alone to Nuremberg on the day before the event. Nuremberg, as everyone knows, is famous for famous for two things; The Nazi war crimes trials and their Car race track which held over 150,000 spectators and was famous for both testing the speed of new cars and holding races. I arrived in Roth, found my digs, registered and got all my gear so I was all ready for the event the next day, Here I was in Roth, the night before I competed in my first Iron Man event and not knowing the script for this kind of event, I just headed for the bar where I had heard all the competitors were gathering. When I got there, as we were competing the next day, I was looking for orange juice. This huge guy says to me 'Is this your first one?' I tell him that it is and he says 'Get a couple of those down you and you'll be fine'. He's pointing to a type of beer, so I have one with food and I like it so much I end up having three. I stagger out of the place as the beers are 6% proof and I don't usually drink in the lead up to competing. I was out cold in bed as it had simply knocked me out. I was up and at them for the race the next day and I didn't feel too bad but, being my first Ironman, I was apprehensive about the physical and mental challenges and during the course of the day we were going to find out if I could handle them or not. We had collected our gear and numbers the previous day so was all set to go. I'd love to be able to describe the build up to the race and me setting things up with the bike and the transition stages but quite honestly I don't remember a thing. It's my first ever Ironman and you would think that I'd remember it all but it went in a flash. Professional footballers get to the FA Cup final and are warned by other players to enjoy it as much as they can and savour every moment because it passes by in instant and they won't remember most of it and that is exactly what happened to me. If you were to ask me about racing in an Ironman in Lanzarote. I could tell you everything to do with my preparation. For example I picked up some great advice preparing for stages of that race from very experienced competitors. Two of the best tips I ever received were from experienced people while I was prepping the night before my very first Ironman race in Roth Germany and putting my bike into the transition stage area so it was all set. There was everyone doing the same thing and checking the pressure in their tyres was perfect. Not to get too technical, the correct tyre pressure for the race was 120PSI (pounds of pressure per square inch). A fellow athlete asked me if this was my first one. I told him it was and he said to me, don't put 120 in now. Put 80 in. I asked why and he said "because when those guys arrive at their bikes tomorrow they may find that they have repairs to do. During the night, the pressure will rise by 20 and you'll arrive at your bike and it'll be 100 because the temperature change through the night and into the morning will have an effect on the tyre pressure and you just add a quick 20 to each tyre or whatever is needed and off you go. He also told me to make sure I had a can of coke in my bag because he said " when you arrive at your bike you will be desperate for something to get the salt water taste out of your mouth and deal with

266

the amount of salt water you've swallowed. A can of coke will taste like nectar and will dilute the salts you have swallowed'. He was bang on with both. The following morning people reported hearing a series of bangs from the bike section as some of the tyres burst having gone up 20 PSI overnight and boy did that can of coke taste good when I got out of the sea water and it did exactly as he had predicted and dealt with all the salt I'd swallowed. Back at Roth for my first Ironman though it was a different kettle of fish as the weather was less demanding and it was canal swimming and not open sea so much easier to navigate.

I arrived at the starting point well in time and it was so well organized. The swim was staggered into pens. You got yourself in the pen that suited your swimming speed and time. It made perfect sense because if you exaggerated about your pace you would soon be found out in the water as competitors overtook you and it got crowded for you so it was to be to your advantage to be as accurate as possible. I placed myself in the right pen for my sort of time, which I do actually remember as 'One Hour & Thirty Minutes' and readied myself. The race started as all races started with a Klaxon

I've completed the swim and the cycle stages and I am on the third and final section of the Marathon and I feel good. As I get well into the marathon and at around the 30 Kilometres mark I can see a guy called Terry in the distance ahead of me, who I have met the evening before in the bar. He is one of the many forces or ex forces athletes that are competing in the event and is very distinctive in his Union Jack vest and shorts. I caught up with him and started to run at his pace with. As we pass food stations I am taking food on board at every opportunity and making sure that I am getting a drink. As we leave a food station, I ask Terry 'where do we hit this mental wall that I have been warned about?'

It was a genuine question. As the race had gone so well for me so far, I expected that I would hit a mental challenge at any time and had been warned about "a wall" that you simply had to run through or it would finish you. Terry didn't look at me, he just replied " You won't hit the wall mate". "Why" I say " Why?" he says "because you've not stopped fucking eating!" As we hit the next eating station he has started wincing with every step and when I enquire what's wrong with him, he tells me that his cruciate ligament has given way. I'm guessing that this is probably an older injury coming back to haunt him. I say to him "Don't you think you need to pull out ?" He replies "I can't do that now Chris. There's only two ways I'm getting out of this race and that's either by completing it or in a body bag". It sounded dramatic but I knew he meant it. "That's a bit extreme" I say but he explained "I select lads for the special forces so I push lads to their breaking point and it's a question of carry on or go home, there is no in between. When the average guy competes in these things or other events and think they have reached a point where they have no more in their locker it is well known in endurance circles that they have only tapped into 40% of what's in their locker and they either push on and they realise this or they pull out and never know". I knew exactly what he meant. I'd wondered about this for a while but it took me spending more time with people who were clearly of that caliber to realise that I was special forces material myself. That's not saying that I was at their exact level, I just knew that if I had been healthy enough when younger without my arm and head injury, I could have been operating at the same level as these guys. I felt little pain and I knew that I would be prepared to risk my life to achieve a goal and that fear would never stand in my way. I was prepared to go to any length to achieve what I needed to achieve. Most other people think people like me are mad and I understand that because they cannot comprehend how straightforward it is for me to risk everything to achieve a goal. I said this to one of my customers one day. I said to him that I'd realised that I was special forces material. The customer said to me "Yeah you've realised you're a fucking nutter'.

I completed the event in 12 hours 4 minutes. That's a two and a half mile swim, One hundred and twelve miles on a bike and a 26 mile marathon in 12 hours 4 Minutes and I felt elated. I now had an Ironman under my belt. I went to the pasta party after the race. The pasta is to replace everybody's lost energy. A plate of pasta and a beer will get 1000 calories in you. At the presentation I am talking to a guy (I can't remember his name) and he says 'Just a minute Chris I need to talk to the guy who's won the race, Ulrik'. This guy called Ulrik is walking towards us and it's the same guy who told me to get a beer down me the night before. I was in awe of him and said to him ' I know you're secret - plenty of beer'. He just started laughing. We had a full on conversation about beer and it's important to note for anyone who wants to drink and still wants to compete at this level as It's got to be proper beer. None of this chemical crap. Beers like Erdinger, Franziskaner or Leffe (mainly barley) do not have harmful chemicals in them and don't leave you the same way afterwards or more importantly the next day. I still drink a bottle of one of these nearly every day to take the edge off the day but it doesn't interfere with my training and fitness

Since that first Roth Iron Man, I've been back there many times to compete and I must have competed in well over a dozen Ironman events in some fantastic locations but nothing better than the Lanzarote Ironman. They were right when they told me that if you haven't done the Lanzarote Ironman then you've not really done an Ironman. I did it four times eventually and it was fantastic but could be perilous too. When you start the swims you've got pens to make it safer and they are based on potential finishing times for the swim section. There may be 2000

269

people at the start but they are all in roped off pens, 30 metres across then 50 meters deep. At the front there are guys one hour or under then the next pen one hour and ten minutes and so on. You decide what pen you're in and God help those who miscalculate as they may end up in a right mess. All the swimmers then start walking into the sea and swimming and its safer and get less clogged. That's the theory anyway. I was in a Lanzarote Ironman and by this time I'm quite experienced., It's about my 8th Ironman event and I'm behind this guy swimming and as I get near I catch his foot by accident. It happens a lot and most people can handle it. I barely touched his foot and he kicked me in the face deliberately. You can't help catching people sometimes until people get their own rhythm. The best approach is to just go with the flow and trust each other that these light touches and accidental knocks have to be accepted. If I'd have kept touching him or got in his way a lot I would have understood his reaction but unfortunately though some people panic and some people kick and bite. This guy booted me as hard as he could in the mouth. He drew his leg back in nothing resembling a swimming technique and kicked out. I was stunned for a few seconds but then I'm afraid that he got the treatment he deserved. I drew up alongside him and punched him. Just in case he thought that I'd done that by accident I punched him again. He swam sideways to get away from me and I didn't feel an ounce of guilt. He was totally out of order and was relying on the fact that the person he kicked, man or woman, would be a wimp and accept it. What if an inexperienced swimmer got into difficulty as a result of it? Well, he got a shock didn't he? I don't want to harp on about negative experiences like that as there were so many positive ones to by far outweigh the bad. I also don't like painting a picture of me using my fists willy nilly because I don't. I can hand on heart say that since I calmed down from post-accident rage incidents, incidents like this were far and few between and would all be instigated by the other person. I wouldn't have liked myself otherwise. But I'd like to end this section with a massive positive.

That first Iron Man in Roth, Germany was a huge turning point for me in my attitude to what I was about. Mixing with the special forces guys had a big influence on me as I was convinced that I was of the same calibre as them, I just hadn't had the same desire or opportunity when I was younger to go into the forces. They welcomed us mixing with them and never treated me with anything but respect because of what I was doing given my age and fitness background. There are also many other people who you could refer to as 'special forces' in Ironmen events just by what they are achieving against the odds. Anthony Lowe and I were in Roth one year for the Ironman event and were stood at the start line looking at the swim ahead of us and no matter how many times you'd done these things, that first challenge of not drowning or being knocked out by a foot or a stray elbow in the 'washing machine' was still daunting and it was healthy to be nervous and not complacent. Anthony was drawing my attention to the distance we had to swim around a bend in the Roth canal before we could turn around to come back to complete the overall distance. As he's talking I'm tapping his arm trying to get his attention and when he looks at me I discreetly point to the guy next to us. He's blind and he's tethered to another guy and they are both looking excited and keen to start the race. That means that the sighted guy has two jobs, he has to get himself through each stage and be the eyes of the other guy too. The blind guy is about to get into the washing machine and can't see where the legs and arms that could harm him are. I turned to Anthony and said "What the fuck have we got to worry about when these guys are prepared to take this on?" Anthony nods his agreement and we were ready to go. It was extremely inspirational and drove me on for a lot of that day. Those guys are true Ironmen. I once high fived a blind guy in the middle of the marathon in the Lanzarote Ironman. I'd passed him on one leg of the marathon. I was coming back on the first stage of the run and he was going out for the outward leg of the first stage and as we passed I shouted 'well done mate" and I clapped him as I passed as I know he's done the bike and the swim and like everyone else must be lifted by the fact that it was only the marathon to go. He smiled in my direction. On the next leg, we are about to pass again and are just close enough to do it. I don't know how he knew that I would or what his partner said to him but we perfectly high fived and slapped each other's hand. It wasn't like he put his hand up and I slapped it, we exchanged the gesture with perfect timing and accuracy. It put the widest smile on my face as I raced on. I wish someone had taken a picture of my face just then. I can remember feeling so uplifted. It was one of a thousand great moments that I have experienced in the last 22 years of competing.

Chapter 22 – Going Ultra

Iron Man events were another level completely from what I had been doing beforehand but it wasn't long once I had handled competing in Iron Man events before my desire kicked in to push things further and as far as I could physically and mentally. I was aware of Ultra events through a book I had read called 'Fitness for Life' by Sir Ranulph Fiennes. The book is excellent for learning about how to train for Ultras and what to eat and the chemical balance and imbalance of foods etc. If you wanted to step up your fitness and general health, this book was excellent and did a lot for me.

I started competing in Ultra events much later in life than most. I have fellow competitors in their thirties wanting to shake my hand when they see me competing at this level. They were impressed that someone in their late fifties was ready to push their body to those limits. Because of my age and because my fellow competitors see me competing in these endurance events, people often think I'm ex-military and when I tell them I'm a Barber they say "What?" They expect me to be in the forces or a job that demands that level of physical activity and mental state. The kind of mental state that military people have and the sort of mental state you will need to compete in any way in the kind of extreme challenges that Ultra runs or Iron Man events throw at you. It's hard to explain but the experience that these events give you help you prepare for the kind of mental challenges that face you at certain points of the event. For instance, hallucinations and other tricks of the mind are common and recognising them are key to being able to continue and drive on in the events to complete them. Training for the mental barriers that you will have to go through in these events is very difficult as some of them you can only really experience by doing the races themselves.

My first 'Ultra' event was actually the Rotherham 50 Race. I did it with Dave Smith, Tony Maddocks and Anthony Lowe. As you've already gleaned yourself reading all this, I am definitely a 'Crank' as my dad used to say. If you look up the definition of the term 'Crank' it can mean two things:

1. ***Crank is*** *a pejorative term used for a person who holds an unshakable belief that most of their contemporaries consider to be false. A* ***crank*** *belief* ***is*** *so wildly at variance with those commonly held that it* ***is*** *considered **ludicrous.***

    Or

2. ***Crank*** *(verb)- to increase (loudness, output, etc)he cranked **up** his pace. to set in motion or invigorate news editors have to **crank up** tired reporters.*

So whichever of these best suits me, why on earth would any of these so called 'friends' want to wind me up any further? But they did. They decided to tell me one week "We are doing this run this weekend". So I said "OK I'll do it with you. Where is it?" "It's just a run around Rotherham and you can enter on the day" they say, so I think, nothing special to prepare for then just a light run in the Rotherham area. What they fail to tell me is that they have been training for this and it's an Ultra run called the 'Rotherham 50' because it's a 50 mile run. The day comes and of course when I get there it soon becomes apparent what the race actually is. They say "we forgot to tell you the details" The race had a 6.00am start for power walkers, 7.00am start for intermediate runners (Us) and 8am start for the elite runners. So we kick off at 7.00am. They all pick up speed and race on ahead so I did my best to keep up with them but even then it was clear that they had trained for this and I hadn't. Eventually I catch them up and they are laughing. I said to them "you need to slow down" and they say "yeah right Chris" but they pick up the pace and I end up on my Jack Jones again.   Eventually I catch them again and I am in a foul mood so I say, "give me the map you twats and I'll do it myself" and off they went. We are now about 13 or 14 miles into it maybe a little less and I am going on and off course. Map reading was never my best skill but eventually I end up at the 25 mile check point which is at a rugby club. It's a well organised event this. There have been a couple of feed stations in the first 25 miles providing water and sweets but when we get to this 25 mile check point there are beautiful soft seats, its lovely and warm, there's hot soup, and a carvery of lovely food. It all smells great and to me after running 25 miles that I've not trained for, it's like I've checked in to a 7 star hotel. I finish my food and stand up, There's two doors to get out. One to the right and someone will give you a lift back to the start, one to the left is to carry on in the event. I take a look back at the food and I see this guy looking at me. He says "what's it to be? Left to carry on or right to get a lift back to the start? I stare at him and I realise that I've got an option to grab a bit more hot food and quit. I stare at him and stick my left arm out and say confidently 'Left'. Now I have just committed to the next 25 miles. So on I go and without much incident I end up at the 40 mile checkpoint and I'm on a country road in the pitch black and I can't see my hand in front of my face. I knew I had to find a style to turn right to cut across a field. The map confirmed this for me earlier but it was now dark and I had no torch or anything that could help me. Why was that the case? Because I thought we were on a light run around chuffing Rotherham not a 50 miler. I thought to myself that I'm here until morning now and I sit down on the edge of the main road. In the distance I can see headlights bopping around. About 20 or 25 minutes goes by and then this light starts coming towards me. I can't see what it's attached to but eventually this guy appears in front of me who I think is a Marshall and who I later find out is called Terry. He says to me 'I think you had better follow me" and I said " Strange that's what I was thinking". He's following the map himself and I now realise that he's not a marshal, he's a competitor. He's actually a power walker and he's caught me up. He's telling me that this is his 10th Rotherham 50 and he's due to get a tee shirt for completing the 10th one. I shared my background with him and we chatted as we power walked all the way to the 45 mile checkpoint. I can see the checkpoint in the distance which is a van with a tent coming off it. I couldn't keep up with him as my legs were seizing up. When we get to the van I say to Terry "I'm calling it a day Terry, my legs have seized up". Terry says "I don't think so son. 45 mile and you're calling it a day? No chance." I was embarrassed by my real reasons which were that I didn't have any kit with me to cope with the lack of light. Eventually I said to him "I haven't got a torch". A Marshall stepped in immediately and said "Here you are son, have this one" I took it gratefully but said to Terry that I still had to deal with my locked hamstrings. Terry was one of those wise old guys that you need when you have a problem. He said to me "As soon as we hit a clearing you need to do some running". "Running?" I say "I can't walk Terry never mind run!! and he said "Look son, you've been power walking with me for the last five miles. You've been using different muscles in your legs. As soon as you start running you'll feel tons better. It works a treat and sure enough running is a lot easier but he can't keep up with me now. We finish the 50 Miles with this combination of running and walking which, as I've written in an earlier chapter is called fartlecking. It's a Swedish terms for using two different paces and translates as 'speedplay'. We arrive at the finishing line and head for the canteen. Tony Maddocks, Anthony Lowe and Smithy are laughing and I throw my trainers at them and tell them to fuck right off and headed over to the food. Terry found me and wanted to thank me. He'd just done his 10th Rotherham 50 Power Walk and done it in his fastest time which he attributed to our fartlecking. We stayed over at a premier inn in Rotherham and went and got beers and a curry. We slept well and all went down for breakfast the next morning walking like we've shat our pants. The woman serving was looking at us as if we had shat our pants but was relieved when we explained to her about the race the day before. It was my first Ultra event and I hadn't trained for it but I'd got through it.

My second Ultra was the VOTWO ' Atlantic Coast Challenge' which was three marathons in three days around the fantastic looking coast of Cornwall. Not only do you have to face the challenge of three marathons in three days which is 78.6 miles, this is a race that provides you with some incredible weather challenges, specifically the wind against the fantastic backdrop of the Cornish coast. The race starts in Padstow and finishes at Lands End. The organisers state, very tongue in cheek, that when you enter that you can complete the race by running, walking or crawling. They also say that completion of the race will get you a challenge medal and a Cornish pastie. VOTWO is actual VO2 and the organisers say that VO2 Max is the gold standard measurement of an athlete's cardiovascular system. VOTWO was founded in 2004 and their objectives are to provide Challenging, fun events, coaching UN sports science support to athletes at all levels; from beginners to professionals.

On the third marathon on the third day I was on the first leg of 10 miles which was quite demanding running along the cliff pathways. I came across some fellow competitors sat on a ledge on the edge of the cliff which reminded me of the film 'Cliffhanger'. I'm not big on heights so I didn't like where they were sat but also wondered why they were just sat there. I walked past them along the narrow and steep pathway and sat down for a few moments myself. A paramedic was sat there too with food and water for everyone. I didn't see the competitors at the next checkpoint though, I realised later that they had just reached their breaking point back at the ledge so had stopped. There are no failures in Ultra events, just people who reach their breaking point. I sat there for a while and then left them. I came to some clearings and started running again.

My third Ultra Event was the Jurassic Coast Challenge. Again this was 3 marathons in three days along the Dorset coast and again run by VOTWO as part of their coastal marathons series. This event had the added bonus for me of having Rhys participating too. Rhys was 21 at the time and although I was made up that he was competing in a race with me, I had the added pressure that my son would be hell bent on beating me. How did I know that? Because he is my son and he gets that competitiveness from me. Add to that, Rhys was in great shape and well capable of beating me dependent on how the race goes for both of us.

The race started in Weymouth harbor for the first marathon. Rhys is giving out to me that he's going to burn my arse in this event. I laughed at him but in my mind I kept thinking about what a good friend and customer of mine called Peter Scraggs (Scraggsy) had said to me recently. Scraggsy was as funny as fuck and a great lad who was famous in Middleton for his plastering. When I told him that Rhys had entered the same race as me, he said "Have you seen your lad run? He runs effortlessly" He was trying to warn me that I might have my work cut out. I just said to him 'I'll burn his arse mate' but in my mind I'm thinking, this is going to be very interesting.

I'm giving him 36 years in age and he looks like an athlete so I know this will be a challenge for me but I have the experience. On the first day Rhys is about an hour and ten minutes ahead of me at the end of the first race. When you finish the first Marathon they give you a time. Then you all start the second day together. I've now got two guys, Jason who lived in California and his mate Gerard an ex USA marine and they are both saying to me "Have you seen your lad. He's like the wind' "Yeah' I say to them. At breakfast on the second day, all the Ultra runners are gathered. Rhys has got his knee strapped up. We have been in separate digs. I'm booked into a hotel and he's at a camp site at Weymouth with other Ultras. I say to him 'What's up with your knee?'. 'It's alright dad it's nothing' he says. We all had breakfast and got to start line and it's a mile flat to the first climb. Rhys is off like the wind and Jason and Gerard are looking at me as I am semi-walking as we build up to the first climb. I can see well ahead that that first incline and I am getting prepared for it just as I see this lad stood at the base. It looks like Rhys but all I can see is the back of him. As I get closer I can see that it is definitely Rhys and he has broken down. When I get to him, he is in bits but at the same is saying to me 'Dad – I've got to do this' I just take one look at his knee and say to him "Are you for real? Look at the state of it' as I point to his knee. Obviously he has played the injury down when I've seen him at Breakfast because now it is so badly swollen it looks like it is going to burst. I say to him ' Look Rhys even if you got up this next climb without that knee popping there is much more climbing to come and then tomorrow it gets even harder. There is no disgrace to call it a day. Live today to fight another day. Go back and speak to Simon.' Simon is an ex-marine organiser. Most ultra runs are arranged and officiated by ex-forces because of their background but Simon is also a banker in Switzerland. They don't really make a lot of money out of these events but it is their thing. It's what they do and how they exist, It floats their boat as they say.

Rhys goes back and I carry on. I am now interested in what Rhys will do when he goes back to speak to Simon. He can either get some rest, get his gear and head to the next train home or he can take a more positive decision and stay. His world has just temporarily collapsed and there are a number of reactions he could have to that. I finished the day's Marathon and headed back to the hotel. I was just grabbing some food and my phone rings and it's Rhys. 'Hi Rhys what are you doing?" I say. He tells me "I had a great chat with Simon he said I've got the bug for this Dad' 'Really' I say 'What are you doing then ? 'I'm staying Dad and I am going to marshal instead so that I can still be part of it and he tells me that as a Marshall, I can have discount off the next event'. I am buzzing about this. He's made such a positive move. I've met many people with all the gear and who talk the walk but can't walk the talk and my son isn't one of them. I couldn't be more pleased with his attitude. It's a proud moment.

The race goes reasonably well for me and as I approach the second to last checkpoint of the third Marathon, Rhys is there and we are coming down this steep incline where the checkpoint is. He is looking right at me and says 'Dad are you cheating?' 'Cheating?' I repeat. He says 'I've had ultra runners coming through here saying to me that my dad looks too fucking fresh and that he's getting taxis to the last mile' "No" I said "I'm not cheating but I'm doing a 200 miler in 6 months time from Southport to Hornsea so if I can't get to the last checkpoint in this marathon on the third day and be fresh enough to run back if I wanted to, then I am not going to be ready for the 200 miler mentally am I?" Then, before I know it, there's the finishing line in a place I think is called Lulworth Cove. I'm not even out of breath. I've done three marathons in three days and I am fine. I now know that I can step up to tackle the GB Ultra 200 mile cross country race from Southport to Hull – bring it on.

The GB Ultra 6 months later in August 2017 was not just my first GB Ultra and my first 200 mile event . It was to provide me with one of the most pivotal moments of my life outside of my marriage and having children and I guess the crash. It was a two hundred mile foot race across the width of the country from Southport to Hornsea, famous for its pottery, near Hull. It was a 6.00am start so I travelled by train to Southport planning to stay in digs the night before. There was a cock up immediately. When I got to the digs they wouldn't accept cash (sign of the times) so I was stuck as I didn't have a bank card. Luckily I sorted it as I rang Jourdana my daughter and she paid it over the phone using her card and I just gave her the cash when I got home. It sounds straightforward enough but when you are about to go into an extreme distance race you are already on edge and don't need any hassle and this mix up stressed me out for a while.

I went for a walk to clear my head and got back to my room for about 10.00pm to try and get my head down. They had given me a room at the front of the hotel which during the day looked fine but now at night I could see that my room was directly below the floodlights that lit the name of the hotel on the front. It was like there were spotlights into my room. Not only that but there was a fucking disco on that night in the room directly below mine. No matter what I did to try and keep the light out and the sounds, it was like there was a disco in my room.

I don't know how much sleep I did get but it was very little because I got up at 4.00am and of course that was too early to get any breakfast. They were just not up yet. I remained upbeat about the race and eventually made my way to the promenade where the race was to start. There were about 100 or so people competing and there was me; No food, lack of sleep - Not the greatest of starts to a 200 mile run.

So off we go and I start the race quite well considering the bad preparation. After about 20 miles I went past a black girl called Loveness who was already walking. As I passed her I noticed she had a GB Ultra top on. At the time nothing registered with me and certainly not that she was an experienced GB ultra runner. A short distance later I started to ask myself 'what am I doing here? I've got 200 miles to run and I'm running off here like it's a short distance. I stopped and went for a pee in some bushes and as I came out again there was Loveness again. This time I could see her tee shirt clearly. '200 Mile Ultra elite athlete'. She was still walking and knew exactly what she was doing. I said to her ' Do you mind if I tag along with you it's my first ultra?' She had no problem with that thankfully as I really needed the coaching. Leading up to that race I had completed various Ultra events but in this race, the first 80 miles has to be completed in under 24 hours. We ran into the night through Liverpool and Warrington over to the Greater Manchester area through (name some places) and I was picking up information from her all the time. She had a GPS with her otherwise I would have definitely been lost by now. We were both carrying drinks and snacks for energy like fig rolls and energy bars. I realised then that I could also help her because at times her head was in bits too and we encouraged each other. We reached a checkpoint at around 60 miles and as we got in Loveness was at a low and she told me that she was on her way back from a stress fracture of her hip. I was shocked. 'Are you for real?' I said. She'd just run 60 miles after just recovering from a stress fracture of the hip. She told me that she was trying to find out now if her hip could handle it. We had 21 miles to go to complete the first stage and she's calculated that we are not going to make the cut off time and very quickly decided that she's pulling out. I think to myself well if she's pulling out then so am I. We were in this room at the checkpoint and Loveness says to one of the race organisers, Wayne Drinkwater, that she's pulling out and I said immediately, so am I. I told him that I was stressed and it hadn't gone right for me. Wayne said 'look, don't worry about it. I'll give you extra time you need to get food in you and get going to the 81 mile checkpoint. It took a lot of pressure off us. I was going through a mental bad patch and I'm only just starting to understand these things. Another competitor then walks in and throws his gear down on the table and says 'I can't deal with this anymore'. Wayne then takes his tracker off him. I'm thinking, Wayne's going to say the same thing to him now. But he doesn't. He just pulls his gear off him and then looks at me and Loveness and says ' Are you right you two?' and we just jump up and say 'Yes' straightaway and off we go through the night. We ran through Stockport town centre in the middle of the night when only taxi drivers and drunks are on the roads. We've got these head torches on and a few miles after the town centre we're going through some woods. This young lad comes out of nowhere right into our path and stops up in our tracks. He is totally spaced out and takes one look at us and say 'wow man - I thought you were fucking Daleks'. 'No mate' I say. 'We are runners'. The lad looks like he is high on drugs and he asks 'Where you running to then?' 'Hull' I say. He has an expression on his face like we've asked him a very hard question and he says "Hull?' Now bearing in mind we are still in Stockport he then says ' You're running to Hull mate?. I work in Hull. Do you know that it's a long way?' He was looking at us as if we were mad. "Yeah I believe so" I say. He comes back with " do you not know you can take magic mushrooms and experience this without running. I'd give it a whirl" Here's this guy on a path to nowhere as far as we can see, advising has that we are mad and should try magic mushrooms! 'I need to shake your hand mate' he says 'I'm impressed. 'I've just been to Tescos but they're shut'. It was 3am in the morning and we just thought he was off his head on something but when we'd said bye to him and run on we came to a Tesco at the end of the path and it looked like he was telling the truth as it wasn't a 24 hour store and was shut.

The next thing I know, Loveness is on her mobile talking to her boyfriend. She turns to me and asks if I want a coffee. She is obviously giving her boyfriend an order and he is going to meet us somewhere. It's now 3.30am and I haven't a clue where we are. 'Yes' I say and she tells her boyfriend to make that two coffees. He boyfriend turns up in his car with two take away costa coffees. I had some biscuits in my rucksack so we are stood in the middle of nowhere drinking coffee and eating biscuits. The sounds in the early hours even in a large park or in the middle of nowhere are totally different to anything during the day. That sounds obvious but you have to experience it to understand it. For instance, the middle of Heaton Park empty at 2am sounds totally different than empty at 2pm. No birds chirping, total silence with the odd sound. I am drinking my coffee and eating my biscuits and can only hear the crunching of the biscuits in my mouth when suddenly feel a wet kiss on the back of my neck. I absolutely shit myself. What the fuck is happening? I turned around and it was a horse. A horse had crept up on us in the middle of nowhere in the dark and first thing it thought to do was to give me a big fat wet kiss on the back of my neck. I'm guessing that it smelled the coffee and biscuits and crept over but it made me jump a mile. It was the last thing I was expecting but it woke me up for the rest of the race stage I can tell you.

We knew we were not far short of the next checkpoint and found ourselves running through some woods. It's August 2017 and I'm about eighty miles into my first British Ultra event which is a two hundred mile cross country foot race from Southport to Hornsea near Hull. I have been running for the last fifteen miles with one of my fellow competitors who I knew only by her unusual first name 'Loveness'. It was her first ultra event after coming back from experiencing a stress fracture of her hip and I was supporting her through some of it. It's what Ultra competitors do. You are as interested in getting others through it as you are getting yourself to the finish line, or in this case the next checkpoint. Running in a GB Ultra is as much about following map readings as it is about the physical challenge because you're not going to achieve anything running the wrong way or an extra twenty miles for no reason other than you've read your map wrong. These events have deadlines for every checkpoint and if you don't make the deadline, then forget it. You can compete in the event and get a tee shirt if you want one with 'GB Ultra 200' on the front. You'll even get the tee shirt for participating, no matter whether you finish or not or you reach the checkpoints within the time limit. If you are a true ultra runner though, you want the GB Ultra Belt Buckle. To be awarded with one of these, you need to reach the checkpoints by certain times and the finish line by the maximum time allowed. I'm getting that buckle and, if have anything to do with it, so is Loveness. Suddenly my phone goes and it was one of the marshals. "Right, where are you now?' he said. I tell him roughly where we are and he said 'Oh right I can see you.' I thought he may be able to see the head torches we each have to wear because large sections of this type of event take place at night across some difficult terrain. What he is actually looking at is us on his laptop as we are all carrying a GPS Tracker attached to our rucksacks. That didn't quite click with me at the time though because I still couldn't see him or the checkpoint. He instructed us to keep going on the path we were on until we get to a main road and then turn left. He said that their Marshall's station, was a short distance down that road. We get to the main road that he had described and as we turn left, suddenly, this incredibly overwhelming feeling comes over me. Sometimes in Ultra Races a lack of sleep can give you hallucinations and strange experiences so initially I put it down to that but the feeling remained and as we made our way towards the Marshal's station, the feeling was getting stronger and it had started to dominate my thinking. It was similar to the feeling you get when you experience Deja vu but the thought was so overpowering and I said out loud 'I've been here before'. I'm confused because its early hours of the morning and I don't even know where I am so how can I say I have been here before but the feeling is getting stronger. We walk towards a bend in the road and Loveness can see something is wrong. 'What's up?' she says but I'm not really listening to her so I don't answer. We walk around the bend and I'm looking down a dip in the road and there in the dip is a bridge and above it in the background I can see a GB Ultra flag. I should be excited to see the flag as it is clearly our marker for the eighty one mile checkpoint which means much needed rest and something to eat and drink but I can't take my eyes of the bridge as I go towards it. "I know this place". The bridge is made of steel amongst other materials but as I near it, strangely, I can see it in my memory as a brick bridge. I look over the bridge and there's a drop down to a railway line and I suddenly realise where I am 'Fuck off' I say out loud and then I spot the road sign 'Mottram Hall Road'. 'Fuck Off' I say again. 'What is it?' says Loveness, who by this time is beginning to get freaked out by the way I am behaving. I finally answer her "It's a long story" I said "but I died here on this bridge in 1980!".

Loveness must have thought I was having an episode and that I needed food and a drink and some sleep because we didn't discuss it beyond that point. Things were racing in my mind about what had just happened and I guess it was that experience of being back on the bridge that made me want to write about my life and tell my story to others. I had come such a long way since the day of the crash but I felt that I had come a lot further mentally too and people need to know that it can be done and that whatever the physical injuries and whatever the mental challenges they can be overcome.

Eventually I snap myself out of this eerie feeling around the crash site and we go to check in and get food down the road at this cafeteria. Within another twenty minutes or so, we leave to run through Glossop to Penistone which is 103 miles into the event and where our sleeping bag is. Before we left I took my sandwich outside and sat on a bench now looking up at the bridge that changed my life. The accident was 36 years ago and my life could have easily ended at that point and yet here I was running a 200 mile Ultra race past the same point. It freaked me out a little. I had a flashback to a moment when I bumped into the Ambulance crew who attended the scene of the accident. They passed me in the hospital after I had recovered and the first thing they said to me was 'Fucking 'ell - your alive!' They told me how they had dragged me out of the car as my legs were stuck and they had been concerned about damaging my legs but I was losing a lot of blood so they felt they had to get me out of there. How ironic that they were worried about my legs as since then they had literally run thousands of miles in training and races and they hadn't let me down yet. Now I was an Ultra runner and I wished I could go back and tell those ambulance guys what I had achieved.

Thirty six years ago I had left this scene unconscious and fighting for my life. Now I was sat in silence looking up at the bridge. I literally died up there I thought to myself. I knew then I wanted to write about my life and how grateful I was for the achievements I had made since a night where I was given little hope of surviving by the ambulance crew. What I couldn't comprehend for the moment was how I had been brought back to the scene by this race and what that meant. I since figured out that it was a reminder of how lucky I had been to survive and what an eventful life I had since. I knew then that needed to write about it before I forgot most of what had happened to me in life.

My fitness as a young lad had played a major part in my survival back in 1979. Medical science wasn't what it is now and things would have been touch and go for me in terms of survival but I was strong. Adrian was in a bit of mess too but he had escaped the major injuries I had suffered. I was told that my cousin, Stephen, Adrian's brother, had said to the staff at the hospital that I was young and fit and didn't smoke or drink and that I was a fighter and to give me a chance. They did do and I proved Stephen right. I am sure that my fitness got me through it. I was besotted with martial arts at the time and trained seven days per week. I was a fit as a fiddle. They operated on me and saved my life and I am grateful that they did.

Back in the race in 2015, I've got to get going again both physically and mentally. It's been an incredible half an hour or so and I've just reflected on 36 years of my life that may not have happened but now it was back to today and this race. We have to run the next leg which is from Mottram to Penistone to hit the hundred and three mile mark. Loveness and I headed out again with two other girls (Helen and Ann) who also appeared to be experience long distance runners. After a while I was getting frustrated with the pace. They were going too slow. I ended up building up my pace and leaving them and heading out on my 'Jack Jones'. This meant that I was without a GPS system but I had some vague directions from Loveness about how we were to negotiate the rest of the stage and I knew that we had to cross a lake and then run across the Pennines to Penistone. I got to the point where I've negotiated the lake and I know that I need go east but when I spot a young couple I decided to ask to make sure. " How do I get to Penistone' I say. They directed me to a path that seemed to go west. I thank them but I'm not happy with the direction they are sending me but I've been up for 25 hours now so I accept that it might be me that's confused and I continue.

I climb a hill and when I hit the top I stop. Now which way? I'm convinced they've sent me in the wrong direction. I end up running all the way back to where I met the couple which must have been (x miles). They are still there so I say to them "Sorry to bother again but I'm trying to get to Penistone. Now the lad is starting to get a little pissed off with me. I say to him " I need to be heading east and you sent me west'. I was shocked but relieved when he says ' I know where Penistone is. I work there. I go there every day!' Just as he told me this I see an Ultra runner coming towards me called Adie. As he passes he shouts ' Chris it's that way" pointing down the hill. He is running in a different direction to the checkpoint before heading out the way that he had just shown me. I end up at the end of one path with three paths to choose from. I get a compass out and it's going against everything in front of me and what my head is saying. I've always been good directionally but all the common sense is saying that I should climb and my compass is saying I should continue downhill. It's throwing me off as the compass never lies and I start to think my brain is playing tricks on me. I decide to follow the compass. It takes me down the hill but then the road starts to wind and eventually directionally we are running in the right direction. Running back down hill my legs started to give way as my shins are a mess. So I had to traverse to stop the pain in my shins.

I eventually get to the bottom off the descent from the Pennines and there I see a partner of one of the girls. He directs me into the right path towards the checkpoint and my sleeping bag. I see an ultra flag marking the direction. I follow it and then beyond it I have tried at least two buildings to see if they are the checkpoint and after going a mile too far I then realise it was the building with the Ultra Flag on itself - Penistone Hall. It cost me another 2 miles and I thought all the others would now have beaten me back but no they hadn't. I walked into Penistone Hall and saw I was still ahead of them which lifted me tremendously.

A girl called Gemma looked after me at the checkpoint. She was an ex forces Marshall and for the ultra runners the canteen had food and drink laid out on a table. I was asked what I wanted and I said 'a pint of Guinness please'. Gemma told me as it was a Church hall they couldn't sell alcohol so she asked again and I said pint of Guinness please and she tipped me off that there was Spar around the back. I told them to put some pork pies aside for me and some canelloni and that I would be back. The Spar was open and I bought two tins of Guinness. I drank my Guinness and ate my food and then got my head down. When I awoke I was again disorientated. I thought I was homeless from Manchester then I realised I was in a race and heard people moving about so I got up and got ready. Gemma came in to wake me but I was already nearly ready. She said to me 'Chris you look fresher than anyone this morning and you're the only one that's had alcohol. As it was the Guinness just took the edge off for me. It had been a very eventful day and I was clearly stressed with it but the two tins had taken that edge off and relaxed me. It also gave me a few calories that I needed to crack on to the next stage.

Neil Rutherford, a fantastic Scottish ultra athlete , won the first Ultra race that I took part in, Southport to Hornsea, in about 47 hours. In an Ultra, participants always want to either win the race or win their age group , which was always my intention on entering a race. Everybody is awarded a metal GB Ultra belt buckle with the details of the race on. When I say everybody, I only mean everybody that completes the race in the allotted time. The allotted time in the race from Southport to Hornsea was 100 hours. So basically you have to complete the course in under 100 hours to earn the belt buckle. All those that don't complete in under 100 hours just get a tee shirt with the race details on proving they have been in the race. I don't enter just to get a tee shirt.

After about 170 miles, I hit a checkpoint and I'd caught up with a guy I eventually got to know very well called Joe Wood who was an army PT Instructor. He'd gone at the first 50 miles too quickly and he'd fucked his shins up badly. Shin splints can be really painful to say the least and once the pain starts getting worse the only thing that's going to help that pain is rest and ice. When I'd caught him up he looked very pale. He was in terrible pain with them. I couldn't eye ball him because I felt nothing but sympathy for his situation and initially I was worried for him. Here he was having run 170 miles and it might be the end of the race for him and he didn't look well to me. A marshal was looking after Joe and said to him "do you want to tag along with Chris? Come on I want you to go with Chris'. I knew that he wanted me to act like a pacemaker for Joe and if there was any chance he was going to finish this race it was being with someone else to drive him on. I was half decent and would have liked to have cracked on and get the best time I could but this was my first ultra so I was happy to go with the flow. The Marshal ran with us to start with and then he left us to get on with it and we did the next 10 miles to Hull together. It was a real struggle but he was doing it. This was really pushing new boundaries for both of us. He was running through excruciating pain and I was running my first ultra and having to hold back for him and get him through it. It was hard but pushing these boundaries is what life was all about for me. Dealing with the highs is easy. It's how you handle the lows that defines you.

We reached the checkpoint at Hull under the Humber Bridge. We had time for a quick nap and Gemma, who was a marshal and ex-army, tells us to get in the parked car just to rest up. I feel I could run on but Joe needs sleep and just to grab a short amount of sleep for an hour, which we can afford to do and still meet the time, is going to be very helpful. We get in the car and my legs are all over the place because there's no room. Joe has managed to stretch his legs out because he's a lot smaller. I didn't realise how cold it was and I am drifting in and out of consciousness. Eventually after the 60 minutes Gemma came back to the vehicle to tell us that time was up. We got out of car and ate a sandwich and drank a bottle of water. I can't believe how fresh I feel. I was keen to get going and said 'We will smash this'. Joe said ' You might but I won't' His legs were bad. Despite how he felt we set off again.

As I'm running with Joe wood (well walking because he is such a bad state) he says to me out the blue 'Chris, do you want a coffee?' I looked around and think 'Where's the costa coffee?' I'm starting to think that he's now hallucinating but then I realise that he's got his headphones in and he's on his phone. Again, I go with flow 'Yeah Ok'. A short while later, as we are going along a path I see in the distance a bloke and a woman looking at us. As we get in closer, its Neil Rutherford, the race winner. Neil bear hugs Joe as they are good pals. He's with Joe's wife and they have parked on a dirt track road and were waiting for us with coffee and Chocolate Chip Cookies. It's then that Joe and I find out that Neil has won the race in a time of 47 hours. I said to Neil 'Wow - I'm Impressed mate'. I'm at 190 miles now with about 10 miles to go. Neil turned to me and said 'No Chris - I'm impressed with you. One hundred started this race but only 42 can now finish it and you and Joe are going to be two of them. That meant 58 have already dropped out or not made the cut off times. By this time Joe was losing it a little. He was convinced that he'd rung his wife to say that he was pulling out and she said he hadn't rang her!

So here we were having completed just short of 190 miles and a bit fucked up physically and mentally, drinking coffee and eating biscuits to try and get a sugar rush that would see us across this next 10 miles to the finish. The biscuits didn't last long though, we hadn't set off yet and my energy levels weren't high enough. I talked with Neil for a few moments about energy and diet and it was this conversation that inspired me to look into being a vegan. I was still a little concerned about my low energy level for this last part of the race and Neil came over to me and said "here you are Chris". And he hands me a bag of Cashew nuts baked in Marmite. I started to put the nuts in my mouth and I went 'Wow what's happening here?' It was like somebody injecting fuel into my body, but it stayed there, the sugar rush didn't drop. Neil starts laughing and says come on you've only got 10 miles to go and as we readied to set off he said 'you owe me a bag of nuts'

We set off again to tackle the last section and Joe started to fall behind me. I'm getting such a rush of energy from the marmite nuts that I'm now holding myself back. I'm not even thinking about the clock. The more I pop these nuts in my mouth the more I needed to run and Joe was just walking. I think to myself, hang on a minute, Joe is a PT Instructor and current forces, he's tough enough to do this and I need to crack on and clock the best time I can but I'm not leaving him. I walk back to Joe and I say to him put your head phones on and shut the fuck up and let's finish this race. And that's exactly what we do. We plough on and complete the race together in under the required 100 hours. We joked as we neared the finish line as to who would cross it first but as we had been through the hardest sections together we crossed the line together. I'd love to tell you exactly how long it took us to finish but that's not what is in your mind when you get through the finish line all you want to know is whether you've made the cut off time, the actual time didn't matter to me at all. Then my next priority was whether Joe finished within the allotted time. He had done and it became a very emotional moment for us both. The sense of achievement was incredible. It was hard but I expected a lot harder. Wayne Drinkwater said to me "what next?" I said "The Marathon Des Sables". The Marathon Des Sables is a real step up. It's a six marathon race of 156 miles across 7 days in the Sahara desert. It had recently come into my sights and was fast becoming a driving ambition of mine but it costs over £4,000 to enter. I'll explain more about this shortly and I dedicate a chapter (26) to it. Wayne said "It's a lot of money to pay just to participate". I was taken aback at him saying that but he suggested doing the Scottish Ultra 200 miler first. I reluctantly agreed with him and entered the race which was Stranraer to Cocksburn near Edinburgh.

At the end of the race, one of the leaders was a Navy Seal from Washington called Trevor. I saw a Paramedic take a tick out of his ankle that he didn't even know was there. He'd presumed he'd been bitten or something as his ankle was red and swollen but the Paramedic pointed out clearly that it had the markings of a tick in that it looked like a bullseye on his ankle. The Paramedic cut into the ankle and took the tick out by turning it anti clockwise because, he told us, ticks go in too your body and lock themselves in by spinning clockwise into the person's body. This little creature, if not treated properly, could have ended up costing Trevor a severe infection and worst case scenario, costing him his leg.

My first 200 Mile GB Ultra completed and I wasn't sure what I expected to feel like but I was surprised I felt so good. In fact I felt great. I'd kept a room booked in Southport with some of my gear in as a sort of insurance if it didn't go well so Wayne Drinkwater said he'd give me a lift back there. He was also surprised at how well I was feeling. He kept asking me "Are you alright Chris" I was so chilled about the whole thing it was slightly concerning. Thoughts of the event quickly turned to getting back to Southport alive as I realised that Wayne was also a human being and had gone without much sleep over the whole event as he was a marshal. He also kept re-assuring me that he was alright and I plied him with Red Bull and Coffee but it was clear that he desperately needed sleep. It was quite comical really, two blokes in a car saying to each other "Are you alright?" "Yeah are you alright?" "Yeah I'm alright are you sure you're alright?". Eventually I persuaded Wayne to pull into some services and get some rest as he was so close to nodding off at the wheel. I told him that I didn't want him on my conscience after he dropped me off. He agreed and I went into the services while he had a nap. He said "Just give me half an hour". I left it two hours and went back to the car and he was totally out for the count, head back mouth open. I left him to sleep for a while longer and then went back and got into the car. He woke and said " Alright Chris? How long was I asleep? ten minutes – something like that?"

The Marshalls do such a great job and go through the same sort of sleep deprivation as the participants of the race.

A few weeks after completing the Southport to Hornsea event, I was in the bath. It was a Wednesday. Work had been quiet all day so I had no bouncing off any customers. My legs were still confused so I was sat in a cold bath to help the healing process. All of a sudden I start crying my eyes out sobbing and feel suicidal. I snapped myself out of it immediately. 'You dickhead' I said to myself. 'You've just done the GB ultra with about 11 hours kip in 4 days and you are still recovering. Go and get yourself another beer and get back in the bath. I ended up laughing my head off. I had gone from a massive high to massive low and then sorted my head out all in the space of a few minutes. I was learning from all this experience of competing at a high level and therefore the massive lows afterwards would be something I'd have to deal with whether I liked it or not.

My next GB Ultra Event was an even bigger challenge and provided me with further evidence that when competing in extreme events, there would potentially be extreme highs and lows. I had signed up and trained hard to run the Scottish Ultra which was a 212 miles run across the width of Scotland from one coast to another. The race started on the west coast at Fort Patrick close to Stranraer and would involve 25,000 feet of climbing across the entire run over to Cocksburn path, just south of Edinburgh on the east coast.

After the first seventy miles I had developed two medical issues. One of them I thought to be nothing but should have been the reason for me pulling out. At the seventy mile checkpoint I was struggling with an ankle injury that when I looked at it made me say out loud to myself 'this is not good" as it was badly swollen after I had gone over on it on the rough terrain and caused me to hit the ground. The other injury was that I had some cuts to my knee from the fall which I thought were minor. The organisers of an ultra race are top notch and extremely experienced in relation to assessing the welfare of runners and making tough and sometimes unpopular decisions about pulling people out of races. The brave thing to do was to take the pressure off the marshals and withdraw from the race yourself. My ankle looked a mess and at 70 miles in a 200 mile event, it was only going to get worse. So I made the decision and pulled out. Later, one of the Marshalls said to me "You do realise Chris don't you, that if you had not made the decision yourself, we would have had to do it for you?" I told him that I agreed with him because my ankle was in such a mess. He told me that it wasn't my ankle that he was referring to. It was the cuts to my knee they were concerned about. You see, when you are running these kind of distances and you are pushing your body to absolute limits, your immune system may not be able to deal with quite simple cuts and there is a risk of infection and at worst septicemia. It was for that reason that they would have pulled me out. I'm glad they didn't tell me that at the time because the competitor in me may have objected and lost sight of the risk of both injuries.

When you pull out of an Ultra race through injury and there is no need for you to go to hospital, your experience can still be very useful to the race and your fellow competitors and you are quickly recruited to be a race marshal. I was immediately sent to the next Checkpoint at the 150 mile point by car. When I got there I thought that there would be plenty of time before the ultra runners would hit the 150 mile mark so I decided to grab some sleep in a hut that had been set aside for the marshals. Some of them were already in there grabbing some kip. Have you ever woken up in a strange place and had those split seconds between asleep and awake where a bit of panic sets in? Well add to that, that when you have just run 70 miles you are also at risk of hallucinating because of the way you have pushed your body. I awoke to partial darkness and was convinced I was dead and in a temporary morgue with other dead bodies. I was absolutely convinced that I had been killed in a terrorist attack and that I had been left for dead with these dead bodies. As it was, the dead bodies were sleeping athletes and a few seconds after I awoke it all started to fit together. I told this story to an experienced ultra runner and he said to me ' you've had a stage one experience - hallucinations - wait until you hit the second stage of the mental challenges of an ultra runner'. That intrigued me. What could be weirder than thinking you are dead and in a morgue? I met Neil Rutherford again. He had been winning that race too but had pulled himself out with injury. I met him at the checkpoint I was Marshalling and he said to me " Chris - you've done the right thing by pulling out of the race. You have to override your ego when you have a serious injury and live to fight another day" He was right, I didn't want to pull out after 70 mile because I felt great but my ankle was a mess so it was definitely the sensible thing to do. I took the opportunity on seeing Neil again to hand him a bag of marmite soaked cashew nuts from my bag and say 'anyway here's your nuts back'. He laughed and said thanks. Bizarrely another memory that sticks in my mind was that as I arrived at that same checkpoint, I saw two paramedics leant against their ambulance smoking. I remember thinking how odd it was that someone in that occupation, saving lives daily, could contemplate smoking. Then I thought that maybe they've seen enough about sudden death to realise that you may as well live your life as you want to.

Chapter 23 - Will The Real Iron Man Please Stand Up!

I am very keen to get across in this book that I do not write about these things in an attempt to make people say 'wow – look at what Chris Duoba has done. Isn't he amazing?'. That's the furthest thing from my mind and quite frankly if anyone thinks that this was my aim then put the book down and go and read about someone else because if you are not getting me at all by now, then I'm not sure you're going to get me by the end of the book. I am talking about my life story for two main reasons.

Firstly and most importantly if this book inspires just one person not to give up on their life at their lowest point and give it a shot at living on and take that chance, then that will be enough. It doesn't matter if you then go on to be the Prime Minister or an Olympic Athlete or a Hollywood star. Yeah that's great and it helps sell a book and get peoples' attention and there's nothing wrong with that at all. I take my hat off to those people who then go on to achieve greatness but everyone needs to know that it's that first step back from walking out onto the road in front of a truck that's the heroic act. The courageous act is to make the decision to go on and not give up and I want this book to try and get that message across. I came so close in 1980 and yet something pulled me back. Whatever it was, It gave me my marriage, it gave me my four children, it gave me owning my own business and it gave me my drive to be fit and compete in these wonderful events around the world and meet some wonderful people. Despite me cocking up some of those things, I am grateful for all of it and want to pay that forward to at least one person and hopefully many more.

Secondly I wanted to get some positive messages out to my mum, my siblings, my ex-wife, my children and my wider family about how much they all mean to me. A man born in 1960 and living through the macho years of growing up might not be able to articulate just how much he feels love and appreciation for his family. I am so grateful that this book has given me a platform to do that and it has been a huge release and very emotional experience to get some things off my chest that rightly or wrongly, I may not have had the opportunity or the know how to do without this book.

Those are the two main reasons but I do also want to say a little about who inspired me through my life. I always loved my Dad. Everyone should have a father that they look up to and I did. He was hard working and always provided for his family as we grew up and I hope I did the same for my family when they were young. My grandfather Walter was also inspirational to me. It seemed to me growing up that he was as strong as an ox but he also had great wisdom and simplified his advice for me and he was always right. He was right about becoming a barber and that it could be the making of me when I had doubts. But my main source of inspiration was my Uncle Joe Ross. He was a genuine Iron Man to me in so many ways. A great athlete and sports man and yet never wanted recognition or fuss. He would run a million miles away from a medals ceremony or the award of a cup and yet he won so much. He served in the Merchant Navy and was well respected by his colleagues and friends, He was a man's man but never one to boast about his capabilities. On leaving the service of the Merchant Navy he joined the Mounted section of the Police in the Greater Manchester Police force at their Hough End headquarters on Princess Parkway in South Manchester. He was one of their most respected officers and they have photos of him at exhibitions and he won some awards whilst serving there. He never brought those awards home though because he didn't like the fuss so none of us have seen them. We only know about them through third parties. I recently took a trip down there to ask about him but the COVID pandemic makes it difficult to speak to people directly and they already have a busy job but I actually met a former colleague of Joe's who must have only been a young man when they worked together. He told us that there is a famous photo of Joe on the back of a police horse in full uniform and with a police woman sat on his shoulders. It sounds like an incredible picture taken from an exhibition to the public. When I think of his life of service in the Merchant Navy, joining the police force, being an athlete but disliking any accolades and awards, I think that there was something in both of our genes that connected us. In my life I skirted close to all of those things in some way but clearly was more fortunate in some more than others. He was someone who I looked up to and still do in his memory as a person I would have liked to emulate.

My Grandad told me that Joe was so good at athletics that he had the chance to compete for selection for the Olympics in a track event but refused to attend. He hated the limelight but he was competitive so the last thing he wanted was to end up qualifying for and competing at the Olympics in the spotlight where he would want to win but not take the podium . I'm told that he used to win competitions all the time but never turn up for the prize giving. His mates or other members of the family used to pick up the trophies for him. He just wanted to compete and wasn't in the slightest bit interested in the prizes. His dad, my granddad, Walter Ross, was gutted that Joe didn't want to follow the path to the Olympics though. It's sounds so much that my competitive genes came from this Ross side of the family because I identify so strongly with all of this. The drive to compete but not for the spoils. Purely for the competition itself.

Joe took on challenges at work too. He was at the pinnacle of his career as a mounted policeman when he took on responsibility for a horse that everyone else had given up on. The horse was unruly and unpredictable. The force saw it as a liability and decided to remove it from the mounted police section as the horses with them were fantastically disciplined and did not react to loud noises or sudden movements, otherwise they would never be able to operate in crowds like at football matches.

Joe saw the horse as a challenge and asked for time to work with it. He was making great progress with the horse when one day as he led it into the stables and into its own particular unit within the stables, the horse went crazy and was bucking and kicking out. Joe was kicked several times and was badly injured. Initially, it was thought that Joe may never walk again but he, like me, didn't accept the prognosis given to him and he recovered. Unfortunately, he didn't recover well enough to return to work and so he was forced into retirement and he and his wife, Jane, left their home in Walkden and went to live in Southport.

After a short time, Joe got into a way of living in Southport and used to borrow a small fishing boat and spend a lot of time out at sea, fishing. One day he went out fishing alone which was not the safe thing to do. He cast the nets over the side alone and it would have been a hugely difficult job. When he threw the last of it into the water, his foot had been caught up in the net and the weight of the nets took Joe over with them. He was found drowned when the search party went out looking for him. The news spread quickly amongst family and his colleagues as he was a popular character. Only one week ago, an officer asked me what had happened to Joe as he had heard that he drowned.

I attended his funeral and it was a terribly sad time. After the funeral, Joes wife, my aunty Jane, came and had a chat with me and at the end of the chat she said to me "You'll never see me again" before I could ask her what she meant she had started talking to someone else. I never did find out why she said that to me but sure enough I have never seen her again. I'd love to find her and catch up with her to talk about mine and Joe's similarities. They had two children both from Jane's first marriage , Steven and Graham, and they loved Joe like he was their own dad. If I could catch up with them before we all pop our clogs I'd love it.

I did manage to have a couple of nights out with Steven when he was older and had his own place. I remember being impressed that his home had underfloor heating and a car that everyone used to talk about back in the day, a TR7, which was a flash car to say the least. Unfortunately though we lost touch and I've never been big on social media so it is so easy to drift away from those who I would still consider close relatives.

Chapter 24 – Anorexia is for Models isn't it?

The only person on the planet who I allow to push my buttons without risk to their health is Philomena. Anybody else would be brown bread. The times I have walked away from an argument with Mena, got pissed out of my head and then gone back and apologised to her whether I was right or wrong. Mena could give as good as she got and we were both strong characters. She had to be tough to put up with me for so long. I remember when she worked at Ungars, she had a supervisory role and was known for her tough approach but she was still very popular with her work mates. It's tough to get a balanced approach like that but Mena managed it.

Mena and I simply grew apart. To both of us, getting divorced seemed the right thing to do from many aspects. In the end it was an amicable split and we agreed not to involve solicitors and conducted matters ourselves. There still needed to be grounds on the divorce papers and 'grown apart' didn't meet the kind of grounds required for a judge to grant a divorce so Phil went into more detail on the papers. She put down that I was isolating myself from her and getting drunk all the time. I didn't agree with that description as I thought I was just a hard working person who, when I got home at night, wanted to relax with a couple of beers and watch a film or whatever but I understood what she was saying and why she needed to say that, so I didn't contest it. The Divorce was completed in 2012. We agreed that she had the house and I moved into a flat owned by my mate, Jason, which was on Baguley Crescent less than a mile away from the shop. I couldn't have the flat above the shop as we had tenants in there who had 12 months left on their tenancy. We gave them 12 months' notice and Jason was good enough to fill the gap for me.

Divorcing from the love of your life is not going to be easy for anyone and although I thought I was handling it all very well mentally, combined with other things in the weeks and months following the divorce, it eventually took its toll on me. I didn't realise it at the time but I had become more obsessive about getting fit. To me I just thought that because I was living on my own and had more time to myself, I was now taking the training more seriously but even Philomena said to me 'More seriously?' as she knew better than anybody how obsessed I could become. 'You were serious before weren't you? she asked.

I was still of an attitude that my training had stepped up because being away from the family home meant that I now had more of an opportunity to train and prepare my own food. I was in the flat above the shop and I'd bought myself a serious bike for racing. Costing £4,500. I already had a bike for training, this was an all singing all dancing 'Boardman' racing bike. The cyclist, Chris Boardman, had developed bikes for less money than some of the bigger brands whose prices for similar kit might cost up to £7,000 or more for the same. This Boardman TT bike (TT meaning time trial) is a proper racing bike. Digitally Integrated gears meant that changing gear was accurate and slick at the touch of a button. The bike was aerodynamically designed to get maximum speed in different positions on the bike that had go faster solid wheels. It was a serious piece of kit that meant that I was able to step up my training and competitive edge even further. I had also virtually become vegan over a two year period leading up to the divorce but I was now more like a vegetarian. I had always been a healthy eater but now as I stepped my training up I had to structure it properly and introduce other things into my diet. If I was doing a run I'd make sure that I would have more vegetables and possibly mackerel because of its Omega three which assists in the repair of damaged tissue. Same for salmon and tuna. If I was having fish I would have lots of vegetables with it.   Similarly, if I was having potato, even chips, I would combine those with some other vegetables. I would never though, have fish and chips because it would create a chemical Imbalance in my digestive system and effect my recovery the day after an event. Instead of waking on the day after an event or extensive training, feeling energetic you would feel bloated and lethargic. It was also important to eat the right food for different kinds of activity. For instance, a long bike ride would need a high carb intake because that would give you the energy you need but the sensible thing would be getting the balance right. A perfect example of how getting the balance wrong once can affect you even when you are eating well for a long time, is the day I went to a barbecue at my friends, Jason and Beck's house. They are not veggies but they are like me in that they normally eat very healthily. Jason is a triathlete and operates at a very high level. We went through a good few beers and had a great night. Their food was top notch and Jason had made his own burgers, so they were really good quality. After a few beers, I'd shouted over to Jason 'Heh Jason where's my burger?'. He's shouted back 'Duoba – I don't know how to break this to you but you're a vegan' ' Not tonight I'm not' I shout back. We carry on drinking and I polish off two absolutely superb burgers accompanied by quite a few more beers. I wake the next morning with Beck's reaction to finding me fast asleep on the garden furniture under the canopy on their decking in the back garden. Apparently, I am the only guest who has not made it home and I'm guessing that Jason must have told me to crash out in the garden as it was a reasonably warm night and he must have just thrown a blanket over me. Becks had come down the next morning, not knowing anything about me sleeping over and got the shock of her life being faced with what she thought was a dead body. I jumped up shocked at her reaction and we all saw the funny side of it. They offer me a coffee which I gratefully accept and I start to plan how I am to get home. I'm in Norden near Rochdale and I have to get back to Blackley, North Manchester which is a 9 mile walk but I can still feel those burgers inside me and I feel heavy and bloated. Jason, being the guy he is, offers me a lift home but I need to get these burgers through my system so I decided to walk it. I felt too heavy to run so I didn't eat much breakfast as I knew I had enough fuel in me to burn off but not the sort of fuel you needed to be going fast. It probably took me between 2 and 3 hours to walk it back but it was well after I had arrived home that I felt clean again and that I'd managed to empty my stomach of the burgers. This was a great example of how the fuel from the night before would have affected my performance if I had been in a race the next day. I think I am very fit but someone who is unfit might take 48 hours to get rid of that lethargic feeling after a night drinking and over eating something like burgers. And that's when they are home-made and you know what is going into them! What it must be like for those eating poor quality food that isn't good for you, I don't even want to think about. Just after my divorce and while I was trying to get really fit, my friend, Brian Silk, had a small unit built into my shop where he could work as a masseur. Brian was also a triathlete and knew an awful lot about fitness and getting in shape. He also knew me very well and what I was about but he was the person who first brought my attention to my problem. He said to me one day "Chris you're doing too much. You're overdoing it'. He was basing his judgement on my appearance and lack of body fat. I look at him and say 'really?' He was right of course. I remember vividly one evening before Brian said that to me where I had to go upstairs to the flat to get my bike for training and I just glanced into the mirror at first and then turned and faced myself. I started to pinch my side and had a chunk of fat in my hand and I was saying to myself that I had to get rid of this fat. I'd convinced myself that I was still overweight and that what I had in my hand was fat but the reality of it was that it was only skin. There wasn't an ounce of fat on me. Mentally, I was getting really confused and yet the one thing I was clear on was that I needed to work harder in training. Even when going out for something to eat with family I thought I looked fat and that people were looking at me and saying how fat I was getting. I didn't want anyone to know that I was suffering inside and see how it was bothering me so I started to go to the toilet in places where we had something to eat and once I was in private I would made myself sick to prevent my body from gaining any more fat. In my mind at the time was that all I wanted was a lean body. I was driving myself crazy pursuing a lean body that I already had and the people that knew me best were noticing. Brian's comment made me think though and somehow instead of sinking further into an Anorexic state , I snapped myself out of it. I know that generally I am a mentally strong person and that it was the stress of the divorce and moving into a flat away from the family that had affected me at the time but I'm told that this is quite natural . Once I had forced myself out of it, looking in the mirror became very different and I started to see a guy in his mid-fifties and I could see his ribs and a six pack. If there was any excess fat on there I couldn't see it. I feel for the many people suffering like this in private and who carry on despite what people say and think but somehow I'd managed to snap out of it. There is no doubt in mind that I was fast becoming anorexic which could have had a devastating effect on me. Although I do agree with people, that I do have a self-destruct button, I also have an ability that once I am convinced of something, I can see it through like no one else to the extent where it might help me or hurt me in some way. I tell myself that It's never too late to introduce a change to your life and I have followed my instincts where that has been possible and it has worked for me for the last 40 years after the crash. Now, because of that experience, I manage things properly. Being an ultra-athlete is the same as being a boxer. You don't want or need to be at your fighting weight all year round but in the lead up to a fight you need to go to boot camp and get ready. It's the same with racing and you form your own bootcamp around your own needs. You need to peak your fitness for the events that you are in and above all if one of your close friends says you are looking good then you can be confident that you are doing something right. Equally if one of them says to you that things are not quite right then you listen to them and do something about it. They will only have your best interests at heart and you should only have the right people as friends anyway. The people I feel for are those that will face these mental dilemmas without their family or the right friends around them. We should all watch out for mental health issues amongst the people we love, the people we work with, the people we work for / customers and those people around us. Mental health is as big and dangerous a thing as physical illness or damage. You wouldn't let a man or woman drag themselves past you in the street with a broken leg and especially if it is someone you know or love – would you? Mental illness is harder to spot but just as damaging and the first bit of dialogue about that may be the most important stage of their recovery. For me it was Brian Silk who spoke up first and made me realise so I have him to be grateful for.

Chapter 25   Captain Fantastic - Making Up For Lost Time

London

On the week leading up to the 2019 London Marathon, I wasn't competing in the race but I was planning to run to London to watch it. The plan was that I would do Manchester to London along canal / tow paths of to test my ability to complete the 200 miles plus with minimal sleep and to go through the various stages of mental tests that this will put me through. I need to do this because the Marathon Des Sables will put me through a test like no other. A friend of ours was running in the London Marathon on Sunday 28th April as a result of an invite they had received and this was also an opportunity to go to London to cheer him on. It was this friend and others that had given me the burning desire to complete the Marathon Des Sables. Myself, Debbie Robinson, Jason Henson and Andy Preston who was an ex-marine, were sat around a table at Jason's wedding in June 2015. It might have been me, because I did know about it, who had first mentioned the Marathon Des Sables. As we sat around that table at the evening function of the wedding, we formed a pact that we would all do it together. Events have moved on since then and circumstances have changed. Jason had a hip operation in 2019 and can only now really run in up to 50K races before the hip would trouble him. Only 50 Kilometres? I know most people will say what do you mean 'only 50 Kilometres?', that's a distance that would be impossible for most people to run. Debbie is hugely successful in business and is an inspirational person who has held a number of high profile roles and is now the Chief Executive of Central England Co-operative. I'm absolutely certain that Debbie will still be running as she has set fantastic times in marathons in the past and it is a bit of bug to get out and run but Andy Preston and I are the only ones daft enough currently still planning to do it. Andy had entered and was about to do it but it was cancelled because of world events - I'm also fairly certain that I'm the only other one daft enough and still able to plan to do it.

I had two thoughts in my mind for 2020 onwards. Firstly I wanted to get my entry finally sorted for the MDS, and train in anticipation for the 2021 event. Secondly and more importantly, I wanted to try and spend more quality time with my four children. The second objective isn't as easy as it sounds because my kids are always busy with something. Then I had the idea to combine the two. Some of them had already said to me that they would like to go on some of my jaunts so I started to talk to them about what I was planning.

The first was to be with Arron and Rhys and was to run / walk to London to see our friend compete in the London Marathon. Initially I set my stall out to tackle it myself and try and run to London. This was perfect in more than one way for me. Not only would it give me the right kind of distance to tackle but it would enable me to see just where I was in terms of sleep deprivation and how it would affect me. That wasn't the only reason it was a perfect trip. When Arron and Rhys heard about what I was planning they insisted on coming with me because they didn't like the sound of sleep deprivation combined with running near canal tow paths on my Jack Jones. They insisted that they come with me for my safety. I'd not even thought of that so I was grateful. They were of course right; I would be running down a lot of tow paths at the side of canals and I didn't want to end up being found in a canal somewhere. So we agreed that the lads would come on their mountain bikes and marshal me and then when we got to London we would watch the marathon and get the train back to Manchester. They agreed and I was over the moon. It would be an opportunity for me to have a bonding session with Arron and Rhys together which excited me even more than the event itself.

Planning the route along canal tow paths can be done on line but it is based of course on being on a Narrow Boat, so the speeds and estimated timings are based entirely on that. According to the best planner I can find, the trip from Manchester to London could be as much as 240 miles and 185 locks and take over 7 days but that's Narrow Boat speed operating at 18 hours per day. We need to do it in four and a half days running and walking with the lads cycling in front assessing the route so we can take the best pathways and behind me watching my back. It was ambitious but we love a challenge.

My plan was on the first stage to do thirty plus hours with Arron and Rhys on bikes to push me along and support me. That required us going for a 6.00am start on Wednesday 24th April 2019 and running through to 1.00pm on the Thursday afternoon approximately 31 hours or maybe a bit longer. Then I would be telling them to go and get some proper food and rest and catch me up on the bikes after they have slept for a short time while I crack on. The plan will be for them to be back by my side for the night time so that they can keep an eye on me front and back with their headlamps so I don't take any wrong turns and fall in. I've warned them that I will be a different person as time goes on and not to spit their dummy out if I don't recognise them or I am a pain in the arse in any way. They can feed back to me later what I've said and done and how I have behaved and see for themselves what's going to happen to me while I have little or no sleep. I want to push myself through this by way of preparing for the Marathon Des Sables as running in that heat with probably limited sleep in the desert at night is going to test my mental approach considerably and the more that I can train to handle things when I get confused or fatigued, the better.

The cost of entering the MDS is four thousand seven hundred pounds which covers the whole thing, flights, hotels and medical support. After an Ultra event I had competed in, I had mentioned me planning to enter it and a friend of mine Wayne Drinkwater had said "It's a lot of money just to participate" I just don't believe you should enter anything without the intention of trying to win it whether that's far too ambitious or not. Once you have this mentality built in then it's the most natural thing to enter any race to win it and never think more of it, even when you don't. I can liken it to a customer of mine that's a Man City fan and has been for a long time. During the bad days for City in the nineties they took a real drop and could have been in big trouble. My customer told me that he and his son were watching Middlesbrough and Man City on Sky at Middlesbrough's ground. Middlesbrough scored after only a few minutes and my customer said 'Right , that's it, it's going to be about 5 nil now!' and his lad who is about 9 years old turns round to his dad and says "It can't be 5 nil now Dad, they've scored so it can only be 5-1. It's that kind of belief that keeps people pursuing things in sport. Despite any setback, there has to be a determination to succeed and a belief that you can succeed.

So the run to London is going to be a great test of whether I can do that kind of distance with little sleep and also give me the benefit of experiencing the various psychological effects sleep deprivation is going to have on me so I can prepare myself properly both physically and mentally. I've been in too many races where people around me have looked very capable physically and then disappeared out of the race. I've found out later that they have hit mental barriers that have prevented them continuing. That's not going to happen to me in the Marathon Des Sables.

When you tell people you are going to run in The Marathon Des Sable at 60+, the people who don't know the sport and the event look at you as if you are crazy. Those that do know the sport and the event look at you as if you are a raving lunatic. The race is unforgiving to say the least. It's the sort of race that will destroy you if you're not ready for it. I stopped listening to some of the comments that come back at me when I tell people that I'll be running it in the near future. They look at me knowing my age and they say 'what about the heat?' or 'what about speaking to someone who has already run it?' I say bollocks to that. Do they really think I would enter a race like that without knowing all about it? So it's hot! So fucking what!! I'll get a tan!! People may doubt what I say but I am 110% clear that I am not entering this race just to participate. I am not entering this race just to complete it and I am not entering this race to win my age group. I am entering The Marathon Des Sable to win it. Aiming for anything less is just not acceptable to me.

On Tuesday 23rd April, the day before the start of the run, I went across to see them at the family house on Mainway in Middleton. As I've said earlier, Philomena and I are divorced but get along well and I just wanted to nip round and get the message across to them that the sleep deprivation may make me behave differently and even badly towards them and that they needed to understand this and not react in a bad way. When I got there the brotherly tension was high and they were rowing about something trivial. I knew that this tension would cause at least one incident between the lads before we got to run itself. But my hope was that we would pull together as the run developed. I left them and said that I'd meet them early the next morning at the McDonalds next to Man city's Etihad stadium which was at the start of Ashton Canal and the start of the 200+ mile trek to London.

The next day, I'm there at the meeting point at 5.30am and I get a phone call from them. They are still at home and behind time. Rhys says they will get to MacDonald's for about 6.15am. It's not a race but I do want to get off at a reasonable time and I do want to get a photo of the three of us together before we head off so I can't start without them. I get myself a McDonalds breakfast and when they eventually arrive around 7am they can't believe I'm having McDonalds Sausage and Egg Bagel, hash brown and coffee before I start the run. I stress to them that it's not a race, we leave when we leave but I wanted the photo before we set off. They took one of me having a McDonald's breakfast as they were so shocked. I said to Rhys 'are you for real – a greasy burger? I've been looking forward to this for months to give me the energy to start off'.

So they had breakfast too and about 8am we set off on the main road with cars hooting us and laughing at how I looked particularly and some people even taking pictures. Next thing a truck goes by. I call it a 'Grabber' but it must have a proper name. It's only one of my best pals, Tommy Mitchell, and he beeps his horn. 'What the fuck are you doing?. I couldn't speak to him properly as he drove past so I waited until the following week when he came in the shop and explained it all to him. He couldn't believe it. So we were off and the adventure began.

My first checkpoint is Marple which is about 10 miles away if I were on foot using roads but it may be a little longer along canal tow paths. This first section of the challenge is pretty uneventful and nothing to write home about. We are just establishing a way of doing this as Arron and Rhys ride ahead as reconnaissance to watch out for particularly difficult areas of the road and also to look for any ideal spots as checkpoints to stop and eat and drink.

When we hit Marple, we see this guy and ask him to take a photo of the three of us. He is out walking his dog and we end up with the dog in the photo with us. As we are having the photo taken my phone goes. It's my good pal Daz McGuire who says 'Where are you now?' 'Marple" I respond and he says 'you are only at Marple?". He thinks we have set off at 6am. It couldn't have worked out better than him ringing at that point because he tells us that there are canal works at Marple and that I need to come off the path and go through a local park and then rejoin the tow path later. If he hadn't rung at that time we wouldn't have had a clue of the obstacle ahead. So we do exactly as he suggests and he is spot on.

After the short diversion, we headed on to Macclesfield. I had totally underestimated just how rough the paths would be and how uneven they were. Only a few sections are half decent but most are rough and this run was going to take a lot longer than I thought. Bearing in mind that I was up well before 3.30am and left the flat at 4am on the Wednesday morning to get everything ready and get myself over to the meeting point, I hit the 40 hour mark with no sleep and visibility getting increasingly difficult and needed to find a place to camp. We have deliberately not booked anything en route as we don't know where and when we want or need to stop so we decide to do it rough. Rhys is taking the lead and we come to this a bit of clearing and he says "How about we stop here now and set up a camp?" Arron responds with "Are you for real? Have you heard that car in the background broadsiding and screeching of tyres - we are in the middle of a council estate somewhere in Staffordshire' but still on the tow path of the Trent and Mersey Canal We need to find somewhere better. So Arron leads the way down the canal and Rhys and myself followed on.

It was about 11pm when we came to these woods near Stoke City Football Club's 'Brittania Stadium', one of the new out of town stadiums that football clubs have been developing into over the last 20 years. There was an overhanging tree. Rhys looks underneath the overhang and says "perfect." We begin to set up camp and go about collecting suitable wood to start a fire and make it through the night. Then we begin to prepare food and get a drink. Once finished, Arron and Rhys both look at me and say 'how are we going to do this' I say to them 'You two get your heads down and I'll look after the bikes' as I've now realised how tired they were. I stay awake and kept the fire going as best I could. Around 3am Friday morning I'm running out of wood and I'm not happy with how close we are to the canal. If I go and fetch wood in the dark, I could easily lose my footing and fall in. So I work hard to keep the fire going without having to fetch more wood but it eventually runs out and there I am wide awake without sleep for coming up to 48 hours in the pitch black with just the sounds of the night to keep me company as Rhys and Arron catch some sleep. Rhys wakes up around 5.30am. It's light and it's freezing cold and he is close to hyperthermia. He looks at me and says 'Dad have you had any sleep?' 'No' I say 'I couldn't keep the fire going either' He then jumps up and collects a load of wood and then he uses the inside of a tampon to catch the smallest ember to get the fire going. A trick he's learned while training in the Marines was to use a tampon because the innards are so light and very inflammable. He gets a cracking fire going. It's absolutely awesome and we all get warm and start getting food out. I think one of us had Pot Noodle but I remember eating cheese, crackers and olives. To be honest I'd have ate worms I was that hungry.

After our makeshift breakfast, Rhys says 'Dad do you want to get your head down? but I refused. I was ok to continue and I wanted to crack on.

317

We packed up camp, put the fire out and they cycled ahead and I run behind them. We are now well into Friday morning and they are both enjoying the ride and are also able to warn me of anything coming up.

At around the 60 hour mark without sleep I am behaving very differently. We have done about 70 miles along these winding tow paths and I get a call on my phone from my mate Daz MacGuire. I'm having a conversation with him and he can't understand me. He said to me 'you dickhead, you are talking double dutch. Go and get a premier inn and go and get proper food down you and get your head down for 6 or 7 hours' I said OK but I had no intention of doing it. Then shortly afterwards Arron said to me 'Dad are you alright?' 'No' I said 'I'm not alright. I need to get my head down for half an hour'. Even though I wanted to push myself to absolute limits and put myself through the experience of hallucinations and the predicted out of body experiences that people say they have with lack of sleep, I'd realised that this trip was not just about me, it was changing shape and was becoming about me and my two sons. They had come along to look after me and were doing so but I also had to make sure that I looked after them by co-operating with them.

I found myself a spot near a bit of a tree and got into the sleeping position. I can hear a train passing and the wind. I thought I'd just grab two minutes sleep and I'd had twenty minutes and my phone goes and it's Daz again. I walked on a bit further looking for a better spot and we come to a spot near some Oak Trees. It was Arron who said they were Oak Trees and explained that the theory is that they give off energy so I've put a sleeping bag and a space blanket on the ground and it's perfect to get my head down with nature. I feel the Sun and the wind around me and I'm much happier. This is better than any premier inn I've nodded off for about half an hour and then when I wake up, I need the loo badly.

This is not something you plan for because those kind of plans can change rapidly. I find a way of going discreetly and making sure some local plant life get the manure they need to grow. I then manage another half hour sleep in the sleeping bag and that's enough.

We cracked on from there and by now were on Coventry Canal and were passing through the area of Atherstone which is in Warwickshire having just left Staffordshire.   Arron and Rhys got on their phone maps and found an Aldi nearby to the route so we went and got some more grub. We stopped on the canal bank and made a bit of fire and it started to rain. Rhys said 'next time let's build the fire under a bridge where the rain can't get to it'. The lads had come well prepared though and Rhys had a back-up gas fire and we cooked the food on that having some chilli beans and kidney beans along with more crackers and olives.

As we were cooking the food, a local woman, who Arron and Rhys had just seen getting a sandwich in Aldi, was back on her narrow boat and passing us as we cooked our food. She shouted to us that she'd rather be eating what we were cooking than the crap sandwich she had bought and jokingly asked could she join us.   Rhys shouted 'Course you can – for a tenner!' and she laughed.

As we progressed through Friday afternoon along the Coventry Canal, we were determined to make the most out of the daylight hours that were left. Arron and Rhys kept going backwards and forwards describing what was up ahead and keeping an eye on me as planned. At one point Arron says to me 'We could do with a bit of tarpaulin to set up our next checkpoint and put together a makeshift tent' Shortly afterwards we passed through Nuneaton and we spotted a Jewson store. Arron went and got some tarpaulin and rope. By this time Rhys was well behind us.

319

Arron brought the gear back and says to me 'Right, I'll crack on and find somewhere now to set up base' I said to him 'Remember, we are not going through the night because I could lose my footing and end up in canal' I'd been up since 3.30am wed and it was now Friday evening which was approximately 66 hours and I'd had less than an hours sleep in total. Forecast was rain too. So I insisted he find a spot suitable away from noise. Arron set off. Rhys was still behind us at this point because he had veered off into an immaculate looking allotment a few miles back and had chatted to this woman fishing on the canal bank. He was asking about the allotments as they looked so well looked after and she had told him that they were owned by Ghurkas. Rhys caught me up to tell me about this and then he says. 'It'd be a good idea if we had a bit of tarpaulin dad' and I went 'Yeah I know, Arron has already got some' 'What?' says Rhys 'Arron has bought some rope and tarp? 'Yeah' I said 'from Jewsons'. "Where was Jewsons' he says. 'Back there where you went off talking to that woman about the allotment owned by the Ghurkas'. I said. Arron is now in front leading to find a good spot and set up camp. He's taken charge now and Rhys is following. Both are natural leaders but they can't both lead at the same time but I'm loving the way that they are getting on and allowing each other to take the lead. I was in my element watching them.

Rhys and I came to what looked like a good spot and Arron's not there. We keep going and hit another good spot and he's not there. Rhys and I agree we need to stop soon and make camp. I remember that I have given Arron a brief and he must be sticking to it. I had told him that we needed to make the most of the daylight hours and then find a quiet spot away from any noise. So I said to Rhys 'When he finds that spot that suits he will set up camp'. We carry on saying' I hope he has set up camp and all we have to do is sit down and have a beer'.

Eventually we catch him up and we are in these woods near a car park and some narrow boats around us and he has just about got this tarpaulin spread out and rope linked through We bear hugged and he told us that he'd gone on and tried to find somewhere better but he had come back to this point. I said 'It's perfect'. I asked Rhys to help Arron finish setting up the camp and they start to work together. I got changed and Arron says 'Dad you deserve a beer' so I got one out. I'm sat down and I've got the beer in my hand and they are setting up camp and I heard Rhys say 'wow that's good cord you've got there Arron - I like your knots' Arron has done his Duke of Edinburgh award and doesn't talk about it at all. Rhys doesn't see that normally. I'm just sat there with a beer watching my two sons get on working together and supporting each other. I'm sat back content with life at that point. This trip was turning into a real bonding experience and my initial objectives were now becoming secondary and I was getting much more out of this experience than I thought I would. This was no longer about me – It was about them and it was about us.

The camp began to take shape. We had a great fire going and loads of wood to keep it going through the night and our makeshift tent was up and looking good. We were all sat with a beer in our hands and as a Dad I can't tell you how good this felt. Outdoors with a fire in front of us with my two boys was such a great feeling. I needed some solid food so I asked Arron where the beef burgers were that we had brought? They were tired and said 'we can't be arsed making them dad'. I needed something substantial so I got the burgers and threw them in a pan with some olive oil and they soon started to sizzle. The pan I used had a removable handle that you withdrew and left the pan on the fire. I turned the burgers and they were looking good. As I am working the food with the warmth of the fire on my face, I must have nodded off for a split second and my hand went forward and tilted the pan and the hot oil in the pan came over my hand and badly burnt my fingers. Whereas someone else might have been jumping around in pain I just withdrew my hand and said calmly 'fucking hell'. The lads were shocked. One of them said 'Dad they are severe burns we need to get to an A and E' I looked around and said 'we are in the middle of nowhere son. Arron has an idea and gets out a jar of coconut and puts solid coconut onto my burns. At some point he has heard that coconut is good for burns. I start to move my hand around which is moving the coconut around as it melted on my hand which was piping hot. The lads were just staring at me and I said 'what's up with you two?' They thought this was bad and that the run was over but it never entered my head. "Who wants a burger?' I said because they were done. We ate the burgers and got our heads down. My hand was throbbing throughout the evening but I knew I have the mental strength to let my body deal with it.

The morning came and when we woke up they wanted to see my hand. They didn't believe what they saw. There were just blisters on my knuckles. They expected to see untreated burns that needed hospitalisation but I had blisters and no pain. The coconut had done the trick. We started to pack up as Aaron told us a story of someone he had met when on his own the day before. A guy was gathering wood along the tow path for his log burner on his Narrow Boat which was only a few hundred yards away from where Arron had decided to set up camp. Aaron had got talking to him and told him what the three of us were doing. The guy had said "right then I'll expect you knocking on my Narrow Boat door tonight when it gets chilly'. Arron had laughed. The guy was good enough though to give Arron a box of matches just in case we needed them for a fire. I thought I'd have a walk around to his

Narrow Boat before we left. It was called 'Living The Dream'. I already liked this guy just from the name of his boat. He came out and we chatted and he said "I really expected you three to be knocking on last night in that cold". We laughed about it as I told him we were trying to get the full bonding experience of being on this trek to London together without the usual home comforts. He went on to tell me his story and how he'd had enough of stress and had got out of the rat race and was getting in touch with the natural world. I was envious of him. It's exactly how I'd felt recently and this guy had done something about it. He resembled Victor Meldrew out of 'One Foot In The Grave' but he was anything but negative like old Victor and was a cracking bloke. He told me that now and again his grown up children would come and spend the night with him on the boat and he loved the life he was living. In my head I thought 'I fancy a bit of that'.

We set off again and It's now Saturday 27th April, the day before the Marathon and due to the arrangements we had made for the return journey we were now on some time constraints. The journey down has taken much more time than anticipated and we needed to get Rhys to a nearby station at Rugby to get a train to Euston so that he can get his pre booked train back to Manchester. At this time, although it will be tight Arron and I are still planning to continue our journey to London on time to make our train later on the Sunday. We were on different trains already because originally Arron and I planned to stay and watch the London Marathon but we had run out of time for that. So we all bear hug and Rhys is gutted that he's got to leave us because really things have only just got going in terms of us all getting into this trip but the clock was ticking so off he went off heading for Rugby train station. He gets in touch with us and we find out that he's made the train and we carry on our planned route. We continue into Saturday evening and our train tickets mean that we have to be London by Sunday 6pm.

We carry on the canal paths and end up on the Grand Union canal on the way towards the Daventry area in Northamptonshire and we met a guy filing up water from a standpipe. People who have narrow boats have a key for these standpipes so that no one else can draw water or leave it running. It is a stroke of luck for us as we have run out of water so we ask if he'd mind us filling our water bottles. 'No problem' he says. We chat to him and his Mrs for a while and he asks me where we had come from and when we tell him Manchester, he's impressed. He looks at our gear and says 'and you've done all that with no tent'. At that point Arron had thrown the tent away in a bin that morning (never used) because it weighed a ton and we had no further use for it. We had binned it hoping that some homeless person would claim it with a bit of luck- we hope so anyway.

The guy says to us 'I'm Impressed with you lads doing this by bivying up'. 'Well yeah' says Arron and he starts smirking and we realise that he is ex forces and there's some sort of connection there. He says 'There a lovely pub called the Lord Nelson. Really friendly some lovely rooms and a hot bath' and he's looking at us and I said 'That's called cheating' and he starts laughing and his Mrs looked a bit puzzled. She doesn't understand but the three of seemed to be interconnected. The more he's laughing, the more she doesn't know why. I say to him 'I can see two pints of Guinness going down well' and he starts smirking again and says 'have a great trip lads'

We say our goodbyes and crack on but after a bit the mention of Guinness has got me going. I say to Arron 'do you fancy a Guinness

Arron ? he says 'Dad the first one won't touch the sides' He's right but I say 'but we are only having 2 son'. We can see this pub in the distance at some locks. It's a lovely looking pub and we head down to it. As we stand outside the place we realise that to go on our journey afterwards, we cannot go any further down the tow path on what we think is still the Grand Union Canal because it heads into a tunnel. We can only go through the tunnel on a narrow boat. The only option is a two kilometer hike around the tunnel to pick it back up again. So we went into the pub as it was getting darkish on this Saturday night and that's when we decided that we would have to grab a train from Daventry to London to make our train home. As soon as we got in there we took our jackets off to dry them off and got two pints of Guinness. We know roughly where we are on our GPS and where we need to get to for the train and it looked like trains were frequent so we sat down and had our pints and ordered another. There was a guy at the bar with old English sheepdog. He looked like ex RAF and his mannerisms supported that. Arron says to me 'Dad stop judging the book by its cover' I said 'I can't help it son'. This guy is like a Basil Fawlty character and he stands up and starts feeding his dog biscuits and shouts really loud to the dog 'STAY' but he's looking at me when he says it. In a real Sargent Major style his shouts 'STAY' again to the dog and then one final time 'STAY' and off the guy goes to the toilet. The dog starts to follow him then the dogs head jumps back. His lead is tied to the chair. He comes back from the toilet and is looking at me proudly as if his dog is obedient and hasn't budged. I found this so comical. By this time I'm looking at Arron and saying 'Shall we have a third' and needless to say Arron is up for it as its lovely Guinness. Next thing a group of lads walk in who look right knobheads and a karaoke sets up. Well that's put a nail in that coffin for me. "Let's disappear' I said. It's gone from being a nice pub to being a knobhead's pub in seconds so we left.

We climb some steps away from the pub and it's getting dark now and we've put our head torches on. Arron turns to me and says "Good job we didn't have that third pint' as we were getting tired now. It was way too late to try and find that canal path so I said let's get our head down so we are fresh for the morning - we head up this lane and see this guy coming towards us with his dog and we tell him we are trying to get on to canal path to London and he starts talking to Arron and he is one of these guys that once he realised what we were about he wanted to tell us in great detail. Eventually he says 'if it were me I stay in that field there until morning'. He goes and we do just that and start to get ready to sleep in the field and he comes back and starts reiterating what he's already told us. I'm getting impatient with him because I'm tired. I want to tell him to fuck off but we are too polite. We get set up and I wanted to do it differently but we are too tired and impatient and got a blanket around me and in the sleeping bag. When I woke the next morning I'd ripped the blanket in the night because I'd got it the wrong way around.

I ended up getting cold. Arron was ok 'ish because he had a sleeping bag but it was a difficult night because of the cold. When Arron realised how cold I was he got closer to me and I was able to get some body heat. As the morning approached I realised I was cold and wasn't getting any warmer so I got up and woke Arron. 'We need to get moving' I said. We sat up in this field with a piece of tarp over our heads and it was still very windy. We need to get some food in now. Arron says 'I'm not hungry dad' I got all the food out that we had left and put it in the middle of us. We had some cheese falafels, crackers – other bits of food all this food soon disappears and I said to Arron' not bad for someone not hungry'. We decide to make ourselves as light as possible and get rid of some of the remainder of our provisions. We tidy up and leave the place as if we haven't been there. We head for the canal path and know we now have 6 miles to go. Arron used the sat nav to guide us and we end up going through this estate and come to this road but we can't find the canal.

We are looking to head for a place called Long Buckby near Daventry and we come to a roundabout and I can see a vehicle coming towards us. I step out and stop the vehicle. He puts his window down and it's an Indian guy. I say to him "excuse me sir (I always say that to a bloke it's the way that I have been brought up I use sir not mate)) we are trying to get to Long Buckby which way shall we head? And he says 'back that way a mile to the canal over the canal bridge - train station 3 miles further down' I thank him and Arron says 'thanks brother'. As he drove off, Arron says to me 'So you don't really need GPS do you dad?' 'No son' I say GPS didn't exist 20 years ago so you just aim to ask a local and they know in most cases.

We head towards the train station. I work on the principle that if someone says 3 miles its six. You always have to double it. Arron is still worried that we are heading the wrong way as we have travelled three miles and there's not a land mark or anything to go on. Eventually we see the train station or what we think is the train station. It's just a bridge and we have to go further to the town centre. It's an unmanned station with a ticket machine but we sort it and after a two hour wait we are heading for Euston. I looked a few days later at what we had achieved before we got on that train and according to the canal routes we had followed, we had covered 137 miles in four and a half days and been through 89 locks on 11 canal ways through 6 counties. It wasn't London as we had aimed for but it had been a fantastic educational experience which was what I needed. The MDS is 156 miles in 7 days in blistering heat but no canal to fall into so that's a bonus!

We arrived in London Euston and found a cafe which was a bit on the quiet side and Arron meets a girl there and gets her number. She wants to visit Manchester and he the other way. We head back to Euston and go to our reserved train's platform. We got to the train and are in the queue to get on with our tickets that have been given to us by one of my customers Mark and fucking hell its perfect like VIP treatment. We get shown to where we will store the bikes which is near the driver and very secure and then we get shown to our reserved seats. When we got on the train I was wide awake. We had two bottles of beer between us for the train. Next thing I know I'm twitching and getting restless. My muscles are all confused with the activity we've had for the last few days of little sleep and at strange hours and Arron's wide awake but on his head phones now. He's there chilling with his bottle of beer. He says 'Do you want that beer?' I just take a couple of sips and say 'that'll do me' and give him it back and I'm totally relaxed.

As the train pulls into Manchester and stops, we get out and all I then see is Arron absolutely panicking and running past me the wrong way on the platform. He's frantic thinking the train will pull out with his bike on it but what he doesn't realise is he is running to the wrong end of the train. I'm stood there thinking where is he going? so I start shouting 'ARRON, ARRON' and this guy with a rucksack on his back stops walking down the platform towards the same end Arron is heading for and looks right at me. I say to him 'You're not called Arron are you?' "Yep', he says "I'm your train driver". What were the odds ? I just apologised to him and explained that my son Arron was heading to the end of the train to get his bike. Arron the train driver says 'his bike is down here". I say "I know where his bike is mate, when you catch him up will you say to him "hey you Dickhead your bike is down that end!" We walk into Piccadilly station and Arron has already phoned ahead to his mum. Rhys has already got home the day before and he's gutted that he's not stayed with us. He'd told the Mrs everything that had happened and the plan is that we get the tram back to Bowker Vale but in the end the Mrs picked us both up from Picadilly and dropped me off at the flat with two bottles of beer and pudding chips, peas and curry and a fish (told you we were still friends). When we get to the flat, the Mrs says to Arron. 'look after your dad make sure he gets into the flat safe' I said 'I think I can look after myself but thanks anyway and I give Arron a massive bear hug and say "Alright son" as we bump fists. I get into the flat and put my back against the radiator and poured myself a beer out. The next thing I know I am waking up Tuesday morning on the floor with a duvet over me and half a glass of beer in the fridge and the food still in the kitchen. Wow, what happened to Monday? I must have been out for the count as soon as I sat down. Amazingly I suffer no after effects whatsoever of the run and my hand was healing nicely. I went out for a walk in Heaton Park and I started to get lots of calls off customers to see where I am and how I am feeling. I just say to them "See you Wednesday and I'll tell you all about it" I've enjoyed the experience so much I just want another day to savour it before going back to work. I really hoped that Arron and Rhys enjoyed it as much as I did. I did learn some things that I needed to learn about regarding the sleep deprivation so this was a good exercise from that point of view but it had turned into something much more and as simple and crazy as it was It was a brilliant few days with both my sons. Now, what can I plan for Jourdana and Lily that'll get me ready for the Marathon Des Sables?

Hadrian's Wall

Since I've been involved in Ultra running, whenever I've entered a race, I always try and recce (reconnaissance for the posh) the area first in order to get an idea of what I'm going to be faced with. There was a 70+ mile foot race along Hadrian's wall planned for June 2020 which I was planning to enter so thought I'd go and 'recce' it In September 2019 and I invited my eldest, Arron, to come along. I enjoy bonding with my sons and daughters whenever I get the chance and the trek to London with Arron and Rhys had worked so well that I'm keen to get them out again when the chance arises. So on Friday 6th of September 2019, We are both booked one way on the 9.30am train from Victoria Station in Manchester to Newcastle. The train was on time and took us through Leeds and York before arriving in Newcastle around 12:30pm. As soon as we arrived I told Arron that I needed to find a McDonald's to get some fuel in me before setting off to find the start of the wall. We found a McDonald's but it was crowded and I couldn't cope with that so I asked Arron to go in and get me a Cheeseburger French fries and a coffee. Arron didn't want to go in or have any food from the McDonald's because he doesn't agree with their principles and was adamant it was totally the wrong thing to do before we set off on a journey. I told him that he'd regret not getting some fuel inside him so we had to look for something suitable for him to eat. Arron's a veggie so it wasn't easy but he knew that Greggs did a vegan sausage roll. We got to Greggs and when he pointed them out to me I said 'oooh they look nice' and so I got one too. People look at me and I am about as lean as you can get and still be very healthy so when I talk to my customers about eating McDonalds and sausage rolls as fuel they look at me and say 'what you Chris? Eating McDonalds and sausage rolls?' I can tell you though its perfect food to fuel you on the morning of a long trek or bike ride. I don't go to McDonalds every day and I probably don't go near one for months at a time while I am training but just now it was perfect and so was the sausage roll! We decided to stock up on snacks so we went on the hunt for a Tesco's or Sainsburys and ended up going into a Waitrose and getting marmite cashew nuts. They are perfect as fuel on the go as they give you energy bursts and Arron was happy because we were back on 'ethical' trading. We finally set off about 1.30pm and were using Arron's phone for a map. I don't have a smart phone as they call them. I've still got a simple Nokia. When someone asked me recently what kind of a Nokia phone did I have, I told them it was a Tesco one. They laughed and I thought what the fuck are you laughing at as I understand now that they all have codes apparently. To be fair, I don't really know how to use that either. I can answer it and I can hang up and that's all I need. I don't have to ring anyone as they always call me and I can just about read a text if someone sends me one. I really don't really know 100% what I'm doing with a text to be honest so it's a fifty-fifty chance of whether I actually read it or delete it by accident. I can't tell you how many important messages I might have deleted trying to read them. I'm hoping I won't be doing that on this particular day because it's my birthday and I'm expecting a few calls and messages off family and friends. As a write this I have 93 unopened messages on my phone.

It starts to rain and we have a bit of a struggle finding our way on to right route but we eventually find the relevant signs for it and leave Newcastle along Hadrian's pathway in what is now becoming heavy rain. We are going for quite some time before the calls start coming in from family, friends and customers and it lifts the mood for both us as we pick up the pace in order to make good progress. It's a 73 mile trek from Newcastle to Carlisle along the route of the wall and here we are, mid afternoon in Newcastle on Friday 6th September with a coach to catch at 11.00am on Sunday 8th September in Carlisle to get home. So we've got roughly 50 hours to trek approximately 73 miles across various sections of very differing terrain. Game on!!

Our enthusiasm for the start of it all gives us a decent pace and before we know we've been at it about five hours and have covered over 15 miles. It's early evening and we are in the Corbridge area and we come across this pub with cracking views of the valley. I turn to Arron and suggest that as it's my birthday we treat ourselves to a swift pint of Guinness which will also double up as food for us. Just as I say this my phone goes and its Jourdana wishing me a happy birthday. The weather has picked up a bit and this pub has such impressive views and the first pint of Guinness has gone down that well that we end up spending a few hours there and having a few more pints of Guinness. We have relayed to the landlord and landlady what we are up to and they were both impressed and in order to look after us they put some food out. Just snacks to go with our drinks before our hot food arrived. Eventually we set off again but by that time we were nice and merry from the Guinness unless they put something in the cheese or peas. We know we have about 50+ Miles left to hike to Carlisle. Its late Friday evening and we come across this field around the area of Corbridge. I said to Arron that we needed to get our heads down at this point and set off again in the morning. I spotted an ideal location for us both and said to Arron 'See that Tree over there?' 'Yes' He said. 'well, you've got a groundsheet, Get that down and then get in your bivvy' (bivouac for the posh). So that's what we did and slept under the stars. We both set up for the night and got comfortable and as we lay there and looked upwards Arron was blown away by the night sky. Being in total darkness gives you a fantastic view of the stars including the milky way and some shooting stars thrown in. I said to Arron; "That's the best cinema you'll ever go to. 'Interstellar 'and 'The Martian' are great films but this is real life and wherever you are in the world the same fantastic film is on. You won't see it in the cities with all their street lamps but out here you have the best seat in the house"

We slept quite well and when we woke on the Saturday morning we didn't say much to each other we just automatically started to pack our gear up to get going again. We started walking, realising that we still had approximately about 55 miles to go. After just a few minutes we came across a guest house which advertised 'morning coffee' on a sign outside but it looked deserted. As we started to nosy into the place a woman came out. Talk about lucky, we couldn't have landed at a better place. The guest house was called The Robin Hood Inn (Corbridge) and we'd highly recommend this place to anyone. A woman who worked there said to us 'Can I help you?' 'We were looking at your sign advertising morning coffee and were wondering what time you opened? It was just before 7.00am and we thought they might not start serving until 8am or even later. She responded 'Is that all you want a coffee? We are only really open for guests at the moment and don't normally open to the general public until 10.00am but come in then'. She shows us through and tells us to sit at any of the tables that are not marked as reserved for guests. She does us a coffee and then cracks on preparing for the guests' breakfasts. Both of us haven't said a word but we are both thinking the same thing. We'd love a breakfast here for our 'fuel' before we set off. She must have seen it in our faces as she carries on preparing the tables for the guests but as she passes our table she says to me "I suppose you'd like a full English wouldn't you? 'Just what the doctor ordered' I say and I looked over at Arron, who remember is a veggie and said 'And I suppose you would like to join me?'. Arron didn't have to answer as his face said it all. So she brings both of us a full English including Sausage, Bacon, Eggs, Mushrooms, Tomato, Beans Toast, butter and Marmalade -the full monty. Despite Arron being vegan you could have put his plate straight back in the cupboard as he'd cleaned it completely. We drink more coffee and then she collects our plates and says quietly ''£18.00 and don't tell the owner'. We pay and then say our goodbyes and as we get outside I turned to Arron and said 'There's a time to be vegan and a time not to be'. Arron replies "and I should have had McDonalds yesterday too" 'All day long' I say. Well fueled with breakfast we set off and put a solid stint in and walked well over twenty miles through the Northumberland Countryside before we stopped for a coffee and cake at a pub come shop come café in Hayden Bridge. It's around 1.00pm before we set off again but now the terrain is now getting a little tougher as the hills are getting steeper. We plough on for a further 10 miles and we find ourselves on a ridge close to a place called Haltwhistle and we can see some abseilers and climbers on a cliff face. We make our way towards some of them and ask ' excuse me - where is the nearest pub from here?' It's a question that's common in this country and very rarely will you ask someone who either knows where the nearest pub is or has seen one on the way to where they are. This is no exception and one of the guys in the group says "See down there that white building called 'Twice Brewed' (which is famous chain) well down there it's got its own brewery, been there for 500 years" We later discovered that some hikers had apparently stumbled across this new brewery and tried their beer and said it's a bit weak so they brewed it again hence they settled on that process and its name was born. Arron was in there like a flash. 'This ones on me dad'. We had a good few beers and some gorgeous home-made Cumberland sausage. The place had a great atmosphere and its yet again another place we'd highly recommend if you find yourselves in the area. We had a good few hours in there and before we left we planned the rest of the journey. It was now Saturday night and we had a coach booked from Carlisle back to Manchester at 11.00am on Sunday. We worked out that we had another

30+ miles to Carlisle and it would be soon time to get our heads down as it was getting dark. We also agreed that we would probably be up for a very early start while it was still dark so we decided to drop on to the road which would be safer to walk on than the ridge. We made some progress to knock a few miles off the journey the next day and then we managed to get our heads down in a ditch at the side at the side of the road for a few hours. Arron remembers this as an amazingly clear night sky. I don't so I wonder whether it was the twice brewed beer that did it. If you've got a ground sheet and a bivvy bag then you can pretty much sleep anywhere. When we awoke it was still night going into morning. The sun wasn't up yet and so we ended up setting off with our head torches on for the first few miles. We did the remainder in one stint at a very decent pace to make sure we made it on time for the coach. It was pretty impressive going because it was at least a 30 mile trek. We arrived in Carlisle just after 10am. I worked out that as we had set off at about 3.30am we had kept up a pace of 4.5 miles per hour which was good going.

The event in June 2020 was due to run from Carlisle to Newcastle, the opposite way. Now that I've recce'd the route I've got a good mental pictures of a lot of the terrain and the distances between key parts of the route. I also know that the toughest part of the terrain is at the start of the race when I am at my freshest so psychologically I have a very good mental picture of the event so job done so far and the day itself will offer the Physical challenges of a race. Arron felt mixed emotions. We'd done it now and so he couldn't understand why I wanted to come back. It was much easier for me to think about coming back because I was now up for the challenge of doing the whole thing in reverse and without any breaks. That was the real mental challenge. It wasn't the distance or the physical nature of running 70+ miles across mixed terrain, it was how much rest you would need in between and whether you could do it without sleep. Arron phones me up a few days later and tells me he feels it's took him to another level now mentally and wants to do another one. I tell him about the Atlantic challenge and he agrees he wants to do it. I told him that was for next year too, 2020. I'm well pleased that he has enjoyed the experience and when Jourdana hears about it she is envious of the experience so I agree that we will organise something similar very soon. An opportunity comes along a lot quicker than I thought when I'm discussing with one of my customers the trip to Hadrian's wall and he says to me 'it's a shame you didn't have time to see William Wallace'. I know that Wallace is the Scottish guy who was reported to be a giant on the battlefield against the English but I've not heard of the memorial or statue of him not far from Hadrian's wall so he has my interest. He tells me of a statue off the beaten track in Scotland north of the wall overlooking back to England in a menacing manner. I decide there and then that I will do a 60/70 mile trek with Jourdana and Arron to this monument in the next few weeks.

Wallace

Around the end of September 2019, the three of us, myself, Jourdana and Arron, set off for Melrose in Scotland as our starting point. Firstly it's a train to Carlisle from Manchester and then a bus to Melrose. As soon as we arrive Jourdana suggests fish and chips. "Good shout" I say and off we go. When you find yourselves in these smaller locations, wherever in the UK you are, it's like slipping back in time. All they have in the village is a co-op. We ask a local and they tell us that the best fish and chips are in the pub. So that's where we head and within a few minutes I have a pint of Guinness in front of me and Arron and Jourdana have a soft drink before the food arrives. As we talk about where we are going to go I realise that I haven't brought the map. It's a great start. Luckily the reception of the pub had maps of the local area and so I went and grabbed one. The map included the location of the Wallace monument too. Whether it's my appearance or the people were just friendly anyway I got involved in a conversation with a couple of people about the map and where we were heading. They gave me some directions that would help. I get back to the table with Arron and Jourdana and Jourdana says "How come people talk to you and are not wary of you? I tell her that its 50-50 really. We chatted further between us and Arron tells us that by coincidence he's actually been to Melrose before as part of a Callanish Band that played Kaley music at a wedding at Melrose Rugby Club some time ago.

We were on our way before long and before we went to the monument we decide to climb some nearby locations just outside Melrose to get some views in of where we are before we head for the forest where Wallace is. As we get to the top of the second hill, it was as windy as hell but the view was exceptional. I decide that it would be great to stay here for the night and see the sunrise tomorrow from this spot. Arron says "We'll freeze to death. We need to go back down" He was right so we moved down to camp nearer the forest. It wasn't ideal but we made a fire and set up base with the view that we'd. We'd met some people on the first climb earlier and they'd made a point of saying "I hope you've got something in those bags to warm you up". It's funny because I did have and as we were sat around the fire I brought a hip flask out and Jourdana looked at me and said "Don't tell me that you've got Lucozade in that". I laughed "No actually. It's Jack Daniels". Jourdana was pleasantly surprised "Dad. How fantastic is that. I'm gutted I haven't brought alcohol myself" So we had a few shots of Jack Daniels and something to eat. It was getting dark then and it started to rain so we got under the canopy. After a while Jourdana says "Dad can you hear that?"   I answered her by saying "Yeah I hope it's not a wolf". "Wolf?" says Jourdana looking a bit spooked. "Yeah" I say "we are low down the food chain here Jourdana – all the local animals are staring at us now saying look at those dickheads. They see us as spare ribs". She knows I am winding her up. The next morning we get up and pack up and head into the village close by to find breakfast. We found a café that did a Scottish breakfast which Arron and I tucked into. Jordanna is vegan so avoided it. The lady that ran the café was really helpful and pointed us in the right direction for Wallace. The statue that we'd travelled to see was in the grounds of the Bemersyde estate which is close to Melrose on the Scottish borders. It didn't take us long to trek up the hillside through the forest into a spectacular spot where Wallace stands on guard leaning on his huge sword and looking over to England. The statue was made of red sandstone by a guy called John Smith of Darnick in 1814. We were amazed at the size of it, 31 feet high, and tried to visualise how hundreds of years ago they managed to either make the structure here on the hillside or transport it to here. Its structure means that you can't really look up his skirt to see if it's true either. We spent about 15 / 20 minutes admiring this incredible local wonder and the powerful image it portrayed of Wallace standing guard over his beloved Scotland looking over the River Tweed giving out a message to the English. Mission accomplished, we took our last look at this fantastic monument to a giant of a man and began to plan our route back to Carlisle to get the train home.

It was great to spend some time together with Jourdana and Arron. Jourdana is easy going and goes with the flow. To her, if that's what it is then that's what it is. She's 27 years old and laid back but very well organised. We especially had a good long chat around the fire the night before and I loved the quality time it gave us. As we headed back I was thinking, how do I get some time with Lily and maybe Callum too. I'll be working on that one. It's a message to all you fathers out there. Spend time while you can with your kids. I'll make up as much time as I can with them but you'd have to ask them whether it will be enough. We got a bus to Melrose to make sure that we got the coach to Carlisle. The trip didn't have any long treks for us but it did what we wanted it to do. On the bus a lady overheard us talking and said to us "don't get off at Melrose, get off one stop further it will be quicker for you". We did what she said and of course she was bang on. We tried to pay extra to the bus driver but he waved us off saying it was on him. Decent of him that. I said to Jourdana that it could only happen with certain people who are on the same wavelength as you. The lady and the bus driver showed that human spirit is still alive and well. We didn't look local to them and of course I've got a no better than a 50/50 chance that they'll assume I'm a nutter and yet they are both decent with us. At the bus station we get some beers to take with us for journey home then an hour later we are in Carlisle nice and early.

Here we are in Carlisle, stinking after being out for two days with no shower and now with a few cans of beer. We tried to change our tickets for the train to leave earlier but it was ridiculously expensive so we sacked that off and decided to wait. We found a comfortable spot in the station and sat down like a bunch of down and outs as we drunk a little beer. We decided to get a few more for the train and headed around the corner to the local Tesco. As we headed back to the station we passed a pub. By this time it was now mid evening on a typical city centre Saturday night. A few lads that spilled out the pub onto the pavement and there I was. One of them decides to try and caress my beard saying "oh look it's Father Christmas". This proves just how different I am now to how I was soon after the accident. If this was 1981, we all would have been on Cumbrian television that night with World War three in the town centre. As it happens I just said "yes mate" and walked on.   Aaron was left absolutely open mouthed because he would have put money on me dropping the guy and he is amazed at my level of patience. Don't get me wrong If he had have kept hold of my beard then it would have been a different story but my patience was obviously influenced by having Jourdana and Arron with me. I wouldn't have wanted to put them in a difficult position. I would have rather been alone if anything was going to happen like that and the guy would have definitely got this year's main present off Father Christmas!! That said, I'm glad that I have some control back and that the red mist doesn't descend when it's not necessary. David Banner would be so jealous. He'd be green with envy!

On the train we got chatting to some lads who were heading to Manchester for the evening and one lad particularly asked what we'd been up to and had a chat with us about walking as he said he was a walker himself but not on our scale. Mena came and picked us up from Picadilly and dropped us off at the flat with a few beers and chippy. All in all another great couple of days. I'm hoping for lots more of them going forward.

Chapter 26 – The Marathon Des Sables

Because I've competed in Iron Man events and Ultra events, people often think I'm ex-military and when I tell them I'm a Barber they say "What?" They expect me to be in the forces or a job that demands that level of physical activity and mental state. The kind of mental state that military people have and the sort of mental state you will need to compete in any way in the kind of extreme challenges that Ultra events or Iron Man events throw at you. It's hard to explain but it's the experience that these events give you help you prepare for the next event and so on. Hallucinations and other tricks of the mind are commonplace and recognising them as such are key to being able to continue in the events to complete them. Training for the mental barriers that you will have to overcome in these events is very difficult as some of them you can only experience by doing the races themselves. It's a little like England training for penalties. It's OK but until you are in the moment you do not know what it feels like. I started competing in Ultra events much later in life than most. I have fellow competitors in their thirties wanting to shake my hand when they see me in these events. They are impressed that someone of my age is ready to push their body to those limits but I have now reached a point where I am ready to go beyond that take my journey to the next level.

The run / walk to London from Manchester with my lads was a test for me and I learned a lot from it. Ironically, if we had completed the whole journey then it would have been over 200 miles. As it stands we completed a distance probably around two thirds of that but without very much sleep. It wasn't the Marathon Des Sables and it wasn't the Sahara desert but taking one thing at a time there's very little I can do to prepare for desert running other than doing the thing itself. I've started so late in life competing in these types of events and once I'd participated in a few Ultra events, I haven't the time to put in years and years of Ultras to work my way towards one of the most challenging in the world. If I am going to do these things, I have to do them now. I know that even Chris Duoba can't compete with Mother Nature and I respect her. I know what I am capable of now at this moment in time and how far I am prepared to push myself. At 60 years old I feel great. I've never felt more capable of facing such a challenge and I don't want to wait. There are some incredible Ultra events around the world but it is the MdS that attracts me because of the additional challenges it offers. Let me tell you a little more about it and what it means to me personally.

There are many foot races you will find on line that claim to be the toughest foot races on earth. They all sound fantastic to me but the one that I have had my focus on for five years and the one that has become my main objective is The 'Marathon Des Sables', or MdS, which is French for Marathon of the Sands. It's also known as the Sahara Marathon. This is a six day Ultramarathon event of 251 Kilometres which is approximately the distance of six regular marathons. The longest single stage of the event is 91 kilometres (57 miles). The event is held every year in southern Morocco in the Sahara Desert and claims to be the toughest foot race on Earth. This is now my goal. This event will complete my journey from being dragged out of that car in Hyde back in 1980 when I was just a 19 year old kid. They told me after the crash that my injuries would limit me physically. The medical staff seemed to be indicating to me that I should have been grateful to be alive and that to live would be a reward in itself. I knew that simply surviving would never be enough. I knew that I would continue to challenge myself and that my goals would always be the near impossible for someone who had come through injuries like that and for someone who had started competing in these events later in life than most. I am proud of what I have achieved so far but nothing means more to me now than competing in what will be the most difficult of physical challenges a runner can face.

Ever since my recovery from the crash I have ploughed on as positively as possible to challenge myself as a person and as an athlete. When they told me I would be limited in what I would be able to do, that was the best thing they could have possibly said to me because I am so stubborn and determined I was always going to prove them wrong. That just wasn't enough for me though. If you had told me when I was 20 years old and still recovering from my injuries, that I would be competing in cyclocross in my mid 30's competing against teenagers and men in their early 20s in a sport that involved cycling a minimum of ten miles across rough terrain and up to 50 Kilometres in an 'Audax" event in Alderley edge, then I would have been over the proverbial moon with just that but once I had achieved that, I needed to go to the next level and that is what I have done ever since. It has not happened by design, it is just something that drives me. When I stepped up to compete in Triathlons, at first I thought, this is me, this is what I was meant to do. As soon as I had competed in a few triathlons, I was already looking at the 'Iron Man' events to go to the next level. At this point I'm thinking, when is this going to end, because as I complete the Iron Man events I start showing an interest in Ultra events. To be fair, this is when I start to really think that I may have pinnacled in terms of what I could achieve. 200 Mile races cross country is surely the limit for me but when I had competed in a small number of those events, some of which I have not completed due to one injury or another, I started to turn my attention to what I think now will be the challenge of my life, especially as I will be at least 60 when I compete in it if not older. This is now my goal. Everything I do now will be with this in mind. I always need to push though so it's not enough to just compete in the MdS. I'll be dammed if I am just going over there to take part and say that I competed in or even completed the race. I'm determined to win it. I said that to a close friend recently and they said " What? Win your age group Chris?" and I gave them a dirty look and said "No. The fucking race!!" Ridiculous some will say. Let them say it. Whatever position I do finish in, I'll be aiming to win it.

When I was in hospital and close to being discharged back in 1980, the medical staff seemed to be indicating to me that I should have been grateful to be alive and that to live would be a reward in itself. I knew that simply surviving would never be enough. I knew that I would continue to challenge myself and that my goals would always border on the impossible for someone who had come through injuries like that. There have been additional challenges along the way too as I started competing in these events much later in life than most and without a military background as most of the ultra-runners are special forces or ex Special forces. I was forty when I did my first Iron Man which was late to start competing in those kind of events. I gave this to myself as a 40th birthday Present. Starting late also had a knock on effect when I stepped it up but I know now that I can tackle anything. In terms of the MdS, I know I can cover the distance and doing 6 marathons is not the issue to be faced up to. The heat is obviously a factor and but that doesn't faze me either, but if I am to win it, I am going to have to complete the race possibly without much sleep in between due the changes in temperature and the fatigue levels will be difficult to overcome but it can be done. I am more challenged by the fact that the conditions will create mental challenges like hallucinations and such for me. It's one thing competing physically but being mentally strong is another thing entirely. I will clearly have to work to overcome this but overcome it I will.

Being healthy enough and fit enough to complete the MdS seems like the least of my problems at the moment. There are a number of hurdles I have to overcome to just get to the start line. My first hurdle will be the cost. The current entry fee is around £4,250. This of course includes flights, race entry and support and some accommodation. I say 'some' accommodation because during the race I will sleep in a tent provided by the race organisers each night. The organisers will also provide water at the camps but I will be required to bring my own food. All competitors must bring with them and carry in their back pay every day, sufficient supplies of food for the seven days and this will all be checked before starting. The checks will ensure that competitors carry at least enough food for a minimum of 2000 calories per day so I must be carrying at least 14,000 calories in my backpack. Those are minimum figures so larger participants must bring more as their metabolic rate will be much higher.

Each runner will be expected to run the equivalent of six marathons in sevens days. There will be one rest day and that will follow the biggest section of the race which will be between 50 and 60 miles. The race organisers are strict on safety as clearly some ultra-athletes will push themselves to dangerous levels if they have to. There are clear rules on what else is to be in my backpack and contents will be checked before we start to ensure that we have certain items. For example, the temperature will reach up to 50 degrees centigrade so we must all bring supplies of sun cream and ways of hydrating quickly, although water will be provided every 7 or 8 miles or so in checkpoints that medical staff will be based at to keep an eye on us all. Runners enter what's described as a chute where we can pick up water and dump trash before continuing in the race. Runners will be pulled out by medics if they are deemed unfit to continue and I guess we won't be allowed to debate it even though I suspect most ultra-athletes will want to. Previous participants warn anyone looking to take part that they will blister, bleed and hallucinate the whole event and if we forget any food there won't be any assistance during the race with energy gels or sweets. I'll be carrying a back pack that must not weigh less than 6.4 kilograms and no more than 15 kilograms including food. These weight restrictions will not include water as you can carry as little or as much as you think you need between checkpoints. There are other items though that you must have in your pack for emergency desert survival. These will be checked before you start so if you do not have the following in your bag you will not be allowed to start:

A sleeping bag, head torch and spare batteries, a whistle, a mirror for signaling if necessary, a compass (always a good idea), a lighter, safety pins, a knife, an aluminium sheet, a passport and identity card (sounds ominous – why don't they ask for dental records too?), head torch and spare batteries, 200 Euros (well you never know, you might find a camel going cheap!!), an original medical certificate filled in and signed by a doctor (do you get the impression there's a suspicion that we might not all survive?), an original and recent ECG with tracing (OK it's looking like they definitely want a belt and braces job on covering themselves against any blame for me pegging out). Even that lot isn't the most worrying stuff, what about the next item: an anti-venom pump!! You don't get one of those in Boots do you? Apparently there are 10 types of scorpions in Morocco and more than 10 types of snake and all of them are venomous. The good news is that a lot of them only get active at night, what a bonus, they can only get you while you sleep! Here's me thinking about where all that sand will get about my person and that's the least of my worries. I'm joking around with this information but believe me I will take it very seriously as I move towards the race. You have to respect the dangers and the risks and I will be doing just that.

The real difficulty with me is getting to that start line with the clearance of a clean bill of health. At 60+ they are clearly going to be wanting full and transparent clearance for me to start so I'll be getting myself in top shape for those examinations. The organisers themselves are fantastically well equipped to host and support the race and its competitors. Over 400 staff will cover the race with more than 100 out on the route itself and over 50 medical staff. Other statistics just make your mind boggle. These are some of the stats published on how organisers will get people to the race, support the logistics of it and manage the safety of all taking part. Get a load of this. The staff will have at their disposal: 100 all-terrain vehicles, several Quad Bikes and Mountain Bikes, over 20 buses, 6 commercial planes, 2 Helicopters and a Cessna plane. Add to all of that nearly 300 tents, over 100,000 litres of water, a lorry carrying an incinerator to dispose of rubbish, nearly 7 kilometres of Elastoplast, thousands of painkillers, a satellite image station to monitor competitors, satellite telephones, several cameras and 4 camels and you start to appreciate the size and the serious nature of this event. I'm already buzzing about being part of it. I'm ready now but every day will be working even harder towards its completion. I want to stand just before that finish line and close my eyes and see that wall on the bridge for the last time and as I open them and take the step that will complete the Marathon Des sables I will lay that ghost to rest once and for all.

Chapter 27 – 60 is the new 20 (COVID 19

As Auld Lang Syne was being sung across the nation on 1st Jan 2020, I entered my 60th year on this planet and I already knew then that this was going to be a year of huge change and challenge. I understand that when some people hit milestone ages like 50 or 60 it depresses them a little because no one likes getting old but I approached it, as I approach everything now, it's new and exciting and is going to be what you make of it. I am ready both mentally and physically to take on the significant challenge of The Marathon Des Sables and that is my next major physical and mental challenge. I have the legs to complete the race and I have the mental capacity to work through the challenges during the race as they arise. The question is will I get in it? It appears that the 2020 MDS was postponed in March 2020 and then cancelled in July 2020 due to the Coronavirus Pandemic. Those people who lost their entry fees in 2020 will get first refusal on the 2021 event which was the event that I was aiming for. I already have significant hurdles to get over to get accepted into the race, well two specific hurdles really. Firstly I will need to ensure that I can pass any medical tests that are necessary before I am accepted in to the event and secondly, there's the small matter of £4,250 entry fee that I am going to have to find. If all the places that were taken for 2020 are moved to 2021, It may have to be 2022 before I can compete in the Moroccan desert. I won't let that delay upset or deter me from my goal. It just means that I will have more time to prepare and ensure that I am fully ready to prevail over the conditions. That sounds like a bold statement but it is this type of attitude that is required to take on challenges like this one. I am also far too familiar with people that say that they are going to do something and with all the right intentions keep putting it off until eventually it's never done. That will not happen to me when it comes to the MDS. I will be entering and I will be competing in it as soon as that becomes administratively possible. In the meantime, I continue to get myself ready for the event in the simple manner that I have already been following for the last year or so.

I wanted to end this book with me travelling back from completing the MdS but the pandemic has prevented that. It's no big thing in the scheme of things. People have lost their lives over the last six months since the pandemic started and families all over the world have been devastated. The world economy has suffered and many businesses gone out of business and people lost careers. All I have to accept is that I won't be 60 years of age when I complete the Marathon Des Sables. I will be over 61 or more. Its no big deal. It gives me more time to prepare and get even more focused on what I need to do. I have already nailed my colours to the mast by taking some drastic steps to ensure that nothing stands in my way of being mentally ready when it happens. As I sit here and write this, I have just celebrated my 60th birthday and only this week I have made two major decisions in my life to pave the way towards what now might be my greatest physical and mental achievement in my life in 2022 or beyond if necessary.

Firstly I have taken the decision to leave the Barber's shop I have owned and have been working in since 1976. I have also left the flat above it as the place I have called home for about seven years. Strictly speaking I'm out of a job and homeless. I'm guessing that almost all of you will read this and think 'what an idiot. Why would he do anything that would risk leading to being without a job and a home?' All I can tell you is this. For the first time in many years I feel free. The weight of the world has been lifted from my shoulders. I can actually breathe and feel excited about the future. Crazy? I can understand how people would think that but when you have had years of successfully managing your sensitive mental health issues, you know when the need to change what you are doing arrives. I have reached that point now and have acted on my instincts.. I went into the Modern / Barbers, sweeping floors for Henry as a 15 year old boy in 1976. Business then was regular and loyal clients. It was a place to escape to for some men where they could talk about what was on their mind. Outside if 100 cars passed the shop in a day it was a busy day on Middleton Road. Now, to count 100 cars passing would take you less than 3 or 4 minutes. Now everybody in the queue is buried in the screen of their smart phone. Back then, if the shop landline rang, we'd apologise to customers for the rude distraction. I can't stress enough how the atmosphere in and out of the shop was vastly different back then. Clearly the Barbers has been modernised now and after handing over the reins to Faz, he has been doing some fantastic work to attract new clients to the shop and I cannot and will not knock anything that has been changed because I would be the first to say how fantastic those changes are. However, it is not the place for me to be right now. Is this down to my mental health and the way that I am? Well, yes partly, but I simply cannot spend any more of my time sat in the shop waiting for a customer to walk in and listening to the background noise that highlights changes that reflect a sign of the times we live in. I know that by carrying on, this is not conducive to me staying mentally well and ultimately well enough not just to get ready for the `MDS , but for living the rest of my life in the same positive way that I know motivates me and keeps me going.

As you might imagine, leaving the place I have called work and my own business for over 44 years has been a huge wrench but even though that hurts, I am 110% confident that it is the right move for me now even though I can confirm that I haven't got the proverbial pot to piss in and my life's belongings amount to 2 bikes, a coffee maker and a couple of bin bags full of clothes and gear. There's something very liberating about this and as soon as I made the decision and started to act on it, the benefits on my health and welfare were almost immediate. I am going to now spend 100% of my time doing three things. Completing and publishing this book, training and ensuring I am ready when the MdS is open for me and exploring developing my portable skills as a Barber just as my Grandad Walter said to me when I was 15. He said that I would always have my trade wherever I went. He was so right and now to add to that I have my own transport, my bike. Times have changed and just because I'm 60 doesn't mean that I can't change with them. I may have the brain and life experience of a 60 year old but I feel like a 20 year old when it comes to my fitness and the state of my health.

I also believe that I have a lot to offer in advising other people on nutrition and training for different outcomes like general fitness, weight loss or competing at various levels. I am going to explore that avenue as I go I into my early 20s, sorry 60's. Just recently while I was still working in the shop, I was thinking of a customer called Mark that I hadn't seen for a while as I knew he was overdue his regular haircut. I was sat in a quiet moment looking out into Middleton Road and a guy in shorts and trainers and black running jacket is walking across the road and looking at the shop and I'm looking at him and as he gets closer and closer I know him but I can't place him. Bloody hell it's Mark. He's dropped a load of weight. Only recently, he'd been telling me that his cholesterol was high and he'd been advised to get it down and had started running. I'd advised him with a few tips on how to reduce his cholesterol. It's like a passion with me. I love helping other people with the stuff that's like second nature to me. They look at how fit and lean I am for 60 years old and I give them solid advice on what they should be looking at doing. It made my week to see the life benefits that Mark was enjoying because he'd bitten the bullet, took advice, listened and applied it and was now reaping the rewards in terms of getting in shape and he is telling me that he can't believe how good he feels.

More and more people will be looking to change their lifestyle once we are clear of this 2020 pandemic as even more focus has been put on people's health and their ability to fight illness and a virus as powerful as the COVID 19 Coronavirus. This pandemic is very much like my crash in 1980. It's been a bad and painful experience that we would have preferred to have avoided but it is to be the making of us. My crash and its effects have 110% led to the incredible events of my life and have made me a stronger and better person. I love life and never take it for granted because I came so close to losing it 40 years ago. A lot of the human race were taking life for granted until the COVID 19 pandemic came along and now look at how people view the luxuries of being alive and going where they want with who they want when they want. Society will come out the other end as I did. Stronger and better for it. I do not want to detract from those that have lost loved ones or lost their own lives but this shocking Virus has happened and is happening and all we can do to show our character in how we react to that. Amongst the sadness and loss, there are always moments of dark humour. It's in our nature to laugh when we can and it is important to retain a sense of humour. A long standing customer of mine, Brian, who owns the Skip company and who was the person that alerted me to the property on Highfield Road, told me the other day that he had paused at the door of his bank that day and put his mask on and gone in. He said that, had he done that 12 months ago, he'd have had a SWAT team around him within minutes and made Granada Reports that night. Life is too short not have laughs.

For me it's also too short not to continue to have goals and ambition and get as excited at 60 years of age as you might have at 20 years of age about new horizons. In fact, in reality, here I am at 60 years old and with the exception of my wonderful family, I literally have nothing to my name in terms of possessions to show for it but I am genuinely excited about what the future holds for me. Whereas at 20 years old, I was one step away from oblivion. It's just a number. It entirely depends on how you feel and what you are going to do about it. Occasionally we get reminded abruptly of this fact by the loss of a loved one or friend but we should retain that approach throughout our lives. Paul Taylor was a mountain rescuer. He was a long term friend of mine. He came into my shop one day and he was complaining about a pain in his side. This had been going on for quite a while. I asked him 'what's up?'. He just said 'It's my side Chris, giving me a lot of pain. Now I knew Paul he was a triathlete and was part of a mountain rescue team. This was not like him at all . Something was not right so I encouraged him to get checked out which he duly did. They treated him for appendicitis and took his appendix out. A couple of months later he was back in the shop and he was holding his side again. I said to him 'what's up, is this your guts again? I thought they have taken your appendix out haven't they?' This was not adding up. Turns out it was cancer and he died within weeks. He was 56. His wife Sue was devastated. She has gone to live abroad now. In those last few weeks, he was in a hospice so I went to see him and I took Rhys with me. He was about 16 and I wanted him to come with me. I made a judgement call that it wouldn't be pleasant for him but that it might be a life experience that would hold him in good stead to see what someone like Paul was going through and realise that you have to grab life and make the most of it. When we got there, Paul was rigged up to all the monitors and drips and it just looked like it was a matter of time before he died. I said to Rhys 'Go on say hello to Paul' which he did. I had brought two bottles of our favourite beer, Erdinger and two glasses. 'Are you having a beer with me then? One beer isn't going to kill you is it?' 'I suppose not' he says and he drank the beer. When we were going I gave him a massive hug and he yelped. "Sorry Paul' I said as I had hugged him that tight. He started laughing and that's how I wanted to remember him. Rhys conducted himself impeccably during the visit and when he came out, he broke down. I knew how he felt because I was feeling exactly the same. I really hoped that the judgement call had been right and that Rhys had benefitted from the visit far more than the upset had weighed on him. Life is far too short not to enjoy yourself and you should always pursue your ambitions. I think of Paul a lot when I make my life decisions. He was a top top guy and deserved better health.

So what now for me? Well same as you, I can't predict the future but I'll tell you this. I am chuffed to the proverbial bits that I have written my life story down and put it out for all to see. If it helps one person then I'm a winner. I'll no doubt be cutting hair again soon because it's both my trade and my social life mixing with my wonderful customers. I'll be damned if I'm not on that starting line in the Moroccan desert in the Marathon Des Sable within the next two years to rise to that next level and to that challenge. Watch this space as I guarantee I'll be writing about it, success or not. In the meantime, if you see a homeless looking 60+ year old Crank in Manchester with a scraggly looking grey beard carrying what looks like a two ton rucksack on his back either walking, running or cycling, don't cross the road to avoid him, come and introduce yourself and have a chat. I don't bite. Well, to be fair I do bite but only people that deserve it!!

Finally, I've already thanked my mum and Philomena for what they have done for me through some difficult times but I'd like to take this opportunity to thank that one copper, those two paramedics, that surgeon, those nurses and our irreplaceable NHS for your part in giving me the gift of the last 40 years. I can tell you that the recovery was slow at first but it led to me having the gift of my own fantastic family, my own business, wonderful friendships and the most incredible experiences that I couldn't have ever imagined were even possible when I got in the car that day. I believe that everything happens for a reason and it all fits together eventually. Although I have made mistakes, and there are some that I can still rectify and will, I have absolutely zero regrets and I look forward to many more fantastic years and life experiences with my family and friends as I definitely have much more life in me yet. To all those people who helped save me and indeed anyone, family or otherwise, that I have lost touch with, if you ever fancy catching up over an espresso then you can find me easily on Facebook under my name. I'd love to hear from you.

End of Part One

Chris Duoba

Printed in Great Britain
by Amazon

49062091R00210